Cisco Unified Contact Center Enterprise (UCCE)

Gary Ford

Cisco Press

800 East 96th Street

Indianapolis, IN 46240

Cisco Unified Contact Center Enterprise (UCCE)

Gary Ford

Copyright © 2012 Cisco Systems, Inc.

Published by:
Cisco Press
800 East 96th Street
Indianapolis, IN 46240 USA

All rights reserved. No part of this book may be reproduced or transmitted in any form or by any means, electronic or mechanical, including photocopying, recording, or by any information storage and retrieval system, without written permission from the publisher, except for the inclusion of brief quotations in a review.

First Printing June 2011

Library of Congress Cataloging-in-Publication data is on file.

ISBN-13: 978-1-58714-117-1

ISBN-10: 1-58714-117-5

Warning and Disclaimer

This book is designed to provide information about Cisco Unified Contact Center Enterprise (UCCE). Every effort has been made to make this book as complete and as accurate as possible, but no warranty or fitness is implied.

The information is provided on an "as is" basis. The author, Cisco Press, and Cisco Systems, Inc., shall have neither liability nor responsibility to any person or entity with respect to any loss or damages arising from the information contained in this book or from the use of the discs or programs that may accompany it.

The opinions expressed in this book belong to the author and are not necessarily those of Cisco Systems, Inc.

Trademark Acknowledgments

All terms mentioned in this book that are known to be trademarks or service marks have been appropriately capitalized. Cisco Press or Cisco Systems, Inc. cannot attest to the accuracy of this information. Use of a term in this book should not be regarded as affecting the validity of any trademark or service mark.

Corporate and Government Sales

The publisher offers excellent discounts on this book when ordered in quantity for bulk purchases or special sales, which may include electronic versions and/or custom covers and content particular to your business, training goals, marketing focus, and branding interests. For more information, please contact: **U.S. Corporate and Government Sales** 1-800-382-3419 corpsales@pearsontechgroup.com

For sales outside of the U.S. please contact: **International Sales** international@pearsoned.com

Feedback Information

At Cisco Press, our goal is to create in-depth technical books of the highest quality and value. Each book is crafted with care and precision, undergoing rigorous development that involves the unique expertise of members from the professional technical community.

Readers' feedback is a natural continuation of this process. If you have any comments regarding how we could improve the quality of this book, or otherwise alter it to better suit your needs, you can contact us through e-mail at feedback@ciscopress.com. Please make sure to include the book title and ISBN in your message.

We greatly appreciate your assistance.

Publisher: Paul Boger	**Business Operation Manager, Cisco Press:** Anand Sundaram
Associate Publisher: Dave Dusthimer	**Manager Global Certification:** Erik Ullanderson
Executive Editor: Brett Bartow	**Senior Development Editor:** Christopher Cleveland
Managing Editor: Sandra Schroeder	**Copy Editor:** John Edwards
Project Editor: Seth Kerney	**Technical Editors:** Carlos Gonzalez, Alan Quinn
Editorial Assistant: Vanessa Evans	**Proofreader:** Apostrophe Editing Services
Cover Designer: Gary Adair	**Indexer:** Tim Wright
Composition: Mark Shirar	

Americas Headquarters	Asia Pacific Headquarters	Europe Headquarters
Cisco Systems, Inc.	Cisco Systems (USA) Pte. Ltd.	Cisco Systems International BV
San Jose, CA	Singapore	Amsterdam, The Netherlands

Cisco has more than 200 offices worldwide. Addresses, phone numbers, and fax numbers are listed on the Cisco Website at www.cisco.com/go/offices.

CCDE, CCENT, Cisco Eos, Cisco HealthPresence, the Cisco logo, Cisco Lumin, Cisco Nexus, Cisco StadiumVision, Cisco TelePresence, Cisco WebEx, DCE, and Welcome to the Human Network are trademarks; Changing the Way We Work, Live, Play, and Learn and Cisco Store are service marks; and Access Registrar, Aironet, AsyncOS, Bringing the Meeting To You, Catalyst, CCDA, CCDP, CCIE, CCIP, CCNA, CCNP, CCSP, CCVP, Cisco, the Cisco Certified Internetwork Expert logo, Cisco IOS, Cisco Press, Cisco Systems, Cisco Systems Capital, the Cisco Systems logo, Cisco Unity, Collaboration Without Limitation, EtherFast, EtherSwitch, Event Center, Fast Step, Follow Me Browsing, FormShare, GigaDrive, HomeLink, Internet Quotient, IOS, iPhone, iQuick Study, IronPort, the IronPort logo, LightStream, Linksys, MediaTone, MeetingPlace, MeetingPlace Chime Sound, MGX, Networkers, Networking Academy, Network Registrar, PCNow, PIX, PowerPanels, ProConnect, ScriptShare, SenderBase, SMARTnet, Spectrum Expert, StackWise, The Fastest Way to Increase Your Internet Quotient, TransPath, WebEx, and the WebEx logo are registered trademarks of Cisco Systems, Inc. and/or its affiliates in the United States and certain other countries.

All other trademarks mentioned in this document or website are the property of their respective owners. The use of the word partner does not imply a partnership relationship between Cisco and any other company. (0812R)

About the Author

For more than 13 years, **Gary Ford** has been privileged to work for many large systems integration companies, Cisco Advanced Technology Partners, and end customers, designing, deploying and maintaining Cisco telephony and contact center solutions. His introductory role to contact centers started in 1997 while working for British Telecom (BT) as a test engineer tasked with integrating the GeoTel ICR platform into BT's core telephony network. Over the following years, Cisco acquired GeoTel and rapidly transformed the ICR product set to include solutions from other Cisco acquisitions and a great deal of in-house innovation. His role has changed over the years from test engineer to contact center and unified communications consultant. Gary spends much of his time designing and deploying Cisco unified communications solutions for a wide range of customers. Gary also holds a bachelor's of engineering degree in computer systems engineering, the status of Chartered Engineer, and several Cisco, Microsoft, and business-related professional qualifications.

About the Technical Reviewers

Carlos Gonzales, manager of Software Development Engineering, is one of the technical managers in the Customer Contact Business Unit in Boxborough, Massachusetts, where he has been working as an engineering manager for the past year. In his current role, he is involved in quality assurance testing, release engineering, and systems engineering activities with respect to the customer contact applications. Before becoming a manager, he held a software engineer and technical leader position for seven years in the Voice Technology Group Solution Test team focused on solution-level testing of UCCE, CVP, CUCM, CUP, CUSP, CTIOS, CAD, UCS, Outbound in Standalone, Distributed, CoW, and Parent/Child deployment models. During his tenure as an engineer, he had the privilege of leading and participating in validating the UCCE system in an end-to-end Cisco solution, as documented in the Cisco validated design guides (aka SRND). Currently, as a manager on the CCBU team, he has been privileged to work with UCCE development, test, and field engineers in deploying UCCE in a UCS, VMware, and EMC data center environment. Carlos holds a bachelor's degree in computer science and is the recipient of multiple Cisco, Microsoft, and VMware certifications in addition to more than 15 years in the networking industry.

Alan Quinn, NCE Advanced Services Europe, is one of the senior consulting engineers in the Unified Customer Contact team in London, U.K. In his current role, he is involved in developing Contact Center as a Service (CCaaS) that includes Hosted UCCE, CVP, and CUCM; the solution is to be built on UCS technology. Before joining Cisco as an NCE, he held a position with a large European service provider as customer design authority for five years. This role focused on planning, designing, implementation, and operation of large contact center solutions that used the NAM/CICM deployment model. Alan has more than 14 years of experience in the communications industry and holds several Cisco voice certifications.

Dedications

Not only is this book dedicated to my family, friends, and pets but also to all those Cisco engineers, customers, and Cisco partners that I have been fortunate to work with during my career.

Acknowledgments

I would like to thank many people for helping me create this book.

The Cisco Press team: Brett Bartow, the executive editor, for taking time to evaluate my original proposal and giving me the opportunity to turn it into a book. Christopher Cleveland, the senior development editor, for providing excellent feedback and getting me back on track as deadlines were looming. Everyone else on the Cisco Press team who have helped convert my ideas, words, and pictures into the book you are reading today. The technical reviewers: As an engineer, it is always frustrating for accidental technical errors to appear in documentation. I therefore greatly appreciate the considerable time and effort that Alan Quinn and Carlos Gonzales have dedicated in performing their technical reviews for this book.

Contents at a Glance

Contents

Icons Used in This Book

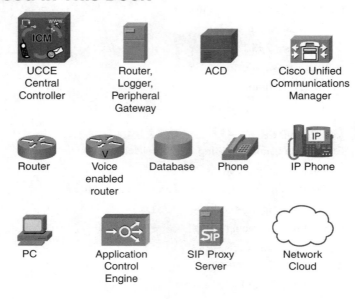

Command Syntax Conventions

The conventions used to present command syntax in this book are the same conventions used in the IOS Command Reference. The Command Reference describes these conventions as follows:

- **Boldface** indicates commands and keywords that are entered literally as shown. In actual configuration examples and output (not general command syntax), boldface indicates commands that are manually input by the user (such as a **show** command).

- *Italic* indicates arguments for which you supply actual values.

- Vertical bars (|) separate alternative, mutually exclusive elements.

- Square brackets ([ ]) indicate an optional element.

- Braces ({ }) indicate a required choice.

- Braces within brackets ([{ }]) indicate a required choice within an optional element.

Introduction

With all the fantastic Cisco documentation available online, why does the world of UCCE need this book? UCCE is such a big topic that it would be easy to think that it is possible to try and cover absolutely everything. Unfortunately, this would turn this book into nothing more than a product reference manual that could potentially be out of date as soon as a new UCCE software version became available. I also feel that I would potentially end up just replicating existing product manuals and reference material already available on Cisco.com.

As I write this section, Cisco has released UCCE 8.5. I actually started writing this book while working on UICM 5.0. It began life as a collection of engineering notes that I would use when deploying UICM with various different legacy ACDs. Many of my earlier notes have been removed because they are not directly applicable to a pure Cisco Unified CM PBX. One thing I have learned during this process is that the majority of tools and techniques I have learned about can be applied to nearly all versions of UCCE. With this in mind, I have also tried to keep this book version-agnostic where possible. As the UCCE product evolves, several great features and enhancements are included. Writing a book about these features runs a risk that the book could become quickly out of date.

UCCE covers many components and applications. Documentation on each individual part can usually be found on Cisco.com. My aim for this manual is to pull together these parts and explain how they can be deployed and used in the real world. To do this, I draw from my experience to detail methods and approaches that I have found to be successful during my career working with UCCE. I am not afraid to say that sometimes I have gotten it wrong. I also highlight the times I did this in the hope that other engineers can learn from my mistakes. I also cover items that I feel have not been covered in enough detail elsewhere, hopefully saving other engineers the time and effort trying to get certain configurations working.

UCCE is a collection of platforms (UICM, Unified CM, CVP, IP IVR, and various other peripheral application servers). I have deliberately kept the focus of this book on the core product and have only touched on the other integrations where essential. I have done this so as not to have too much overlap with several other fantastic books in the Cisco Press catalog.

In the late 1990s, I was fortunate to work at the British Telecom (BT) research laboratories in the U.K. We were busy testing a call-routing platform created by a U.S. company called GeoTel. The GeoTel ICR solution provided an intelligent call-routing platform that could connect various ACD types by multiple vendors. All the call routing and reporting was available in a single common interface.

BT's interest in the GeoTel platform was to modify the platform into one that could be hosted in a service provider environment and allow multitenancy so that the platform could be segregated and allow several customers to be supported on the same hardware.

After the Network ICR (NICR) platform had been created, Cisco stepped in and purchased GeoTel. The number of supported ACD types expanded over time and also started to support the recently acquired Selsius platform, which became Cisco CallManager, or Cisco Unified Communications Manager, as it is known today.

With advances in Voice over IP (VoIP), the Cisco CallManager became the preferred PBX platform to integrate with Cisco ICM. Through various marketing changes, this platform became known as Cisco IPCC.

To support the smaller end of the market, Cisco also released an IPCC Express platform. This solution also uses Cisco CallManager but is a totally different application to IPCC Enterprise. To distinguish the two platforms, IPCC Enterprise was rebranded as UCCE, and IPCC Express became UCCX.

I take a brief look at UCCX in this book, just to point out the differences between it and UCCE. However, the core of this book covers both the enterprise and hosted versions of UCCE.

Objectives of This Book

This book is not a technical design guide, administration manual, or user guide for Cisco UCCE. Although the first few chapters give an overview of various deployments, architectures, and the product history, the goal of this manual is that it should be used by field engineers on customer sites. Technical specifications, designs, and installation instructions can be found in great amounts at Cisco.com. Many of these documents are referenced in this manual, which you should download. This manual has been written to provide you with an engineer's view of how and why to do UCCE things. Plenty of examples are given for configuration and tools that work in the real world. Real-world deployments rarely use the latest versions of software. With this in mind, I have included engineering notes from many different versions of UCCE in case you are maintaining or troubleshooting an old deployment.

Who Should Read This Book

The primary targets for this book are Cisco UCCE deployment and systems engineers installing the platform for end customers. These engineers typically work for Cisco ATP partners. Nearly all these engineers hold several Cisco professional qualifications ranging from CCNA to CCIE. I believe that the required experience level for readers of this book would be a minimum of at least one UCCE deployment, or an end customer that has had experience supporting a UCCE environment.

The secondary target is the actual end customers in charge of day-to-day maintenance and troubleshooting their own platform.

How This Book Is Organized

This book contains 16 chapters that cover the core areas of Cisco Unified Contact Center Enterprise. An overview of each chapter follows:

- **Chapter 1, "Contact Center Overview":** Details an overview of contact center technology and the benefits of Cisco contact center solutions

- **Chapter 2, "Platform Architecture":** Covers the Cisco contact center architecture and its component parts

- **Chapter 3, "Deployment Models":** Discusses the various deployment options available when installing Cisco contact center solutions

- **Chapter 4, "UC Operating Systems":** Covers the different operating systems used by the components that comprise a Cisco contact center

- **Chapter 5, "UCCE Road Map":** Details a historical journey of how UCCE has evolved

- **Chapter 6, "UCCE Platform Deployment":** Documents the stages undertaken when deploying the core UCCE platform

- **Chapter 7, "UCCE Application Configuration":** Provides a step-by-step guide of the application configuration sequence

- **Chapter 8, "Call Routing":** Covers the concepts of routing calls within a contact center environment

- **Chapter 9, "Call Flow Scripting":** Provides a series of best practices that can be followed when developing UCCE call flow scripts

- **Chapter 10, "Reporting":** Details the reporting infrastructure used in UCCE

- **Chapter 11, "Nodes and Processes":** Covers the individual processes that work together to create the core services of UCCE

- **Chapter 12, "Unified CM and IVR":** Details the other Cisco platforms that are integrated with UCCE

- **Chapter 13, "Data-Driven Routing":** Provides a detailed guide about creating database routing within UCCE

- **Chapter 14, "UCCE Databases":** Covers the UCCE database architecture and a series of SQL queries to assist with UCCE configuration

- **Chapter 15, "Management and Administration":** Details several of the UCCE tools available for the UCCE administrator

- **Chapter 16, "Troubleshooting":** Provides a framework that can be implemented when troubleshooting UCCE problems

Chapter 1

Contact Center Overview

This chapter covers the following subjects:

- An overview of the Cisco Contact Center

- An introduction to the benefits and features offered by the Cisco Contact Center

- An understanding of the different products within the Contact Center suite

A call or contact center is often thought of as a centralized office or building with the sole focus on handling customer queries, usually with a high volume of calls typically over the telephone.

The nature of inbound queries varies greatly depending on the type of business operating the contact center, but usually the calls provide product support or information inquiries to the business's customers. Many organizations of various sizes have their own contact center, with the number of agents ranging from a handful to several thousand employees. Some of the organizations that do not have their own contact center or require additional capacity outsource their contact center needs to a third party. This third party handles customer calls as if it were part of the original company.

Most major organizations use contact centers to interact with their customers. In addition to handling inbound calls, many contact centers offer their customers a wide range of options for contacting them. Email, web collaboration, instant messaging (IM), fax, and video chat are all gaining popularity as the acceptance of residential broadband connectivity with higher connection speeds and bandwidth availability becomes more widespread.

In addition to inbound contact, some contact centers also perform outbound calling. For example, telemarketing operations call existing and prospective clients to offer new products and services. Technologies such as Short Message Service (SMS) text messaging have also proved to be popular as a less-intrusive form of outbound contact.

Historically, many contact centers have been built using traditional private branch exchange (PBX) equipment which, over time, has been enhanced and upgraded to what is now referred to as an Automatic Call Distributor (ACD). The ACD is a platform that can handle incoming calls and distribute them to specific groups or teams of agents within the contact center. The calls are usually routed depending on business logic programmed into the ACD. Logical groupings of agents can be defined depending on the business functions that they can offer. For example, a small business could offer its callers two inbound phone numbers. One number reaches agents in the support team, and the second number could be delivered to the sales department. Agents can be selected to receive the calls based on various metrics or formulas. Two of the most popular methods for distributing calls are as follows:

- **Longest available agent (LAA):** This method selects the agent from a skill group that has been sitting idle for the longest period of time. LAA is often considered to be a fair call distribution method in favor of the agents as calls are delivered to the agents who have the longest time period since handling their last call.

- **Minimum expected delay:** This call distribution method could be used when all the agents are currently busy and the caller needs to be queued against a single skill group. The contact center platform would calculate, from short-term historic values of handling times, what the expected delay could potentially be for each skill group. Assuming that each of the skill groups would handle the call effectively, it would be beneficial to the caller to deliver the call to the skill group with the smallest expect delay value.

Many vendors exist that manufacture ACD equipment. Traditionally, the majority of ACD equipment was built around proprietary hardware and software, with the only level of integration being through standards-based telephony protocols such as Integrated Services Digital Network (ISDN). With the emergence of Voice over IP (VoIP) in the last decade, many vendors have redeveloped their platforms to support IP and the various standards-based protocols offered, such as ITU-T H.323 and Session Initiation Protocol (SIP). In addition to this integration, the vendors have also opened interfaces, or application programming interfaces (API), to allow third-party organizations to develop additional products providing enhanced and advanced features.

As organizations grow through expansion or acquisition, many find themselves with several contact centers distributed over multiple geographic locations. With voice and data connectivity between these locations, several companies look to enhance their existing investment in their current platform by creating a virtualized contact center over many sites, including many different ACD types. With the current shift toward VoIP, many enterprise customers seek to renew or replace their time-division multiplexing (TDM) equipment with IP-based contact centers before the support contracts expire on their TDM platform.

After an IP contact center has been implemented, the next step for many organizations is that of business transformation. With the use of intelligent endpoints offering integration with many back-end systems or existing business processes, business transformation not only seeks to reduce costs but also to enable users to be more productive. A large proportion of contact centers uses only a small percentage of the platform's capability. By leveraging existing functionality not currently in use, both end-user productivity and customer satisfaction can be increased.

Contact Center Characteristics

Cisco has a strong track record in providing robust and scalable data network infrastructure and applications. With the acquisition of GeoTel in the late 1990s, Cisco branched out into ACD technology. Through further acquisition and a strong in-house product team, Cisco has an extensive voice product suite and impressive network virtualization strategy that provide the following benefits:

- **Self-service:** Enabling the customers to manage their interaction with the business without requiring human intervention not only reduces the payroll expense for the company but also has many additional benefits, including removing the repetitive and mundane calls from the agents.

- **Dual-tone multifrequency (DTMF) touchtone:** This is the most popular technology used for self-service, but speech recognition has been widely adopted as the performance and recognition capabilities of speech platform have increased. The use of extensible markup language (XML), and in particular VoiceXML (VXML), has also enabled organizations to develop a single back-end platform that can be accessed through many user interfaces. For example, a web page and self-service Interactive Voice Response (IVR) script both have different user interfaces but can connect to a single back-end system through VXML-capable middleware.

- **Call control:** To provide feature-reach telephony platforms offering the functionality expected by end customers, Cisco developed a series of protocols to enable IP phone and voice gateway connectivity. Skinny Client Control Protocol (SCCP)—also known as Skinny—and MGCP (Media Gateway Control Protocol) are still in use today but are also joined by SIP. H.323 has also been supported in gateways since the early versions of the Cisco platforms.

- **Call routing:** An essential requirement of any contact center is the capability to route calls. Having the capability to route calls over multiple vendors, multiple sites, and based on complex business policies demonstrates a scalable platform.

- **Video calls:** The capability to provide a human touch is essential to the success of a contact center's role in customer service. With the advent of video technology, some organizations offer video kiosks to enable the caller to have a face-to-face videoconference with a representative of the company. The kiosk can be located at a branch office or even a remote location over a network. As well as providing face-to-face conversation, the kiosks can also be used as video self-service or enable an agent to "push" prerecorded video to the kiosk to assist the customer.

- **Presence:** Although first-time call resolution is a great measure of customer satisfaction, it is inevitable that a portion of calls need to be transferred elsewhere within the organization. Having the ability to see the real-time status of colleagues or experts, or even using instant messaging to chat to them before attempting to transfer a call can greatly reduce the amount of handoffs experienced by the caller. Federation also provides the ability to extend contact to organizations or staff outside the contact center.

- **Interoperability:** No vendor can be expected to provide the entire stack of applications to do the tasks required by the business for the contact center. Many vendors have comprehensive partnership and development programs with published APIs into the contact center products to enable third-party vendors to provide enhanced applications. This interoperability includes functions such as customer relationship management (CRM) software, IVR, workforce management, and voice recording.

- **Reporting:** Without the visibility of the contact center as a whole, it would be impossible to understand how the business can achieve customer satisfaction. Management information is an essential tool for any contact center manager to visualize performance and ensure that key performance indicators (KPI) are being achieved. A good reporting platform tracks all contact from start to end, also termed *cradle to grave*.

Contact Channels

Traditionally, call centers offered only limited methods of getting in touch with an organization. Although customer contact over the telephone is still the most popular method, various other media channels are now available to enable customers to reach out to the contact center. Many variations of voice contact have emerged in addition to traditional landline circuits, cell phones, Internet-based voice such as Skype, or SIP-based services. These emerging media channels are instant messaging, video chat, email, web collaboration, and fax.

Web collaboration is currently used by many organizations on their support and sales web portals. The sales teams use it to reach out to potential customers currently browsing the companies' websites to answer questions with a personal touch and guide the customer, eventually to a point where the customer is informed enough to make a purchasing decision. The support teams find collaboration useful to guide existing customers to find specific resources that can solve their issues in a prompt and efficient manner, thus improving customer satisfaction.

All channels connect back to individuals or groups of people in the organization. The front-line staff that usually handles these contacts can be the on-site agents or shop retail staff. Providing location flexibility for these staff is important and easily achieved with technology, allowing the agents to be home- or mobile-based. Location independence also comes into play if you have remote resource, such as at a branch office, that you would like to become part of the virtualized team. The ability to provide the same technology and contact handling regardless of location can also become beneficial during disaster scenarios. A second tier of staff also exists for assisting the front-line staff with queries or problems outside of their knowledge base. This is where the experts are used. These knowledge workers are not typically the first responders in the same way as the front-line staff, but are available, perhaps on an ad hoc basis, to assist where possible.

Cisco Contact Center Features

The suite of products within the Cisco Contact Center portfolio offers a wide range of features available to customers. This product suite meets the traditional requirements of call handling with the advanced features available from an IP-based solution.

The features offered include the following:

- Contact center virtualization

- Feature-rich agent and supervisor desktop controls

- Computer Telephony Integration (CTI) and CRM integration

- A choice of client software for call control

- Knowledge worker functionality

- Support for remote and mobile agents

- IVR self-service and call-treatment capabilities

- Reporting

- Platform management portal

- Outbound option

- Third-party integration

The sections that follow cover these features/products in greater detail.

Virtual Contact Center

Cisco Unified Contact Center coordinates an agent's ability to work on multiple simultaneous tasks from various channels (voice, email, and chat) while allowing the agent to be interrupted with high-priority tasks, if required. For example, an agent can handle multiple chat sessions at the same time, or tasks from different channels such as responding to an email inquiry at the same time as handling a voice call. In this way, Cisco Unified Contact Center can optimize the agent's time, helping to allow the maximum amount of customer contact with the resources available.

Cisco Agent Desktop with Presence

Presence information provides a real-time status indicator that displays the ability and willingness of a colleague for communication. Popularized through many of the instant messaging chat clients, the user can publish his presence state, such as Available, Busy, or Away, allowing other presence users to instantly see the person's availability.

Integrating Cisco Agent Desktop with presence extends real-time collaboration into the broader enterprise. Through this integration, agents and supervisors can collaborate with relevant colleagues and subject matter experts outside the contact center. For efficiency and convenience, the contact center defines the view to show only the colleagues who are appropriate for agents to access.

Presence information has also proved popular with front-line telephony users or reception staff that handle a large number of calls requiring transfer to another party. Seeing the presence state of a user allows the transferring party to better handle the call and provide meaningful information back to the caller, such as providing the caller with the option to leave a voicemail if the party is away or even providing a time that the party will return.

CTI and CRM Integration

CTI is a key driver in enabling business efficiency and improving customer satisfaction. Forcing a caller to repeat account information when transferring calls, not having access to his customer records or call history, and having no awareness of simple details such as the time spent in queue before he was answered are surefire ways of annoying callers and leaving them with a bad impression.

Cisco Unified Contact Center provides a wide range of tools and features to perform CTI. The call-routing platform and Agent Desktop combine to provide the agent with enterprise-wide call-event and customer-provided data. This data is screen-popped to the agent on call delivery, providing the agent with all the required information before she answers the call.

Customer Relationship Management (CRM) integration takes CTI to the next level by further improving efficiency and therefore reducing costs. Cisco provides a range of CRM connectors for many of the popular third-party CRM applications, including Siebel, SAP, Salesforce.com, and Microsoft CRM. CRM integration enables the agent to use a single CRM screen with all the telephony controls embedded into it. The agents therefore log in, control their state, and perform all call handling through a single user interface. When a new call arrives, a screen pop appears in the CRM application displaying all the caller's account information retrieved from the CRM database, perhaps based on the caller's Automatic Number Identification (ANI) or account number collected from an IVR. Enabling account data and call control to occur in the same screen saves the agent time that would be spent double-typing information into various desktop applications, thus reducing call-handling times and improving efficiency.

Agent Desktop Options

Cisco Unified Contact Center offers a variety of desktop options for contact center agents, including the following:

- **Cisco IP Phone Agent:** IP Phone Agent provides basic ACD functions on a Cisco Unified IP Phone, and in many cases, it eliminates the need for installing an agent desktop on the agent's PC.

- **Cisco Agent Desktop (CAD):** Cisco Agent Desktop provides built-in agent desktop capabilities that allow agents to perform call-control functions directly from their desktops. CAD offers an out-of-the-box, rapid, easy, low-risk deployment. Desktop workflow and screen pop are natively provided functions that do not require the skills of a development team. CAD also supports presence and web browser integration.

- **Cisco CTI OS Toolkit Desktop:** The CTI OS Toolkit Desktop is available for companies that require specialized, custom desktop capabilities tailored to meet the specific needs of their contact center operations. The CTI OS custom development kit simplifies custom CTI integrations as it provides support for many different programming languages through its software development kit (SDK). The toolkit comes with a compiled agent and supervisor desktop. These are not actually meant to be deployed because they are a basic example of what can be achieved with the toolkit; however, many organizations use them as an initial deployment before rolling out a custom CTI OS desktop at a later date.

- **Pre-integrated CRM desktop:** This is a strategic integration with the leading CRM vendors including Salesforce.com and Siebel. Pre-integrated desktops save customers time and effort that would have been spent performing CTI development.

Cisco Unified Expert Advisor

Many contact centers require the capability to provide agents with the backup skill available from a product specialist or knowledge worker. These specialists typically have work activities other than providing assistance to customers, so the contact center platform requires the capability for the knowledge worker to handle incoming customer calls without the need for them to conform to the rigid business rules of the contact center. Cisco Unified Expert Advisor provides this facility through the use of a presence desktop application, allowing contact center agents to see the experts' availability.

Call context data can be transferred between the agent and the knowledge worker through the creation of specific URLs that can link to data with a CRM system to access all the caller information and call history.

Using knowledge workers throughout the enterprise can improve first-call resolution and hence increase customer satisfaction.

Support for Remote and Mobile Agents

Cisco Unified Mobile Agent enables the contact center to include temporary and remote agents in the business during high-volume periods.

Mobile Agent allows you to use clients irrespective of geographic location. They don't have to be extensions of the Cisco Unified Communications Manager (Unified CM) cluster. They can be on a third-party ACD or even a plain old telephone service (POTS) line at home or a cell phone. All the call control is performed through a desktop client that supports both CAD and CTI OS. When an agent logs in, he provides a contact phone number to which he would like the contact center to deliver the calls. Mobile Agent is also great for use in disaster scenarios or situations where the calls need to be delivered to a system or phone line where no peripheral gateway (PG) connectivity is present. The Mobile Agents are reported active, just as if they are in any other standard contact center agent.

Cisco Unified Mobile Agent adds the capability to bring temporary agents online during seasonal high call volume with reduced startup costs. Agents can choose their destination phone number during signup time and change the number as often as they want, providing both the contact center and the agent with total flexibility.

Self-Service and Call-Treatment Capabilities

Cisco Unified Contact Center offers two options for self-service and call treatment:

- **Cisco Unified IP Interactive Voice Response:** Cisco Unified IP IVR facilitates self-service applications, such as access to bank account information or voice menus, by processing user requests through touchtone input or speech-recognition technologies. Customers can use voice commands to retrieve the information they require without ever speaking with an agent, or to quickly navigate to the correct department or agent who can help them.

- **Cisco Unified Customer Voice Portal:** Cisco Unified Customer Voice Portal (CVP) operates with both TDM and IP-based contact centers to provide a call-management and call-treatment solution with a self-service IVR option that can use information available to customers on the corporate web server.

Note   For example, with Unified CVP, customers can pay a bill, order products and track delivery, locate a dealer, schedule a pickup, change name and address information, make travel arrangements, check payment status, receive notification of unusual activity, or request literature or product information.

Reporting

The Cisco Unified Contact Center solution provides real-time and historical data necessary for contact center reporting. The reporting function provides accurate and timely reports on contact center activity, helping managers make informed decisions regarding staffing levels and contact handling. Standard reporting templates provide automatically operational functions for common reporting needs. Custom reports can extend the standard reporting package to meet specific reporting needs. Reporting data can be exported to external data warehouse environments or analysis tools.

Cisco acquired the company Latigent that created an advanced reporting application, which Cisco rebranded as the Cisco Unified Intelligence Center (CUIC). CUIC provides a single environment for developing ad hoc reports. Users/supervisors also have some flexibility in tailoring the reports. CUIC does not require the same level of expertise to create the reports as with some other reporting packages.

In addition to CUIC, Cisco also has an integrated reporting tool called WebView. WebView has been available since the early versions of Cisco Unified Contact Center

Enterprise (UCCE) and provides a comprehensive range of more than 200 out-of-the-box reporting templates. Custom templates can also be created using Sybase InfoMaker, which is a report generation tool similar to the popular Crystal Reports application.

Over time, the presentation layer of CUIC will replace WebView.

Management Portal

The Cisco Unified Contact Center Management Portal (CCMP) provides the contact center management team with an intuitive web-based administrative interface to facilitate day-to-day tasks. The CCMP interface is aimed at the user who needs to complete common administrative tasks such as adds, moves, and changes of various configurable items including agents, skill groups, phones, and teams.

CCMP not only configures UCCE elements but can also configure some Unified CM end devices such as IP phones.

CCMP is a partitioned system that can support multiple business units with complete autonomy and offers hierarchical administration to support multiple business-level users with specific roles and responsibilities. CCMP provides audit trail reports detailing all configuration changes and usage of the management portal.

Cisco Contact Center Portfolio

The Cisco Unified Contact Center product portfolio (see Figure 1-1) is composed of several platforms of which Cisco UCCE is actually a product suite. To better understand the product placement within the portfolio, it is important to understand the solutions that are available, and then further see how they can be broken down into their component parts.

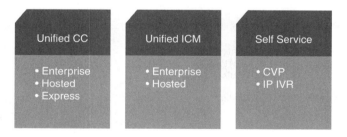

Figure 1-1   *Cisco Contact Center Product Suite*

The three solutions available in the contact center portfolio are based upon sizing:

- **Single-site ACD:** For an organization with a single site and a small number of agents, the Cisco Unified Contact Center Express (UCCX) platform is preferred.

- **Multisite ACD:** Should the organization have multiple sites or require a virtualized platform, the Cisco Unified Contact Center Enterprise (UCCE) for VoIP or Cisco Unified Intelligent Contact Manager (UICM) for TDM platforms are often used.

- **Hosted ACD:** Cisco Unified Contact Center Hosted is typically aimed at service providers to enable multitenant platforms for its customers, but it is also used by some large enterprise customers to provide segregation among several business entities where routing, reporting, and security need to be kept independent.

Before getting into a detailed breakdown, it is important to be aware that as of Cisco Contact Center release 7.0, the following name changes were introduced. However, the name changes have not yet been consistently integrated into the documentation set or the software:

- Cisco Intelligent Contact Management Enterprise Edition is renamed *Cisco Unified Intelligent Contact Management Enterprise (Unified ICME)*.

- Cisco Intelligent Contact Management Hosted Edition is renamed *Cisco Unified Intelligent Contact Management Hosted (Unified ICMH)*.

- Cisco IP Contact Center (IPCC) Enterprise Edition and Cisco IPCC Hosted Edition are renamed *Cisco Unified Contact Center Enterprise (Unified CCE)* and *Cisco Unified Contact Center Hosted (Unified CCH)*, respectively. Cisco System IPCC is renamed *Cisco Unified System Contact Center Enterprise (Unified SCCE)*.

The use of the generic abbreviation *ICM* is intended to include both Unified ICMH and Unified ICME.

The use of the generic abbreviation *CC* in this document is intended to include Unified CCH, Unified CCE, and Unified SCCE, but not Unified Contact Center Express (Unified CCX).

It is important to understand what makes Unified CC different from Unified ICM, and also to understand the demarcation between Enterprise and Hosted. If you disregard UCCX initially as this is a totally different product, you quickly realize that the following three products share the same code base:

- Cisco Unified Contact Center Enterprise

- Cisco Unified Contact Center Hosted

- Cisco Unified ICM Enterprise

The product name is allocated depending on the ACD technology used in the deployment and whether the product is being deployed in a hosted environment.

Unified Contact Center Enterprise (UCCE) and Unified Intelligent Contact Manager Enterprise (UICME) are deployed in similar enterprise situations. The difference between these two products is that UCCE is deployed with the Cisco Unified Communications Manager IP-based PBX, whereas UICME is typically deployed on legacy ACD environments.

A similar product definition could exist for both Unified Contact Center Hosted and Unified Intelligent Contact Manager Hosted. In theory, the former platform would be purely for hosted Unified CM servers and the latter for a mixture of legacy ACD types.

In reality, most hosted service providers actually have a single platform that supports a mix of both Unified CM and legacy ACDs. Some instances of where a pure Unified Contact Center Hosted is deployed are usually for relatively new service providers or out-sourcers looking to provide a pure IP-based multitenant platform. This is because the new hosted platforms usually do not have any old legacy ACD equipment to support, so choose an IP PBX and build up from a greenfield site. A *greenfield site* is generally considered to be a new office or building that the organization moves to during relocation.

Cisco Unified Contact Center Express

As previously mentioned, the entire line of contact center models shares a similar code base with the exception of UCCX. UCCX is a different product aimed at a much smaller-sized contact center deployment. The characteristics of UCCX are as follows:

- Designed for midmarket, enterprise branch, or corporate departments, UCCX provides a sophisticated customer interaction solution for up to 300 agents.

- UCCX can be installed as part of a UCCE solution using the parent/child model.

- Earlier versions of UCCX were frequently deployed as coresident solutions with Unified CM. However, since version 5.0 of Unified CM, the Unified CM platform has ported to a Linux-based appliance model, so a minimum of a two-server solution is now required.

- UCCX also supports Cisco Unified Communications Manager Express (CUCME), which is not supported by UCCE.

- Sharing a similar agent desktop to one of the available desktops to UCCE, UCCX provides an agent environment that is almost cross-platform, enabling experienced agents to work on either UCCE or UCCX without a great deal of adjustment.

- Although UCCX supports both the Cisco Agent Desktop and the IP Phone Agent, it does not come with a development toolkit for CTI OS SDK.

Cisco Unified Contact Center Enterprise

Cisco UCCE is a highly evolved, best-of-breed, advanced contact center routing platform. UCCE is actually a suite of products because UCCE comprises several Cisco solutions, including the following:

- Cisco Unified Intelligent Contact Management (Unified ICM)

- Cisco Unified Communications Manager (Unified CM)

- Cisco IP Interactive Voice Response (Unified IP IVR)

- Cisco Unified Customer Voice Portal (Unified CVP)

In addition to the preceding applications, a Cisco network infrastructure, including Cisco voice gateways and IP Phones, is also required to support these products.

Cisco Unified Contact Center Hosted

Cisco Unified Contact Center Hosted is suitable for both large enterprise companies and service providers. It also works well for outsourced contact centers that host several of their customers on a single platform. For enterprise companies with multiple branches or divisions, the value is a centralized contact center infrastructure that can offer services to remote locations. For incumbent service providers and new service carriers, the product creates a new, high-margin service revenue stream. The service provider hosts the contact center infrastructure software, which is shared by multiple customers (multitenancy) in its central office or data center. Subscribing customers can have IP or TDM infrastructures, or a combination of the two.

UICMH is a high-capacity, high-reliability network service platform that offers a wide range of services for IP- and TDM-based networks. Its services include traditional intelligent-network routing, IVR, and network-queuing services to Cisco Unified Intelligent Contact Management platforms of service provider customers or enterprise branch offices. Therefore, UICMH functions much like a service control point (SCP) to a full set of hosted contact center features. You can integrate UICMH with existing TDM, ACD, and IVR equipment in addition to Cisco Unified CM and Cisco Unified CVP.

UICMH has been deployed in high-capacity carrier environments since 1997 and has proven its capability to handle millions of calls every day. It delivers an excellent service value today as part of a UICMH solution and facilitates a smooth transition to other IP-based voice services.

One of the many early advantages for end customers of using a hosted TDM platform was the ability to preroute calls in the service provider network before delivering them to the most suitable site. Before the advent of voice and data convergence, prerouting in the service provider's network gave multisite contact centers a distinct cost savings normally associated with secondary routing. For example, without prerouting, a two-site contact center has no way of informing the carrier's network of agent or resource availability at its contact center sites. Inbound calls would typically be delivered to each of the sites based on a static percentage split, that is, 50 percent of inbound calls delivered to site A and the remaining 50 percent delivered to site B. Should a call arrive at one of these sites without available resources, the call could either be queued until the next free agent can take the call or it could be automatically rerouted over a tie line between the sites. Even with this routing in place, it does not mean that the other site has free resources to handle the call.

Prerouting changed this poor call handling by providing a mechanism whereby the service provider's intelligent network has visibility of the resources at each site. This was made possible through the use of a UICMH platform in the network obtaining a real-time data feed from a peripheral gateway installed at the customer's site. The ACDs provide the PG with resourcing information that is sent back to the UICMH platform, allowing the service provider's intelligent network (IN) to make a decision about which site to route the call to.

Delivering the call to a site that had free resources, or had agents likely to become available in the shortest period of time, allows the customer to reduce the amount of intersite voice traffic and therefore reduces the number of tie lines required between their sites. For customers with more than three sites, large cost savings can be achieved.

Cisco Unified Intelligent Contact Manager Enterprise

Cisco UICME has the same code base as UCCE. The main difference of UICME over UCCE is that UICME provides an abstraction layer for many different TDM-based ACDs. Cisco UICME was the precursor to UCCE.

Cisco UICME is pitched at the contact center that uses one or more legacy ACDs. By legacy ACD, Cisco is actually referring to any non-Unified CM ACD or PBX. Because of the abstraction layer provided by the peripheral gateway, several different ACD types can be connected by a single UICM platform. This was the original design intention of the platform many years ago—to connect several disparate ACD types into a single routing and reporting interface to be used throughout the enterprise.

As the UICME product has evolved, various different ACD types, vendors, and models have been supported and withdrawn. A popular current use of UICME is for organizations wanting to migrate from their legacy ACD to UCCE. Several enterprise organizations have many different ACD types. This usually comes about because the ACDs have been purchased from various vendors over a long period of time depending on pricing and functionality available at the time. Each vendor has a different management and reporting interface for the business and technology teams to learn. UICME provides a common interface over the different ACDs for reporting and configuration. After UICME has been deployed and successfully integrated with the organization's ACDs, the next step for migration is typically the deployment of Unified CM and its subsequent integration with UICME. Many organizations then take a phased approach to slowly migrate legacy ACD handsets across to IP endpoints.

Cisco Unified IP IVR

Cisco Unified IP IVR is a software-based IVR system that processes IP streams routed to it by the Unified CM and UCCE. These streams typically take the form of contact center queue announcements, prompt and collect menu structures, and self-service applications.

Unified IP IVR has an open and extensible architecture allowing the developer to incorporate out-of-the-box and custom-developed Java classes. This enables a wide range of scalable and portable applications to be developed to meet business needs.

Unified IP IVR was the IP IVR of choice before Unified CVP was introduced into the product suite. It is still a popular IVR choice today and is typically chosen over CVP when single-site platforms are being deployed, or when a low IVR port density is required.

Cisco Unified Customer Voice Portal

Cisco Unified Customer Voice Portal (CVP) integrates with both TDM- and IP-based contact centers to provide a call-management and call-treatment solution with a self-service IVR option that can use information available on the corporate web server. With support for ASR and Text-To-Speech (TTS) capabilities, callers can obtain personalized answers to their questions and can conduct business in new ways—all without the costs of interacting with a live agent.

To protect existing investments in contact center technology assets, you can deploy CVP in both TDM and IP contact centers. More important, you can deploy the application in a hybrid environment that many businesses have as they migrate their telephony networks to a common converged environment for data, voice, and video traffic. Thus when agent assistance is required, CVP can easily provide call-routing and -transfer services over either TDM or IP to route calls to the best location and resource to handle the inquiry.

CVP includes support for agent queuing and multisite call-switching capabilities that use standard Internet technologies to provide a smooth customer experience, even when transferring calls between multiple locations. With support for the UICME and UCCE, CVP delivers self-service as part of a comprehensive customer-contact strategy that attracts customers by providing unique, personalized interactions.

Used with UCCE, CVP is often seen as an advanced IVR and queuing solution that comprises a carrier-grade platform that can scale to support a high IVR port density. Expanding beyond the functionality provided by IP IVR, CVP delivers both voice and video self-service applications. CVP provides callers with touchtone and speech recognition.

In comparison with IP IVR, CVP has a greater degree of complexity and cost but also provides greater scalability and redundancy. Because of the distributed architecture of CVP, one of its often-used features is the capability to handle and queue calls on the network edge (or most efficient location) through the use of a voice browser.

CVP can also be deployed as a standalone IVR without the need to rely on UCCE. It can also be deployed *in front* of an ACD.

CVP applications are created using Unified Call Studio, which is an integrated development environment (IDE) based on Eclipse. The IDE offers a drag-and-drop user interface.

Other Voice Components

Although this book focuses on only the application layer of UCCE, it is also important to understand the other essential voice components required for a UCCE deployment:

- **Cisco Unified Communications Manager:** More than just an IP PBX, the Cisco Unified Communications Manager (Unified CM) is a powerful call-processing platform that is both scalable and distributable. The Unified CM solution supports voice and video at its core and also has a suite of management and third-party tools to provide a rich telephony platform.

  An essential part of UCCE, Unified CM is a powerful call-processing platform that is both scalable and distributable. The Unified CM solution supports voice and video and also has a suite of management and third-party tools to provide a rich telephony platform. Unified CM provides the underlying telephony delivery that UCCE takes advantage of to enable a higher layer of intelligent routing.

- **LAN/WAN architecture:** A key part of voice and data convergence is the underlying network infrastructure needed to support the voice, video, and signaling traffic. IP telephony places strict requirements on network characteristics such as packet loss, delay, and jitter to ensure that voice and video quality is achieved; therefore, you need to deploy quality of service (QoS) mechanisms on the routers and switches throughout the network. As well as server and application redundancy, you can achieve network redundancy through the duplication of devices and links that provide quick network convergence and adaptability or rapid convergence should a topology change occur.

- **Voice gateways:** Providing connections to other organizations, voice gateways allow the enterprise to connect to the outside world. Various types of voice gateways exist. The functionality provided relies on the voice modules configured in the voice gateway. T1/E1/FXO cards are usually connected to the PSTN or other switch types. FXS modules can be used to connect to internal telephony endpoints such as fax machines. IOS configuration allows SIP trunks to connect.

- **UC endpoints:** Unified Communications endpoints are user devices such as a deskphone, a softphone application running on a client PC, or even a video camera connected to the phone and PC for videoconferencing. IP handsets have all the functionality you would expect from a normal telephone but also include advanced functionality such as directory applications and presence running on the phone.

Summary

This chapter has provided a high-level overview of some of the features and platforms that comprise the Cisco Contact Center suite. Although you know that these products share the same code base, you have learned that they have a different focus depending on the end customer's telephony requirements:

- **Cisco Unified Intelligent Contact Manager Enterprise (UICME):** Aimed at customers who have one or more legacy ACDs within their enterprise. Typically, it is for customers who are looking to implement a unified management and reporting interface as an abstraction layer over their existing ACD and IVR equipment. Implementing Cisco UICME is also a common path for customers wanting to migrate to VoIP while still benefiting from their legacy investment.

- **Cisco Unified Contact Center Hosted (UCCH):** Aimed at the customer who wants to outsource his telephony and/or contact center technology to a third party, typically a network telephony carrier. The hosting company provides all the hardware and software to deliver and manage the platform, whereas the customer pays for and benefits from a managed solution.

- **Cisco Unified Contact Center Enterprise (UCCE):** An enterprise solution aimed at the customer who wants to use a VoIP contact center based around the Cisco Unified Communications Manager IP PBX. This solution is the most popular Cisco contact center deployment model and is the focus of the remainder of this book.

Chapter 2

Platform Architecture

This chapter covers the following subjects:

■ An overview of the low-level Cisco Unified Contact Center Enterprise (UCCE) architecture

■ Details about the software components of Cisco UCCE

■ How platform redundancy is achieved

In Chapter 1, "Contact Center Overview," you learned that the enterprise and hosted versions of the contact center products all share a similar code base and that they take their
product name depending on whether they are integrated with a legacy Automatic Call
Distributor (ACD) or Cisco Unified Communications Manager (Unified CM). In this
chapter, you look at a breakdown of the platform architecture into its logical components
to achieve a greater understanding of the individual software components for the solution.

General Cisco Unified Contact Center Architecture

Several components of the contact center architecture are shared between each of the
platform types and are used regardless of the deployment model. Figure 2-1 shows a
generic platform architecture.

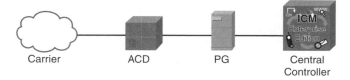

Figure 2-1   *Cisco Unified Contact Center (UCC) Generic Architecture*

Router

The router process is the heart of the contact center platform and is responsible for making decisions on how to route the customer contact throughout the organization. The router holds a real-time view of all the contact center resources to allow instant routing decisions to be made. The real-time view is created by the router gathering real-time data from the peripheral gateway (PG) and combining this information with the configuration data retrieved from the logger database. The router process retains all the information in run-time memory to enable fast processing of call-routing requests.

Logger

The logger process controls access to the underlying Structured Query Language (SQL) databases on the logger servers. These databases contain all the contact center configuration information. The logger is also responsible for replicating data out to the Historical Data Server (HDS).

Figure 2-2 shows a router and logger with their two network connections.

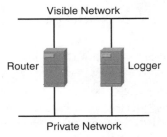

Figure 2-2   *Colocated Router and Logger*

> **Note**   The router and logger processes are often referred to as the *central controllers*. For smaller deployments, they are usually deployed in a coresident fashion. When a router and logger process is colocated on the same server, it is referred to as a *rogger*.

Administrative Workstation/Real-Time Distributor and Client AW

To configure the platform, an admin workstation (AW) or client AW is used. When installing the contact center platform, at least one server is configured as a real-time distributor. The real-time distributor also has a configuration database synchronized with the logger, and call center status is fed from the router to the distributor in real-time. This real-time update to the distributor is used for tasks including real-time reporting and monitoring of call flow scripts. The AW can be located at any central or remote site. It allows administrative users to monitor call handling through the system and allows the user to make changes to configuration data and the routing scripts.

As shown in Figure 2-3, a second type of AW is also available. The client AW does not have its own database but connects to the real-time distributor to obtain and update configuration and UCCE events. When a configuration change is made on a client AW, the client AW retrieves the configuration from the distributor. The change is then written directly to the central controller. The router process then informs all the distributors of this change.

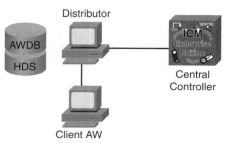

Figure 2-3   *Administrative Workstation and Client AW*

The AW is not a duplex system because it is not critical to the routing of calls. However, many deployments have multiple AWs, not just for redundancy but also to allow multiple users to have simultaneous access. In recent versions of UCCE, Cisco also supports the virtualization of client AWs.

Historical Data Server

Another component with an SQL database is the Historical Data Server (HDS). The HDS is a required component for reporting using WebView or the Unified Intelligence Center. The HDS uses a real-time distributor process to obtain reporting information from the logger. Typically, the logger is configured to store approximately 30 days worth of call records, and the HDS is configured to store several years worth of reporting data.

Figure 2-4 shows two AW HDS servers connected to a duplex Unified Intelligent Contact Management (UICM) platform.

Figure 2-4   *Historical Data Server*

Peripheral Gateway

The peripheral gateways (PG) provide an abstraction layer between the central controllers (router and logger) and the peripherals to which the central controller is connected. Examples of peripherals include ACDs, private branch exchange (PBX), and Interactive Voice Response (IVR), as illustrated in Figure 2-5 and Figure 2-6. The PG converts the proprietary communications from the peripheral into the protocol used by Cisco and vice versa. The PG is capable of sending route requests to the central controller and also receiving a route response in return. The PG has a real-time connection to the peripheral and is aware of calls in progress and agent availability or status. Many of the processes running on the PG are generic and used regardless of the type of peripheral connected. The process in the Peripheral Interface Manager is specific to the peripheral and manages the route request and route response between the peripheral and the central controller. Chapter 11, "Nodes and Processes," presents a breakdown of the subprocesses within a peripheral gateway in more detail. The PG is typically located at the same site with the

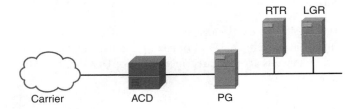

Figure 2-5 *Peripheral Gateway Connected to a Time-Division Multiplexing (TDM) ACD*

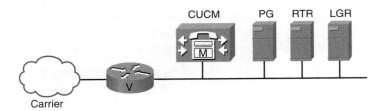

Figure 2-6 *Peripheral Gateway Connected to a Unified CM Cluster*

ACD, and it does not have to be deployed as a duplex pair; however, it often is for fault tolerance reasons. Two PGs work together, with one PG having an active connection to the peripheral and the other PG being in an idle state. Should a fault occur, such as a hardware or network error with the active PG, the idle PG becomes active and maintains the connection to the peripheral.

CTI Server (Including CTI Object Server)

The Computer Telephony Integration (CTI) server process works with the peripheral gateway to collect and control the various functions provided at the agent desktop, as illustrated in Figure 2-7. In early versions of Cisco Intelligent Contact Manager (ICM), applications would interface directly to the CTI server through IP socket applications developed against the CTI server application programming interface (API). In more recent versions, Cisco released CTI Object Server (OS) and provided an object server and suite of dynamic link libraries (DLL) that can be developed against many popular programming languages including C++ and Java. All agent desktop software and applications requiring a CTI interface (including workforce management and call variables for voice recording) are now connected through the CTI OS rather than directly to the CTI server.

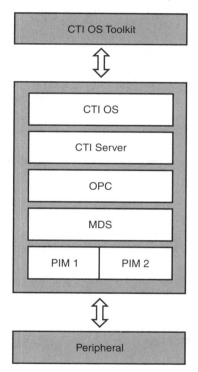

Figure 2-7 *CTI Server Architecture*

Reporting (WebView and CUIC)

Management Information is a critical component of any contact center. Reporting is used to provide a *window* into the business so that analysts and business managers can establish a clear picture of how the contact center is performing. Early versions of Cisco ICM provided a tool called Monitor ICR to perform this reporting function. Monitor ICR was replaced with Cisco WebView. WebView has undergone a series of changes over the years to provide a more robust and comprehensive reporting environment. WebView can be installed coresident on the HDS server, or it can be deployed as a standalone web server to achieve higher scalability, as shown in Figure 2-8.

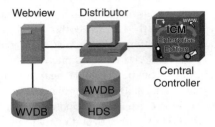

Figure 2-8 *WebView Server*

Differing from WebView, Cisco Unified Intelligence Center (CUIC) provides a flexible reporting portal that enables dashboard-style reports from multiple reporting sources. For example, contact center statistics can be combined with Customer Relationship Management (CRM) data in a single report. The reporting Web 2.0 framework enables flexibility in the report layout to include prebuilt controls, grids, gauges, and Really Simple Syndication (RSS) feeds. The suite consists of two components, both of which require their own standalone server:

■ **Intelligence Center Premium:** Provides the web-based interface for configuring the reports

■ **Archiver data repository:** An external Microsoft SQL database that enables connections to multiple data sources

When developing custom reports, WebView requires a developer or employee with strong SQL skills to create the custom reports using Sybase InfoMaker. The interface provided with CUIC is more business user-friendly, enabling custom reports to be created by users with only an intermediate knowledge of reporting.

Network Interface Controller

The network interface controller (NIC) is used only when the platform connects to a carrier, as illustrated in Figure 2-9. The NIC enables real-time access to the carrier's service control point (SCP).

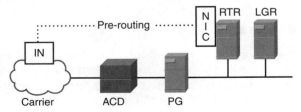

Figure 2-9 *Network Interface Controller*

Cisco UCCE

In comparing the Cisco UCCE and generic architectures, the main difference is that an IP PBX is used; in particular, the IP PBX is the Cisco Unified Communications Manager. To support queuing and voice announcements, an IVR is required. Many IVRs are supported, but the most commonly deployed IVRs with UCCE are Cisco Unified Customer Voice Portal (CVP) or Cisco IP IVR, as shown in Figure 2-10.

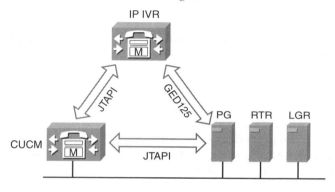

Figure 2-10   *Cisco UCCE Architecture with IP IVR*

Cisco UICM

In comparing the Cisco UICM and generic architectures, the main differences are that a time-division multiplexing (TDM) legacy ACD is used rather than an IP PBX. The legacy ACD typically supports call control to the handsets, queuing, and basic IVR functionality. Figure 2-11 shows a typical UICM architecture that also supports prerouting through the use of a connection to the carrier's intelligent network (IN). In this scenario, when the ACD receives a new call from the carrier/PSTN, the ACD performs a route request to UICM to determine the destination for the call. The UICM platform can provide the routing decisions as it receives a real-time update of the agent/ACD status through the PG.

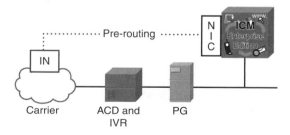

Figure 2-11   *Platform Architecture Including ACD Queuing*

Cisco UCCH

Software as a service, or cloud computing, provides a user or organization with a true hosted platform. The company has little or no knowledge of the infrastructure in the cloud; it is just a user of the delivered service.

Although Cisco Unified Contact Center Hosted (UCCH) is not currently a true cloud computing platform, often termed Software as a Service (SAAS), the architecture could potentially become one.

UCCH was originally developed as an extension to the Cisco ICM platform to enable carriers to use ICM in a multitenant environment. ICM already had the capability to connect to a carrier's SCP to allow prerouting of calls rather than call delivery and then the potential side effect of tromboning the call elsewhere because of agent availability.

Early UCCH architectures required the carrier to host the central controllers and the NIC with its connection to the carrier's voice network. The customer would host its ACDs with a colocated pair of PGs and usually an AW. The PGs connected back to the central controllers over a WAN. An important difference between the UICM and UCCH architecture is that the hosted central controllers are actually split further. In Figure 2-12, you can see that the central controllers have a network logger and router duplex pair, and also a customer logger and router pair. The customer central controllers are segmented to allow up to 25 customer instances per system. Figure 2-13 shows an additional pair of customer central controllers.

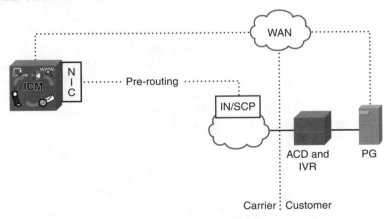

Figure 2-12 *Platform Architecture with Network Prerouting and SCP (Using Customer ACD)*

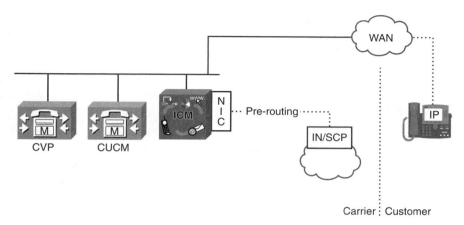

Figure 2-13 *Platform Architecture with Carrier Prerouting*

The NIC uses a C7 (SS7) connection with V.35 cards to the SCP.

With the introduction of IP telephony and the increase in WAN speeds and quality of service (QoS), the location of the ACD/PBX can be more flexible. Many contact center sites now consist of only the end-user telephony device or IP phone and an inline power switch connected through a WAN router back to the central site that hosts the Unified CM server. This flexibility allows the carrier to host both the UCCH and Unified CM servers. This model is more like a cloud computing solution. As more organizations switch to using softphones rather than physical phones, SAAS for voice could become a reality.

Platform Redundancy

Platform survivability is an important feature for enterprise voice architectures. Cisco UCCE natively supports a distributed redundant call-processing architecture.

The core UCCE components, central controllers (router and logger) and the peripheral gateways, should be installed as duplex pairs for all nondemonstration or lab deployments.

Before implementing redundancy into a platform, it is important to consider why redundancy or survivability is required. Typically, redundancy is designed into a solution as part of disaster planning. Disaster planning involves the discussion and documentation of who, what, where, and why:

- **Who:** Which users or customers are affected by the disaster?

- **What:** What equipment, hardware, or software has been impacted?

- **Where:** Is the disaster confined to a single floor or office building?

- **Why:** What caused the disaster? Could it have been a human error caused by an engineer or a countywide power outage?

When exploring potential disaster scenarios, it is easy to stay focused on technology-led problems, such as power cuts or server or hardware failure. Although this section only addresses the application redundancy features of UCCE for disaster recovery planning, it is also important to consider the nontechnology failures or disasters, many of which have become high profile in the media recently. Such disasters include large-scale flooding or hurricanes, countywide power disruptions, nationwide pandemics such as flu, and even software attacks including denial of service and viruses.

The core UCCE components are designed to be deployed in a redundant fashion without a single point of failure. The term *duplex* is often used to refer to the fact that a redundant component or server has been deployed. Not only are multiple servers required, but additional network infrastructure and connections are also needed to ensure the fault tolerance of the system.

The central controllers run in a dual-processing, active-active mode. In contrast, the peripheral gateways run in an active-hot standby configuration. Higher resiliency is achieved by separating the A and B sides over two data centers, as illustrated in Figure 2-14.

Figure 2-14   *Side A and B Architecture*

A duplex central controller uses the synchronized execution approach to fault tolerance. The central controller processes are duplicated and run as synchronized process pairs. In synchronized execution, if one component fails, its peer continues running and the system runs without interruption. The database server is also duplicated, but technically it does not run synchronized. Because all modifications to the database come through the logger, the databases automatically remain synchronized.

Chapter 6, "UCCE Platform Deployment," covers the use of dummy PGs and discusses various failure scenarios.

The duplex servers connect through a network infrastructure. This network infrastructure is composed of a public and private network. The private network sends heartbeat traffic at specific intervals. Should five sequential heartbeats be missed, the UICM node begins its failover process. Only UICM-specific traffic is sent over the private network. The private network between the central controllers is also responsible for the state transfer.

To support the heartbeat traffic, predefined network QoS characteristics must be met. These requirements are documented fully in the UCCE Solution Reference Network Design (SRND) (http://www.cisco.com/go/srnd).

Admin workstations, HDS servers, and WebView servers are not duplex components; however, it is common for more than one of each component to be deployed. Usually, one HDS can replicate from LoggerA and the other from LoggerB during normal running to minimize data transfer over the network, assuming that Logger A is located with HDS A.

Summary

This chapter provided a more detailed view of the actual software components or nodes that make up the Cisco UCCE architecture. The important components to be aware of are as follows:

- **Router:** The router performs the real-time processing of contacts based on its *view* of the contact center, which it builds from the real-time signaling traffic received from the various peripherals connected to the platform.

- **Logger:** The logger maintains database connectivity for the platform and the synchronization of this data.

- **AW/HDS:** Used for management and configuration of the platform and also the long-term storage of contact center reporting information and call records.

- **Peripheral gateway:** The PG provides connectivity among various vendors' ACD types by converting the signaling into a format that the router can understand.

Chapter 3

Deployment Models

This chapter covers the following subjects:

- An overview of the different deployment models
- The two different deployment options
- Notes regarding real-world deployments

Cisco Unified Contact Center Enterprise (UCCE) can be deployed in many different ways to meet the business and technical requirements of the contact center. These deployment models are typically reliant on how the Cisco Unified Communications Manager platform is deployed, rather than by the limitations of the Unified CC components.

This chapter has not been written to give a detailed design of each of the deployment models; instead, it is meant to give an overview of the typical designs on which UCCE deployments are based. The second half of this chapter details some of the real-world deployments in use.

Note Comprehensive details of the official deployment models can be found in the UCCE Solution Reference Network Design (SRND) Guides at Cisco.com: http://www.cisco.com/go/srnd.

Different deployments can generally be classified into one of the four following models:

■   Single-site

■   Multisite with centralized call processing

■   Multisite with distributed call processing

■   Clustering over the WAN

Single-Site

As indicated by the name, a single-site deployment consists of having all the contact center, unified communications servers, and components in a single office building, as illustrated in Figure 3-1. It would be wrong to say that single-site deployments are always small in size, but typically smaller organizations or companies with only one office have a single-site deployment. A deployment that has no WAN connectivity between any of the UCCE components would be considered to be a single-site deployment.

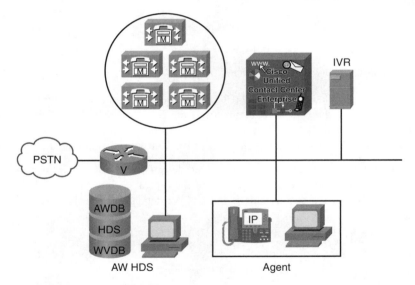

Figure 3-1   *Single-Site Deployment*

Is important to note that even though this is a single-site deployment, platform redundancy should still be deployed to make it suitable for production use. Only lab or nonproduction systems can be deployed as simplex.

Although platform redundancy, such as dual switches, voice gateways, and central controllers are deployed for the single-site model, the main disadvantage is the lack of a second building in a different geographic area as a backup. Without a backup system in a different geographic area, if the overall site suffers from power cuts or other localized issues such as a natural disaster, this could result in system downtime.

An advantage of the single-site model is that no requirement exists to use multiple voice codecs. With no WAN traffic, all the voice encoding can be performed in a high-quality codec such as G.711. This reduces the number of digital signal processing (DSP) resources required and simplifies IP Interactive Voice Response (IVR) and voice recording design.

Multisite with Centralized Call Processing

A multisite deployment with centralized call processing typically caters to an enterprise that has a core central site or data center with at least one or more smaller remote sites, as illustrated in Figure 3-2. Often the smaller remote sites have only IP phones and the agent desktop personal computer (PC) deployed that connect back to the central site over a WAN link. Depending on the number of endpoints and the importance of telephony at the remote sites, a voice gateway with Survivable Remote Site Telephony (SRST) can be installed to support basic telephony functions in case of the loss of the WAN link. All the call-processing servers are located at a single central site.

This model is generally used when the remote sites are sufficiently small or have no or limited IT support personnel. Centralized platforms enable server and voice gateway

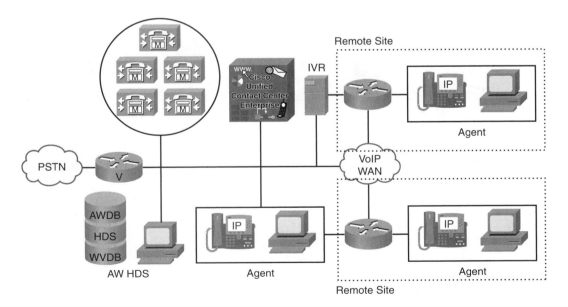

Figure 3-2 *Multisite with Centralized Call Processing*

hardware to be located in fully managed data centers with minimal hardware resources deployed to the remote sites. Depending on the size of the remote site and local laws regarding emergency calls, some remote sites will be deployed with a small router enabled for local call breakout to support localization for emergency calls and general call traffic in the event of a WAN failure.

Centralized voice gateways often provide an advantage when deploying trunk-side voice recording, and also help reduce WAN bandwidth requirements by allowing calls to be queued centrally rather than over the WAN.

Multisite with Distributed Call Processing

The multisite with distributed call processing model is usually deployed for organizations with several large sites, offices in different counties/countries, or offices separated by large distances, as illustrated in Figure 3-3. Distributed call processing refers to that several independent Cisco Unified Communications Manager (Unified CM) clusters are used to provide standalone call handling at the sites. For example, a large enterprise with two major offices could have a standalone Unified CM cluster at each site. Both clusters would typically be connected to allow internal calls between the platforms. As UCCE supports multiple peripherals, each Unified CM cluster would be connected to the UCCE central controllers through peripheral gateways. Even though two clusters are in use, the UCCE platform would see them both as part of a single virtual contact center.

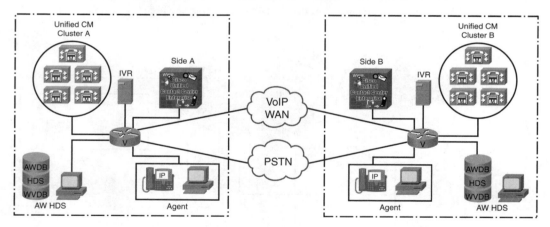

Figure 3-3 *Multisite with Distributed Call Processing, Two Unified CM Clusters, and One UCCE*

The distributed call processing model was often used in earlier versions of Unified CM when several sites requiring a large agent capacity was required. Because of the early sizing limitations of Unified CM, several clusters were required.

Another method of deploying a distributed call processing model would be to use a System CCE configuration at each of the large enterprise sites, and to connect these System CCE platforms to a parent UCCE, as illustrated in Figure 3-4. This type of deployment is often referred to as a *parent/child model* and is discussed further in the section "Parent/Child Deployment."

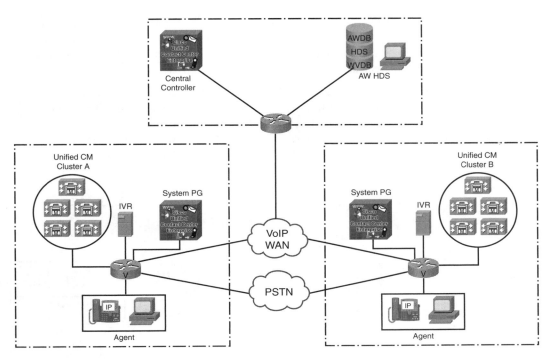

Figure 3-4 *Multisite with Distributed Call Processing, Two Unified CM Clusters and Child System CCE, and One Parent CCE*

A distributed call processing model certainly allows the scalability required for large organizations and provides the survivability required for multisite contact centers, but it does pose several deployment and configuration problems. Common concerns include the ability to use IVR resources across clusters. For example, because of the Java Telephony Application Programming Interface (JTAPI) restrictions, IP IVRs can be associated with only a single Unified CM cluster.

The multisite with distributed call processing model does, however, provide an incredibly scalable architecture. Non-UCCE remote sites can even take advantage of using Cisco Unified Communications Manager Express (UCME). Remote contact center sites can also use Cisco Unified Contact Center Express (UCCX) as part of a parent/child model.

Clustering over the WAN

With the advances in the UCCE applications and the quality of service (QoS) provided by LAN and WAN links, the clustering over the WAN (COW) deployment model is now a popular choice for multisite organizations. Both the Unified CM and UCCE products can be deployed in a distributed manner, which lends itself well to splitting the architecture over multiple sites. Typically, the UCCE components will be distributed as Side A and Side B, and the single Unified CM cluster will be split across data center locations to meet the sizing requirements of the VoIP devices at those sites.

When deploying clustering over the WAN, as illustrated in Figure 3-5, a greater focus is placed on the WAN infrastructure used. The interprocess communications between the Unified CM subscribers and UCCE applications have strict network characteristics that must be met to ensure that the platform is reliable. These network characteristics are documented in detail in both the Unified CM SRND and the UCCE SRND. Typical network characteristics include adequate bandwidth sizing and network latency.

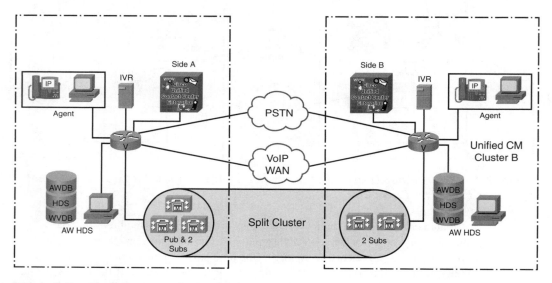

Figure 3-5   *Clustering over the WAN*

Some of the key advantages of clustering over the WAN are as follows:

- Single point of administration for users for all sites within the cluster
- Feature transparency
- Shared line appearances
- Extension mobility within the cluster
- Unified dial plan

These features make this solution ideal as a disaster recovery plan for business continuance sites or as a single solution for up to eight small or medium sites.

Factors to Consider When Choosing a Deployment Model

Unless you deploy UCCE in a greenfield site, the solutions architect generally has to design the UCCE solution around the existing legacy architecture. Many things influence which deployment model is chosen, including the following:

- The location and sizing of existing public switched telephone network (PSTN) connections

- Current data centers or server room locations

- Whether any traditional Automatic Call Distributors (ACD) are in use or require interoperability for system integration or future migration

- How redundancy and survivability should occur during failure or disaster scenarios

This last point, with the number and size of sites, is a key influencer in the chosen deployment model for both greenfield and legacy migration/integration.

> **Note**   Often telephony platforms are deployed in an office to replace an existing PBX. The term *greenfield deployment* is often used to refer to a deployment in a location where no platform has previously been installed. In many cases, a greenfield deployment can be easier than a migration.

Deployment Options

In addition to taking into account the chosen deployment model, it is also important to be aware of the different UCCE configurations that can be implemented:

- Enterprise/System UCCE is the most common deployment model for an organization.

- Parent/child is often used for large multisite customers. Sometimes it is deployed to connect existing child systems, but more often it is used to provide the individual remote sites with redundancy should a failure occur at the central site.

Enterprise/System UCCE

Two peripheral deployment options are available when installing UCCE: Enterprise Peripheral and System Peripheral (sometimes called System PG [peripheral gateway]). The main difference between the two is based upon whether the Unified PG has been deployed independently of the IVR or whether the Unified CM PG and IVR PG are both deployed in a generic PG.

Deploying an Enterprise PG configuration allows greater flexibility for call routing and platform management. For example, it is possible to manually configure the IVRs with a degree of load balancing of calls within the Script Editor application, rather than using the nonconfigurable load balancing of System PG. This often helps during upgrades and troubleshooting. The disadvantage of using an Enterprise PG is that each peripheral is required to be configured independently. This adds a layer of complexity to peripheral configuration and call routing because translation routes will be required to transfer calls between peripherals.

In addition to the ease of installation, System PG uses a different administration interface than the Enterprise PG. A web administration interface is used rather than the traditional UCCE Windows applications.

System PG has been phased out in UCCE version 8.0, but it has been included here as an informative note to make engineers aware that this deployment option might be in use in a system that they have been asked to administer.

Parent/Child Deployment

The parent/child model uses the UCCE Gateway PG to connect a UCCE System PG (the child) to a UICM or UCCE platform (the parent), as illustrated in Figure 3-6.

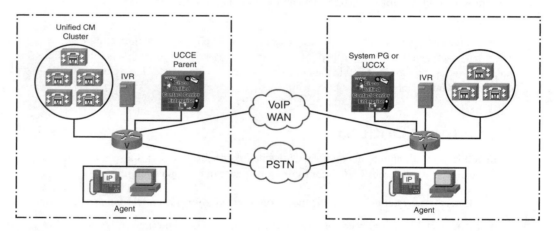

Figure 3-6   *Parent/Child Model*

The Gateway PG makes the child system look like any other peripheral. In addition to the UCCE System PG, it is also possible to deploy Unified Contact Center Express (UCCX) as a child of a UCCE parent.

The child platform is configured to function as an independent platform and therefore does not require the connection to its parent to route calls. This independence provides an extra layer of redundancy to the platform and is therefore ideal for larger remote sites should the WAN connection to the parent or the actual parent platform fail.

As the child looks like a regular ACD to the parent, the parent can perform all the normal call-routing functions such as prerouting and postrouting, and the translation routing of calls. The child, however, is not aware of other peripherals that reside in the parent's domain or other child domains.

Real-World Deployments

Although the previous sections detail the standard deployment models, combinations of these models are usually found in real-world scenarios. For example, many customers that have multiple sites usually distribute the central controllers, call control servers, and voice gateways over two core sites. The remote sites are typically deployed with only phones and agent desktops that connect over the WAN. The larger of these remote sites can also be deployed using the parent/child model using UCCX.

Software, hardware, and platform versions change over time as the platforms themselves evolve. During the software lifecycle, you see new features and products introduced into the product range and older products are phased out. The majority of customers have maintenance contracts on their platforms and receive software upgrades as part of their support contract. Unfortunately, because of changes in support teams or finances, as an engineer, some of the platforms that you will be asked to look at will be running old software versions and possibly products that are no longer supported by Cisco.

Many of the deployments I have worked on consist of a single site, or collection of buildings in the same retail park or industrial estate, that are in close geographic proximity and would suffer the same fate in the event of a natural disaster. Many of the customers fortunate enough to administer multiple buildings in different areas do not design disaster planning into their business planning. They do split the platform architecture to survive failure of a UCCE component, but they do not split the business functions. For example, an outsourced contact center with two buildings might dedicate one building to one area of business and the second building to another. This might seem like a logical thing to do, but it does not provide disaster tolerance to both business areas should a problem occur with one building. Some larger customers, such as financial institutions, are fortunate enough to have multiple central and remote sites, enabling a greater degree of redundancy but at the expense of a platform requiring a design of higher complexity.

When designing, upgrading, or troubleshooting any UCCE platform, there are two software compatibility matrices that you should consult:

- **Unified CM compatibility matrix:** You can find this at http://www.cisco.biz/en/US/docs/voice_ip_comm/cucm/compat/ccmcompmatr.html#wp42029.

- **UCCE software compatibility guide:** You can find this at http://www.cisco.com/en/US/products/sw/custcosw/ps1844/products_device_support_tables_list.html.

Summary

This chapter examined the different playbook UCCE deployment models. Although many real-world deployments are often a combination of different models, the important deployment models to understand are as follows:

- **Single-site:** Easily distinguished from other models as this type of deployment has no WAN connection to other sites. All the required components are resident on the same site.

- **Multisite with centralized call processing:** This model is a popular hub-and-spoke-style deployment that suits organizations composed of a large head office and several smaller remote sites. All the core infrastructure is located centrally with only a minimum of equipment, such as IP phones and maybe a voice gateway, at the remote sites.

- **Multisite with distributed call processing:** This model is often found with large enterprises that have so many phones that they cannot be supported by a single Unified CM cluster, or are geographically diverse and would struggle to meet stringent network characteristics to support a split architecture. This architecture is also used in organizations that have grown through mergers and acquisitions.

- **Clustering over the WAN:** It was not until organizations fully deployed QoS that this model became a viable solution. With the advent of faster WAN links and the intelligent architecting of networks, clustering over the WAN provides an excellent architecture for organizations with multiple sites. The built-in redundancy available with UCCE allows a natural tendency to use clustering over the WAN where possible.

Chapter 4

UC Operating Systems

This chapter covers the following subjects:

- The operating systems in use for the Unified Communications platforms

- The bill of materials (BOM) and third-party applications

- Receiving notification regarding updates

The Unified Communications suite of software applications requires the proper hardware architecture to operate. Various hardware platforms are in use, ranging from IP phones running a firmware build through Cisco IOS—based router and switch devices to high-end Microsoft Windows and Linux servers.

All the different devices require software updates at some stage in their product lifespan. These updates can be required for a variety of reasons, such as a software update to fix a known bug or security issue or maybe a platform upgrade to a new version. The updates can also be from multiple vendors. For example, Microsoft might release a security patch for the Windows operating system, and although the Cisco application does not require this fix, it would be prudent for the systems administrator to deploy it.

It is this platform management that can often cause headaches for systems administrators. Although recognizing that they should review and deploy fixes, systems administrators also need to maintain configuration management and platform stability. Cisco has implemented several measures to assist the systems administrator by creating a custom Microsoft Windows build for earlier versions of Cisco Unified Communications Manager (Unified CM) and more recently an appliance-based server architecture with an underlying Linux platform. The latter is a hardened machine with minimal user configuration to ensure that only the correct updates can be applied. This greatly reduces upgrade and patching issues because Cisco restricts the applications that can be deployed.

Operating Systems in Use

For the core Unified CM servers, three varieties of operating systems are currently in use:

- A standard, user-installed, Microsoft Windows build
- A Cisco-prepared and -configured autoinstall Microsoft Windows build
- A Cisco-prepared and -configured autoinstall Linux build

The sections that follow cover these in more detail.

MS Windows for Cisco Unified CM

For Unified CM versions up to 4.x, the application has been deployed on a Microsoft Windows platform. The actual build of Windows is a custom build created by Cisco that is installed and configured by a series of build disks during installation. The same Original Equipment Manufacturer (OEM) version of Windows is also used by several other Cisco Unified Communications products, including Cisco Unified Contact Center Express (UCCX), Cisco Customer Voice Portal (CVP), and Cisco Emergency Responder.

Several benefits exist for using an OEM build. Not only does it enforce the server hardware to be a required specification, but the operating system (OS) is also preconfigured with the correct application and security settings to ensure that the Unified Communications software can run as expected. The OEM OS setup also requires minimal user input during the entire installation. The OS install boots from a DVD and loads all the utilities required to guide the installation engineer through the process, formatting and configuring the hard drives and also performing BIOS updates if required.

Cisco Voice Operating System (VOS)

Designed to provide an easily deployable and secure platform, the Cisco appliance model is a customized and locked-down Linux OS build for Unified CM versions 5.0 and later. By controlling the base operating system on which the Unified CM application is deployed, Cisco can provide a platform with a reduced total cost of ownership (TCO) and also reduce the cost of delivering a Unified CM solution.

The installation DVD for the appliance model performs all the OS and Unified CM application configuration. During installation, the engineer is prompted only for the essential information, including network configuration and administration settings.

After the OS is installed, the system administrator has limited access to the server through a secure command-line interface. The appliance model is quite a change from previous platforms where the administrator had free reign over the configuration of the server.

Although originally meeting some resistance from the voice community, the appliance model provides many benefits to the organization. The main benefits include

- **Reduced TCO:** The total cost of ownership is reduced in many ways. As the server has no OS to maintain, there is no need for systems administrators specialized in particular OS versions. Upgrades are streamlined with the aid of a dual partition, allowing software to be installed during working hours and then switched over when required. This also allows the facility to switch back if necessary.

- **Increased security:** Restricting access to the OS also prevents the installation of malicious applications or even the accidental deployment of a tool that could damage the Unified CM software. As the server OS is built for a specific purpose, rather than a general-purpose server, any unused services normally installed for a generic build have been removed. This greatly reduces the amount of potential security holes.

- **Rapid server deployment:** A single server image installed from the DVD enables rapid deployment of the OS and Unified CM applications.

MS Windows for UICM/UCCE

Unlike the Unified CM and associated products, Cisco Media Convergence Servers (MCS) ordered for UCCE deployments do not include a customized distribution of the operating system. This is also true for customers ordering non-MCS servers that meet the specification on the bill of materials (BOM) document. Users ordering servers for UCCE must also order the appropriate editions of Windows Server and MS SQL Server. UCCE systems administrators must assume primary maintenance responsibility for their Windows environment. Cisco does, however, provide as a service ongoing Microsoft security patch certification for UCCE.

Bill of Materials (BOM)

Software and systems requirements to support the UCCE platform change over time. Cisco produces a definitive guide for all the hardware and software requirements. This guide is called the bill of materials (BOM). The BOM is an essential document that details all the supported hardware and software that can be used when building a UCCE platform.

At press time, the current Windows OS requirement is to use Windows 2003.

Note   The BOM is updated as Cisco and the supporting vendors release new platforms. The BOM for UCCE 8.0 can be found at http://www.cisco.com/en/US/docs/voice_ip_comm/ cust_contact/contact_center/ipcc_enterprise/ipccenterprise8_0_1/user/guide/icm80bom.pdf.

Third-Party Software

To ensure that the server operates as required to support the Unified Communications applications installed on it, Cisco recommends that only supported and approved third-party applications are installed. These applications, such as antivirus software, are detailed in the

BOM. If a customer is experiencing problems with his system and the Cisco Technical Assistance Center (TAC) discovers that the server has unsupported applications installed, the customer is usually asked to remove those applications before support continues.

Having a strict set of supported applications often causes problems with some enterprises that have corporate standard third-party applications in use on other servers and want to standardize across the data center.

For development of supported applications to integrate with the Unified Communications suite, Cisco has two programs: the Cisco Partner Program and the Technology Affiliate Program. Both of these programs provide the vendor with access to the Interoperability Verification Testing (IVT) performed by Cisco.

Learning About Updates

Because of the importance of staying aware of product updates and issues, Cisco has a series of tools available to ensure that the systems administrator is kept informed.

Of the various tools, the Cisco Notification Service (previously called the Product Alert Tool) enables you to specify the Cisco products that you are using and to receive regular updates through email or RSS newsfeed. The alerts include security advisories, security responses, field notices, end-of-life announcements, known bugs, and software updates.

Note   A Cisco.com login is required to access the various notification tools that can be found at http://www.cisco.com/en/US/products/prod_tools_index.html.

Summary

This chapter explored the different operating systems in use throughout the Cisco Contact Center suite. The main varieties to be aware of are as follows:

- **Cisco VOS:** The Cisco Voice Operating System or appliance model is the latest operating system designed by Cisco and built on a Red Hat Enterprise Linux platform. Cisco VOS is currently used for platforms including Cisco Unified Communications Manager and Cisco Unity Connection.

- **MS Windows for Cisco Communications Manager and Unified Contact Center Express:** Version 4.x and below of the Cisco Unified Communications Manager were called Cisco CallManager. To ensure that the base operating system used for this application and the hardware that it was installed on met certain technical requirements, Cisco released an OEM version of Microsoft Windows Server. This OS is still in use for UCCX, but it has been phased out for recent versions of Unified CM.

- **MS Windows for UICM/UCCE:** Using a native build of Microsoft Windows Server, Cisco specifies only the software revision and required maintenance packs to meet the minimum requirements for the UCCE applications. Cisco frequently advises on which Microsoft fixes should be applied, but it does not bundle the fixes into a maintenance release as it did for the OEM version of Windows.

Chapter 5

UCCE Road Map

This chapter covers the following subjects:

- The Cisco software maintenance lifecycle

- The road map of how Cisco UCCE has evolved into its current product suite

- Key features that have been introduced with each software revision

All UCCE engineers are aware of a customer who is running an old software platform that has never been updated or patched. The customer's server only gets rebooted during a power outage, and he has never had any issues. Fortunately, these customers are few and far between. The majority of enterprises running any type of mission-critical platform pay regular attention to maintaining their systems with recent updates and the latest security and system best practices.

Software support is an essential service provided by vendors. Supporting multiple software versions can become expensive and unmanageable, so vendors typically support only the most recent major software versions of their products.

To give customers adequate notice about new releases and the phasing out of old software versions, the majority of vendors have some form of software product lifecycle.

Cisco Software Product Lifecycle

The Cisco software product lifecycle provides a framework for software availability, its support and maintenance, and eventually the software's end of support and withdrawal from distribution.

Software Phases

The various phases of the software product lifecycle can be broken down into the following (as illustrated in Figure 5-1):

■ **Early release:** Early-release software is usually provided only to Cisco partners and developers so that the third party can get an understanding of the features and changes before customer installations are required.

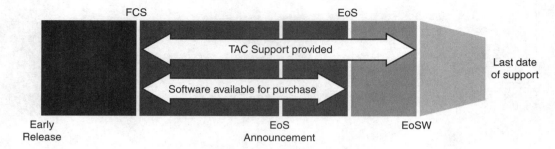

Figure 5-1   *Cisco Software Product Lifecycle*

■ **First customer shipment (FCS):** Also called general availability, this is the first day of release when the software is available to customers.

■ **End-of-sale (EoS) announcement:** The EoS announcement is notification to the customers that the particular software version will be withdrawn from general availability. The announcement usually occurs approximately 6 months before the actual end-of-sale date.

■ **End of sale (EoS):** End of sale is the date that the software release can no longer be purchased or included in manufacturing shipments.

■ **End of software (EoSW) maintenance:** Up until this date, the Cisco engineering teams will actively provide updates and maintenance for this particular software release. After this date, no further updates will be provided, and the customer is advised to upgrade to a more recent version. Recommendations are usually given when these announcements are made. When a software release goes EoSW, you usually get 34 weeks before it goes end of support. When it is the last version of a train, you get 34 weeks plus 18 months to remain supported by the Cisco Technical Assistance Center (TAC).

■ **Last date of support:** Even though the EoSW date has occurred, TAC will still support the software release up until the last date of support, but no new updates will be made available for the software release. After this date, the Cisco TAC will not accept new TAC cases, and all support services will cease. The software release has now become obsolete.

Software Support Road Map

During the phase between FCS and EoSW, Cisco periodically releases software updates on a frequent and defined schedule. To identify the software release in use, its compatibility with new releases, and any necessary migration steps, Cisco uses a consistent software release naming convention.

The format of the naming convention is $x.y(z)$, where

- x is the major release version.
- y is the minor release version.
- z is the maintenance level.

A major release marks the starts of a new software release. Although this software release usually has an upgrade path, it typically requires a full installation or a technology refresh and has implications for data migration. The major releases frequently have nonreversible changes such as database schema enhancements. An example of a major release would be the announcement of the availability of Cisco Unified Contact Center Enterprise (UCCE) version 8.0 when the current version in general availability is version 7.x.

A minor release provides problem resolution fixes and new features to an existing major release. Since version 5.0, the minor releases are deployed using an automated patch installer rather than a manual installation. The automated installer ensures that the minor release is compatible with the platform the engineer is trying to install it on. A further benefit is that the automated installer also has an uninstall or rollback facility should the engineer want to remove the minor release. An example of a minor release for any major software version starting with 7.0 would be numbered 7.1(1).

A maintenance release contains problem resolution fixes for one or more components only for the latest release in the current support train. For example, if the current release is 7.2(1), the next maintenance release would be 7.2(2). Cisco would not provide a maintenance release for a 7.1 train because it would expect the customer to upgrade to 7.2. The automated installer would prevent a 7.2(1) maintenance release from being installed on a 7.1 platform. Maintenance service releases are usually released on a 13-week cycle. The only exception to this release schedule is the first maintenance release for any given major or minor release. You don't have to install every maintenance release; usually they are deployed only if they contain a fix for something that you're experiencing problems with.

In addition to major, minor, and maintenance releases, Cisco also provides ad hoc releases called *engineering specials (ES)*. An ES is a special short-term release provided as an emergency fix for a high-priority defect. Engineering specials are developed only for the releases that are currently supported by the engineering team. The ES numbering scheme is incremental, and the patches are usually installed through an automated installer and can therefore be rolled back if required. Few customers require an ES because they are typically used with a customer that has a fault specific to its deployment.

Platform Upgrades

Not all software releases adhere to the release schedule. For example, a lot of effort has been made by the engineering and marketing teams to bring all the UCCE components into line with a version numbering scheme that is clearer to the customer. This is typical for version 7.x and 8.x of UCCE, where the individual components such as Unified Intelligent Contact Manager (UICM), IP Interactive Voice Response (IVR), Unified

Customer Voice Portal (CVP), and Cisco Unified Communications Manager (Unified CM) have now pulled together under a similar major release number.

With this in mind, it is imperative that the engineer clearly understands the software compatibility matrix and upgrade paths available when planning a platform upgrade. Each software release also comes with a release document that details information that should be taken into consideration before applying the new release.

The latest minor and maintenance releases are available from the Download section at Cisco.com. The major software releases are not available for download and can be obtained from your Cisco support partner based on your product entitlement.

The Evolution of UCCE

Like many enterprise applications, the Cisco UCCE platform has gone through many software revisions over a long period of time. Cisco UCCE originally started as an Automatic Call Distributor (ACD) bolt-on architecture used to provide carrier prerouting capabilities and a single management and reporting interface over different ACD types.

In its original form, UCCE was known as GeoTel Intelligent Call Router (ICR) and was designed and developed by a small company called GeoTel based in Lowell, just north of Boston, Massachusetts.

GeoTel ICR 2.5

When released, GeoTel ICR was the first product to distinguish itself from the competition for call routing. Many interexchange carriers (IXC) and ACD vendors offered the capability to route customer calls between an organization's call centers using public and private telephony circuits. Both technologies accomplish the same goal of distributing and delivering calls to the most suitable agent or team to answer the call. The GeoTel ICR performed this routing by taking a new approach, which GeoTel called *enterprise call distribution*.

Enterprise call distribution involves the intelligent gathering of status information from multiple distributed call centers and collating this "real-time view" of the entire enterprise on a single platform. When a new call request is received from the carrier, the call-processing engine can return information to the carrier to ensure that the call is delivered to the most appropriate ACD or resource. Chapter 8, "Call Routing," delves into more detail about this prerouting functionality.

In addition to enterprise call distribution, GeoTel ICR also introduced several enhanced features:

■   **GeoTel Gateway SQL:** The capability to perform database lookups in real time and influence the call delivery or call data based on the outcome of the data retrieved from the database.

■   **GeoTel Gateway:** Similar to the Gateway SQL option, the GeoTel Gateway allowed external applications to be executed. These applications could return data to influence call routing.

■   **GeoTel Enterprise CTI:** Providing a link between the agents' desktop applications and data held within the ICR platform, Enterprise CTI was responsible for the screen-pop and after-call data. Enterprise CTI allowed this call and agent data to be stored in the routing engine and seamlessly transferred between agents and peripherals as the call passed through an enterprise.

■   **GeoTel Schedule Link:** Schedule Link allowed an administrator to import agent schedule and roster information from an external workforce management platform. This allowed call flow scripts to calculate call delivery formulas against the schedule. It could also be used for agent compliance to verify that the agent's login times were consistent with his roster.

■   **GeoTel Partition:** Most organizations can realize benefits by sharing infrastructure and services. GeoTel Partition allowed a single ICR instance to be split into several business units. Call-routing scripts and resources such as skill groups or agents would be allocated against each partition. This logical allocation of resources made it easier to assign call-routing control to different areas of the business.

■   **GeoTel Network ICR:** The Network ICR feature was requested by British Telecom and allowed a network service provider to host the GeoTel ICR platform in its cloud while extending intelligent call-routing services to the enterprise.

■   **GeoTel Enterprise IVR:** The Enterprise IVR was not an actual IVR platform. Like the ACD functionality, GeoTel left IVR development to the IVR vendors. GeoTel provided an IVR API to which the vendors could develop against. This allowed GeoTel to support a large IVR base.

Note   The Enterprise IVR API is called GED125 (GeoTel Engineering Document) and is still in use today.

■   GeoTel Monitor ICR: Using a series of canned reporting templates, Monitor ICR allowed supervisors and administrators to run reports based on data gathered in the ICR databases.

■   GeoTel WebView: Implementing reporting templates similar to Monitor ICR, WebView allowed users with a web browser to access reporting data from the ICR databases.

GeoTel ICR 3.0/4.0/4.1

Versions 3.0, 4.0, and 4.1 introduced several new features and improvements over previous versions. It was also within the later of these versions that GeoTel was acquired by Cisco, and the product underwent a rebranding from GeoTel ICR to Cisco ICR. ICR 4.1 introduced the concept of an *enterprise agent*.

The enterprise agent provided CTI screen pops, call distribution, and reporting capabilities for remote or home-office agents that were not connected to an ACD. Much of the functionality and advanced call-routing capabilities possible with the ACD-based agents could also be used by the enterprise agent. Two types of agent were supported: the home agent with a plain old telephone service (POTS) line and the branch office agent with access to a private branch exchange (PBX) phone. The agent's desktop personal computer (PC) would connect back to the central controllers through an enterprise agent peripheral gateway (PG).

The enterprise agent never became a popular feature. The requirement to have a music telecom voice card for each PC and the network requirements for the softphone were excessive. Remember, this was in the days before widespread home broadband usage!

Many of the configuration items, such as device targets, that were used for the enterprise agent are still in use today as the concept behind the enterprise agent evolved into Cisco IP Contact Center (IPCC).

ICM 4.5

One of the most memorable features of Intelligent Contact Manager (ICM) 4.5 was the introduction of a Cisco Discovery Protocol (CDP) driver for the Windows servers. This allowed the servers to show up as CDP neighbors from the Cisco switch architecture and also be detected by CiscoWorks. Nearly all the engineers who tried this technology at the time quickly became familiar with the Windows blue screen of death!

Prior to the release of maintenance releases in version 4.6, all updates were through hotfixes. Not all the hotfixes needed to be deployed for every customer because many were specific to the type of ACD in use by the customer. Before the release of ICM 4.6, the number of hotfixes available for ICM 4.5 grew to a large number.

Cisco ICM 4.6

Cisco ICM 4.6 introduced support for Microsoft Windows 2000 and SQL Server 7.0. With this change in OS and database requirements, much of the hardware minimum requirements also changed. To cope with this change, Cisco introduced the concept of Common Ground and Technology Refresh upgrades.

The Common Ground upgrade retains the existing server infrastructure if it met the requirements or could receive additional hardware such as disks, memory, and processors to bring it up to the correct requirements. Each of the servers within the ICM platform would receive an operating system (OS) and database upgrade before upgrading the Cisco ICM application.

The Technology Refresh option involved migrating all the ICM production system to a new hardware platform that met the requirements detailed in the bill of materials.

These upgrade paths are still in use and supported by the latest versions of UCCE, and they have proven to be reliable and robust approaches for platform upgrades. The most popular approach that I have been involved with is the Technology Refresh. This method enables a whole new platform to be built in parallel, which minimizes risk.

Following the acquisition of Selsius, Cisco rebranded its product to become the Cisco CallManager. ICM 4.6 saw the integration of CallManager with a dedicated peripheral called CallManager PG. CallManager 3.x provided the telephony call control, IP IVR 2.2-enabled call queuing, and voice menus, whereas ICM pulled all the products together to provide ACD functionality.

Cisco WebView also received a significant improvement with the addition of 75 new reporting templates specifically for Cisco IPCC.

Cisco ICM 5.0

ICM 5.0 was the first version to introduce multichannel routing, which actually turned the Cisco platform into a contact center rather than a call center application. The multichannel routing included integration of voice, web callback, web collaboration, and email routing. ICM 5.0 gave customers the ability to implement a universal queue, which allowed an agent to receive contacts from each of the channels from a single logical queue. To do this, ICM 5.0 introduced a Media Routing Peripheral Interface Manager (PIM) to manage route requests between the ICM and the web/email collaboration options.

Other changes implemented in ICM 5.0 included the following:

- **Support for Microsoft SQL Server 2000:** Previous versions supported Microsoft SQL Server 7.0. With the upgrade to SQL 2000, many of the database table names were changed to prevent clashes with reserved words used within SQL Server. Customers upgrading from 4.6.2 to 5.0 were allowed to use SQL Server 7.0 as a migration step and still retain support as long as SQL Server was upgraded to SQL Server 2000 within 14 days. This made the upgrade process easier, especially for large enterprise and service provider customers having many database servers.

- **Quality of service traffic marking:** Also introduced in ICM 5.0 to provide further support to customer sites having remote peripheral gateways located at the end of WAN links. This allowed customers to use existing WAN connections rather than having to deploy dedicated Frame Relay links for the control traffic between the peripheral gateway (PG) and call router processes.

- **WebView replaced Monitor ICM** as the tool of choice for providing reporting information.

■ **Outbound dialing became possible** for IPCC customers using Cisco CallManager as a software-based dialer rather than requiring a hardware-based approach.

Cisco IPCC 7.0

Skipping IPCC version 6.0, version 7.0 was launched to coincide with the naming conventions for Unified Communications Manager 7.0. Many new features were delivered with version 7.0, including the following:

■ Microsoft Windows 2003 and Active Directory support

■ System IPCC, for simpler installations and administration

■ IPCC Gateway to facilitate the parent/child model

■ Security enhancements

■ Quality of service (QoS) tagging for all communications

This was also the version that started to distinguish between ICM and IPCC. Both names were retained, but Cisco started to push IPCC as the premier solution as it made sense that customers deploying new contact centers would prefer to implement an IP solution rather than deploy a greenfield site using a legacy ACD.

Cisco UCCE 7.5

Released and rebranded in July 2008, Cisco IPCC became Cisco Unified Contact Center Enterprise (UCCE), whereas Cisco ICM received a slight name change to become Cisco Unified Intelligent Contact Management. Some of the core features and benefits included the following:

■ Support for PGs and client administrative workstation (AW) deployment on virtual servers. These two components were chosen because an enterprise is likely to have many more PGs and client AWs than any other component.

■ Total server reduction through coresidency and increased agent capacity per server. A significant detail for service providers is the ability to run multiple Computer Telephony Integration Object Server (CTI OS) servers on the same server. It is worth noting from a functional perspective that nearly all the components can be coresident; however, from a supportability and performance perspective, it is necessary to split the components over several servers.

■ Windows platform updates to support Microsoft Vista and SQL Server 2005.

■ Doubling the capacity of peripherals to 150.

■ The use of Expert Advisor to allow calls to be escalated to knowledge workers.

■ An alternative reporting interface, Cisco Unified Intelligence Center (CUIC).

■ The support for split PGs to enable UCCE to be deployed with the Unified CM clustering over the WAN architecture.

Cisco UCCE 8.0

Version 8.0 of UCCE was another major release that provided several feature enhancements, including the following:

- Support for Unified CM version 8.0, IP IVR, and CVP.

- An OEM version of Windows 2003 and SQL Server 2005 that can be deployed on Cisco Media Convergence Servers (MCS). This is similar to the OS used for CallManagers version 4.x and below. Eventually it's possible that the core of UCCE will be deployed on the Cisco appliance model, or Voice Operating System (VOS), servers.

- CUIC and Expert Advisor can be deployed on VOS.

- A new web-based installer to guide the engineer through installation. This will be used for the majority of UCCE components with the exception of PGs.

- The old IPCC dialer mechanism, whereby dialer ports are registered on the UC Manager as Skinny Client Control Protocol (SCCP) phones, but new dialer setups can be configured using Session Initiation Protocol (SIP). The outbound calls are then made as SIP from the voice gateway, reducing bandwidth requirements over the network. The voice gateway can also perform answering machine detection.

Cisco UCCE 8.5

Released at the end of 2010, UCCE 8.5 is a relatively new release that is simple to deploy and provides two useful features:

- **Whisper Announcement:** This feature enables an agent to hear a brief prerecorded message just before she is connected with the caller. This is typically information that is useful to the agent, such as the caller's name or perhaps the menu options she selected at an IVR prompt. This feature is often requested for multiskilled agents or agents in an outsourced contact center that handle calls for several different clients.

- **Agent Greeting:** This feature enables a recorded message to be played to the caller on behalf of the agent. Typical information includes a short welcome message, perhaps identifying the agent and business unit to which the caller has been connected.

Both of these new features are dependent on UCCE integration with CVP because CVP provides the announcements.

Summary

This chapter discussed the Cisco software maintenance cycle and walked you through the evolution of Cisco UCCE. The main points for consideration are as follows:

- The Cisco software maintenance lifecycle is a clearly defined process applicable to all the products within the Cisco Contact Center suite. Having this process assists both customers and the various Cisco systems integration partners by setting expectations of when software releases are to be made available and when it is necessary to upgrade to a recent version to maintain adequate product support.

- Cisco UCCE has evolved for more than a decade. During this time, the Cisco product team has worked closely with customers and partners to deliver the enhanced functionality in use today.

Chapter 6

UCCE Platform Deployment

This chapter covers the following subjects:

- Planning for a UCCE deployment

- UCCE software installation

- Deployment testing

The initial deployment and installation of a Cisco Unified Contact Center Enterprise (UCCE) platform is only a small part of the total ownership and administration required to maintain the solution. However, getting the installation correct is an important step to ensuring that the solution remains supportable and problem-free.

As you discover in this chapter, the deployment of an advanced solution such as UCCE can be a long process requiring a dedicated project team with experienced technical specialists.

This chapter briefly introduces the Cisco Lifecycle Service methodology used by Cisco and its partners to deploy advanced unified communications solutions. Although the life-cycle covers the entire deployment process from the initial business ideas through to the solutions optimization, this chapter focuses on the design and implementation of the core UCCE software components that need to be in place before the application-level business requirements can be implemented. Chapter 7, "UCCE Application Configuration," details the aspects of application-level configuration.

It is common practice to split larger UCCE installations among various deployment engineers or several small teams of engineers. This is done because a complete UCCE deployment encompasses several different products or platforms that require specialist skills. The different technical skill sets required for a UCCE deployment include the following:

- **Business analyst:** The business analyst is responsible for converting the business requirements into detailed technical requirements. The business analyst might also be required to collect the end-user data. This includes details such as the agent names,

IDs, skill groups, teams, extension numbers, and locations. **Solutions architect:** Having the responsibility for the overall solution, the solutions architect is aware of the "bigger picture" of the technical aspects and understands all the integration interfaces of how the different components interact.

- **Microsoft Windows specialist:** Many organizations prefer to deploy their own MS Windows architecture for UCCE because of its integration with Windows Active Directory. If the customer prefers that the Cisco partner perform the Windows and SQL Server installations, a specialist is then required with these skills.

- **Unified CM engineer:** Responsible for the installation and configuration of the Unified CM cluster, including voice gateways and interfaces to the PSTN or any legacy time-division multiplexing (TDM) technologies.

- **Unified IVR/CVP engineer:** The Interactive Voice Response (IVR) engineer is responsible for the installation and configuration of the chosen IVR platform and then the subsequent integration of the IVR into UCCE.

- **UCCE installation engineer and application engineer:** Both of these roles can be performed by the same engineer. This is especially true for smaller deployments. For large installations that have hundreds of complex routing scripts, skill groups, and thousands of agents, these roles are usually split to ensure that the project is delivered on time. In practice, the UCCE installation engineer is also often skilled at IVR installations, so he can perform the initial installation of the core UCCE components and then hand over the application configuration to another engineer while continuing with the IVR work in parallel.

- **Third-party specialist:** Several products exist outside of the core components that integrate into UCCE including voice recording, workforce management, speech recognition, and email/web collaboration. These products often require specialist installations by skilled engineers or the product vendors.

Lifecycle Services Approach

To instigate a consistent approach to network implementations, Cisco created a network lifecycle methodology that partners and end customers could use throughout to achieve their network-related business goals. As organizations began to deploy unified communications technologies, many people experienced challenges with implementing UC technology on their existing network infrastructure. Many of these challenges were because of a lack of a structured approach.

Cisco recommends that a proven lifecycle approach is followed when deploying complex solutions. When an organization engages with Cisco and a Cisco partner for the deployment of a UCCE solution, the Cisco consulting engineers use the Cisco Lifecycle Services approach to ensure smooth project delivery.

The Cisco Lifecycle approach is built to the standard of the Information Technology Infrastructure Library (ITIL) and other standards-based frameworks. The approach, shown

in Figure 6-1, comprises six distinct phases, collectively known as the Cisco PPDIOO
Lifecycle Methodology.

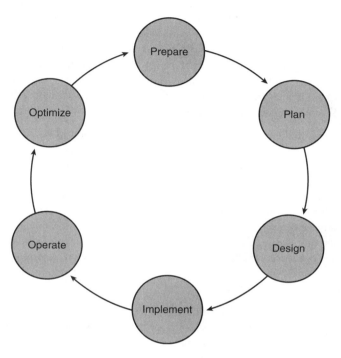

Figure 6-1   *Cisco PPDIOO Lifecycle Methodology*

The aim of the lifecycle is to align the business and technical requirements at each phase:

- **Prepare:** In the prepare phase of the lifecycle, an organization determines a business
  case and financial rationale to support the adoption, enhancement, or migration to
  the new technology. The organization is required to develop a technology strategy
  and identify a technology and a high-level architecture to meet those requirements.
  After the financial and business value of the chosen technology has been assessed,
  the company can validate the technology's features and functionality through proof-
  of-concept testing.

- **Plan:** Successful deployment depends on an accurate assessment of an organization's
  current network and overall readiness to support the proposed technology. In the
  plan phase, a company determines whether it has adequate resources to manage a
  technology deployment project to completion. Certainly for UCCE deployments, a
  Cisco Authorized Technology Provider (ATP) partner is required for deployment, so
  this planning phase would almost certainly be a joint task between the organization
  and the partner. A detailed project plan is created to identify resources, potential dif-
  ficulties, individual responsibilities, and critical tasks necessary to deliver the final
  project on time and on budget.

- **Design:** During the design phase, a comprehensive and detailed design is created to meet the business and technical requirements. A design aligned with business goals and technical requirements can improve network and platform performance while supporting high availability, reliability, security, and scalability. Many of the features deployed for a UCCE solution are out-of-the-box components that require configuring to suit the organization, but UCCE also has several programming interfaces that can be developed against to provide the organization with enhanced, custom features. These should also be documented during the design phase. The design phase can also guide and accelerate successful implementation with a plan to stage, configure, test, and validate network operations.

- **Implement:** In the implementation phase, an organization works to integrate the UCCE solution in accordance with the design—without compromising network availability or performance or impacting the current operation of any existing voice or contact center solutions. The implementation phase is probably the most visible phase to the organization as the project work takes progress. For a solution as large as UCCE that encompasses contact center, telephony, and networking components, the installation, configuring, integrating, testing, and commissioning of the systems usually requires a large team of engineers with a wide range of skill sets. After the solutions operation is validated, an organization can begin expanding and improving IT staff skills through professionally delivered training courses and on-the-job ad hoc training from the Cisco partner.

- **Operate:** Day-to-day platform operations represent a significant portion of an IT budget. A key business driver is to reduce the total cost of ownership (TCO) of a solution's running costs while continually maintaining, and potentially enhancing, performance. Throughout the operate phase, an organization proactively monitors the health and performance of a solution to improve service quality, reduce disruptions, and maintain high availability and reliability. Contact centers typically have a higher staff turnover rate than regular office-based roles. This has the impact that a large portion of work will be performing adds, moves, and changes.

- **Optimize:** Contact centers are generally the first, and sometimes only, point of contact into the enterprise for an individual customer. Contact centers strive to be the best and to provide a high standard of customer service to their callers. Business best practices and contact center technology are constantly evolving to ensure that the caller is given a good experience. In the optimize phase, an organization is continually looking for ways to achieve operational excellence through improved performance and expanded services. This results in the changes to business requirements and the potential to implement new technology. In recent years, contact center technology has advanced so rapidly that occasionally technology drives through business change. Many new features available in recent versions of UCCE have resulted in organizations wanting to upgrade as they can see a direct competitive advantage for implementing the new solutions.

Prepare and Plan

The preparation and planning phases for a UCCE deployment are outside the scope of this book. To achieve success in these phases, it is necessary to engage with a Cisco partner capable of delivering a solution that meets the organization's vision and requirements.

Cisco has a vast product and services catalogue covering a wide range of technologies. It is therefore important that the chosen Cisco partner has a proven background for the planned deployment. To assist with choosing the correct partner, Cisco requires that partners specialize in certain technology areas and prove their capabilities by having an agreed-upon number of trained and qualified staff with access to UCCE laboratory facilities.

For a Cisco partner to deploy and support a UCCE solution, it must have achieved the Authorized Technology Provider (ATP) accreditation for UCCE. The ATP program is an invitation-only program focused on the high-end enterprise contact center marketplace. Only when the partner has satisfied the entry criteria can it then resell and support UCCE solutions.

Design

With the different deployment models available and the various options about the distribution of software components based on the size of the contact center, you can design a UCCE solution with many permutations. However, you needd to consider several key points when creating a design:

- **Scalability:** Is the solution sized correctly for the number of staff that will use the platform initially and for at least 1 year following going live?

- **Survivability:** Does the proposed solution take advantage of the multiple levels of redundancy available with UCCE?

- **Compliance:** Does the design meet or exceed the customer's business requirements? Are the hardware and software compatible with the bill of materials, the Solution Reference Network Design (SRND) Guide for UCCE, and the Cisco Assessment to Quality (A2Q) process?

Software Versions

When creating a UCCE design, one of the initial considerations is which version of UCCE should be used. It would be easy to insist that the customer deploys the latest version of UCCE. However, many customers prefer to wait for at least the first maintenance release of a product to become available. It is also wrong to select a software version in isolation. A key feature of unified communications is the capability to integrate with many different products or platforms. It is therefore important to consider the following before making a decision on which version to choose:

- Does the chosen software version have the required features? Most new features are introduced in the major software versions; however, some features do become available in the minor releases.

- Is the software version first customer shipment (FCS), or has it been available for some time and is known to be a stable, or preferred, release? Are several maintenance releases available that have fixed the majority of known bugs? Good practice is to check the release notes for any known outstanding bugs. Many of these bugs are minor, but is there anything in particular that can affect this specific customer?

- Are specific IOS versions required on the network infrastructure, in particular, voice gateways, CUBE routers and analog interfaces?

- Are there any specific IOS features that need to be enabled on the network, including QoS, firewall ports, and traffic engineering?

- Does a network management requirement exist to ensure that operational support personnel are aware of issues in real time?

- Does the organization already have a Cisco Unified CM platform? Is this software version compatible, or is an upgrade required?

- Which other Cisco Unified Communications products are proposed or are already in use? This includes IVR, voicemail, and Unified Communicator.

- Does the organization require the integration of any third-party products such as voice recording, wallboards, customer relationship management (CRM) integration, attendant consoles, and instant messaging?

- Is any legacy TDM integration required?

As detailed in Chapter 3, "Deployment Models," Cisco produces a compatibility matrix to assist when choosing software versions. Two versions of the matrix are available: a generic Unified Communications matrix that details product compatibility with Unified CM and a contact center—specific matrix for products including Customer Voice Portal (CVP) and IP IVR.

Cisco also regularly performs an IP communications systems test. This is a standard methodology for Cisco to perform systemwide testing of all Unified Communications products in a single laboratory environment. A major deliverable of this testing is a recommendation of compatible software releases that have been verified during this testing process. Organizations that plan to deploy multiple voice applications and infrastructure products can adopt these recommendations in their design.

Note   Although it is outside the scope of UCCE, Cisco also provides a legacy Automatic Call Distributor (ACD) compatibility guide titled *Cisco Unified Intelligent Contact Management ACD PG Supportability Matrices*, which details the major ACD vendors and their respective connectivity support with Unified Intelligent Contact Manager (UICM).

Platform Sizing

When designing a Cisco Unified Communications solution, an essential application for the solutions architect to work through is the Unified Communications Sizing Tool (see Figure 6-2). This tool enables the design team to step through a comprehensive set of questions to specify the majority of components (CVP, IP IVR, Expert Advisor, Agent Desktop software) that make up the UC solution. As well as detailing the software components, the tool enables the design team to enter details including call-handling parameters, software versions, anticipated service levels, and redundancy options.

Figure 6-2   *Unified Communications Sizing Tool*

The tool prompts the user with a large number of design questions and can take considerable effort to complete correctly. The resulting output of completing the sizing tool is an Adobe PDF document detailing design options and performance metrics based on the data entered. This document should also be submitted to the A2Q process.

The sizing tool can also be used for designing expansions to existing UCCE platforms.

Note   Readers with a Cisco.com login can access the Unified Communications Sizing Tool at http://tools.cisco.com/cucst.

Platform Redundancy

You can design redundancy into a UCCE solution in many different ways. The recommended methods are as follows:

- **Hardware redundancy within a component:** Examples of this include multiple disks within each server using a RAID mechanism or dual power supplies.

- **Node redundancy:** This involves distributing the different nodes (loggers, routers, PGs) over multiple servers.

- **Distributed architecture:** The UCCE software architecture is naturally redundant through its use of a Side A and Side B. It is common to separate the core platform over two physically diverse locations. The LAN and WAN connections are also diversely routed to separate the UCCE private and public network traffic.

Server Naming Conventions

Early versions of UICM did not have many of the supportability tools available today. When enabling trace settings, collecting logs, and performing administration duties, the platform required the support engineer to frequently establish remote control sessions to the required servers. To make it easier to identify the role of server, it felt that a standardized naming convention should be used. The commonly used server naming convention combined the customer instance name and the servers role. This naming convention was not mandatory, but many enterprises chose to implement it.

The naming convention used the format of three concatenated acronyms, GEOXXXYYYY, which are detailed in Table 6-1.

Table 6-1 *Server Naming Convention*

Acronym	Description
GEO	An abbreviation of GeoTel, the original developers of the UICM platform.
XXXX	An abbreviation of the customer name, usually the customer instance name.
YYYY	An acronym of the node type, as follows: • For a logger, use LGRA or LGRB, depending on the A or B side. • For a router, use RTRA or RTRB, depending on the A or B side. • For an administrative workstation, use AW proceeded by an integer value. • For a historic data server, use HDS preceded by an integer value. • For a peripheral gateway, use PGnA or PGnB, where *n* is the integer value of the PG as defined by its DMP identifier.

Table 6-2 provides an example of the server naming convention, with GEO being substituted for CSO (Cisco) and using a customer instance name of cus01.

Unfortunately, the naming convention has not been continued in the later versions of the software, so standard acronyms for newer components such as the support tools server do not exist.

Table 6-2 *Example Server Naming for Customer Instance cus01*

Server Name	Server Type	Node	Description
csocus01lgra	Logger	A	Logger Side A
csocus01lgrb	Logger	B	Logger Side B
csocus01rtra	Router	A	Router Side A
csocus01rtrb	Router	B	Router Side B
csocus01pg1a	PG	1A	Peripheral Gateway 1 Side A
csocus01pg1b	PG	1B	Peripheral Gateway 1 Side B
csocus01aw1	AW	1	Administrative Workstation 1
csocus01hds1	HDS	1	Historical Data Server 1

Note   For smaller deployments that combined the logger and router nodes into a "rogger," the acronym of RGR is often used.

Deployment Spreadsheet

Solution design documents tend to focus on the architecture and the services that will be provided by the end solution, but they should also include the configuration settings that will be used. As UCCE is a distributed application that requires installation on several servers, the software setup process will be run many times, and potentially by different engineers, especially if the solution is distributed over several geographic locations.

Before deployment commences, it is advisable to have a node deployment spreadsheet that has been created by the solutions architect and reviewed and approved by the installation engineers.

The deployment spreadsheet is a quick reference guide with configuration details taken from the solution design that covers all the application settings to be used by the installation engineers during UCCE installation.

For simplicity, it is often easiest to represent the data in tabular form within a spreadsheet. Each sheet represents a single UCCE node and the settings required for the entire base software installation process.

Taking a logger installation as an example, the LoggerA sheet would require the configuration settings detailed in Table 6-3.

Table 6-3   *LoggerA Installation Settings*

Application	Setting
SQL Server	SQL Server version SQL Server settings (database and log locations, sort order, service startup accounts) SQL Server service pack version
UCCE Installation	Location and version of maintenance release (if required) Drive destination for installation files Install OS security hardening? Install SQL Server security hardening? A preshared key for Support Tools communication
UCCE Domain Manager (assuming LoggerA is the first UCCE node)	Customer instance name Domain name Customer instance number Facility name Domain usernames to assign to UCCE (Config, Setup, and WebView groups)
UCCE Web Setup	Administration username and password (that are assigned to the UCCE setup group) *NOTE: The italicized comments that follow are example answers for a LoggerA setup.* Deployment type [*Enterprise*] Side [*A*] Fault tolerance mode [*Duplexed*] Router Side A private interface [*csocus01rtrap*] Router Side B private interface [*csocus01rtrbp*] Logger Side A private interface [*csocus01lgrap*] Logger Side B private interface [*csocus01lgrbp*] Enable historical/detail data replication [*Y*] Display database purge configuration steps [*N*] Enable outbound option [*N*] Reboot on error [*N*] Reboot on request [*N*] Do not modify service account [*selected*] Stop and then start the logger [*N*]

This same method would need to be applied to all the UCCE components, including routers, peripheral gateways (PG), support tools server, and IVRs to provide a comprehensive deployment spreadsheet. It is easy to see that creating these spreadsheets for an entire deployment can be time consuming, but doing so ensures that consistency is attained throughout the installation.

It is also advisable for the sheet to have a signoff section so that the installation can append a date and time that the configuration took place. This is useful for establishing a timeline in case retrospective changes need to be applied in the future. It also helps the project manager determine the project's progress.

Network Services

Network services are the foundation protocols and applications that run on the network to provide functionality to higher-layer applications and products. UCCE relies on several underlying network services.

DNS and HOSTS

The Domain Name System (DNS) service and HOSTS files provide device hostnames to IP address resolution. The communication between UCCE nodes is through IP. When configuring the various UCCE components, hostnames are generally used to provide support engineers with human-readable server names to make troubleshooting easier. For IP communication to take place between two servers, the server names need to be resolved to an IP address.

DNS services tend to be reliable, but the loss of the DNS service could have major consequences on the reliability of the UCCE platform. It is common practice to create HOSTS files that are a static list of server hostnames and their associated IP addresses. The HOSTS files usually list both the public and private addresses of only the UCCE server interfaces and are copied to each UCCE server. The servers also have details of the DNS servers configured on the public network interface controller (NIC) so that the UCCE server has access to other non-UCCE servers and services.

Tip An MS Windows server uses the following hostname resolution sequence:

1. The client checks to see whether the name queried is its own.

2. The client checks the local HOSTS files.

3. The client queries the DNS servers configured on its NIC.

4. The client checks for NetBIOS name resolution.

A disadvantage of using a HOSTS file is that the HOSTS file needs to be manually maintained and distributed throughout the necessary servers if any UCCE IP address or server names are changed, including the addition of new servers, such as PGs. Fortunately, the core servers that comprise a UCCE solution infrequently change.

Quality of Service

Network quality of service (QoS) is the ability to provide different priorities to streams of IP traffic for different applications, users, or data flows. QoS can be implemented in different ways. Usually the traffic is classified and marked on entry to the network. It is then prioritized as it traverses the network through the use of queuing or reservation algorithms. Both LAN and WAN traffic can be prioritized.

Although the core UCCE servers do not actually touch any voice streams, an entire UCCE solution comprises three different types of traffic:

- Data traffic consists of general traffic between clients and servers, such as the communication or heartbeat traffic between the central controllers, Computer Telephony Integration (CTI) data sent to an agent desktop application, or database replication traffic.

- Voice traffic consists of Real-Time Transport Protocol (RTP) packets that actually contain the packetized voice streams between IP phones, gateways, or IVRs.

- Call control traffic consists of the protocols used to perform control functions such as the communication between a Unified CM subscriber and an IP IVR, or the SCCP control messages sent when an IP phone goes off-hook.

To understand QoS for UCCE, it is also necessary to understand the two independent communications networks used in a UCCE deployment.

Figure 6-3 shows the distributed components of a standard UCCE deployment. The central controllers and PGs each have two or more NICs. One NIC is connected to the *public* network (sometimes called the *visible* network), and the other is connected to the *private* network. The private network carries synchronization and heartbeat traffic. The public network carries all other traffic. Components such as the Unified CM servers and admin workstation historical data services (AW HDS) do not need a connection to the UCCE private network.

It is important to understand that the PG private network is different from the central controller's private network. The private interfaces for the PGs do not need to communicate with the private interfaces for the central controllers. This, however, does not mean that two separate private networks are required for architectures such as clustering over the WAN. In many cases, the two private networks are combined, but just sized correctly to support the necessary bandwidth requirements. For distributed deployments with both halves of the central controllers located on different physical sites, the private network does need to be physically separate from the public network. This often results in a private point-to-point link being installed purely for the private traffic. This diverse network is required so that two network connections exist between each side of the central controllers to ensure that the central controllers can still communicate and process calls in the event that one network connection fails. If both network connections fail, Side A or B attempts to continue based on an algorithm determined by the *side* of the router and the number of PGs with which the router is in communication. The requirement for the private link is often the most discussed point during the A2Q process!

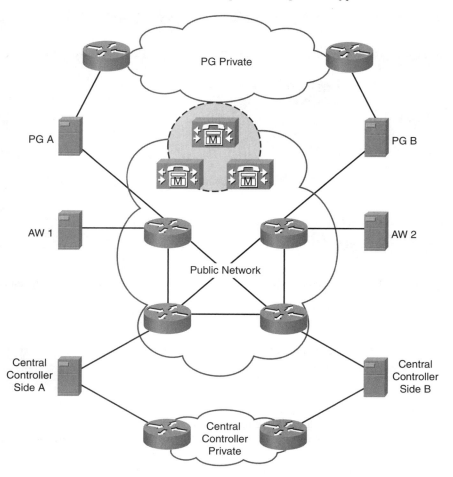

Figure 6-3   *UCCE Independent Communications Networks*

For many smaller single-site deployments that combine the logger and router onto the same server, the private network is achieved by using a crossover cable between both machines.

The UCCE solution supports QoS tagging in the application. This means that the UCCE component marks the traffic with the assigned QoS classification as it leaves the application and therefore requires no further marking in the network. Assuming that the network trusts the QoS tagging, the QoS marking will be retained until it reaches its destination.

In UCCE version 8.5, QoS tagging is currently supported only for the private networks of the router and PG processes. Figure 6-4 shows an example of the default QoS tagging for Router A defined during web setup.

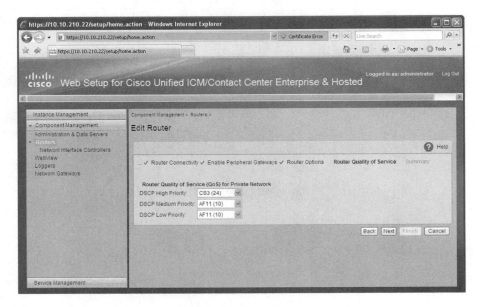

Figure 6-4   *Router A QoS Marking for the Private Network*

Tip   QoS tagging for the router and PG is defined only on Side A. When the two sides establish communications, Side A notifies Side B of the QoS values.

Prior to applications-based QoS marking (and for networks capable of only marking the packets at the network edge), UCCE uses additional IP addresses assigned to the public and private NICs. UCCE applications now actually use three traffic priorities—low, medium, and high—but prior to this, only two priorities were used. These priorities were based on the source and destination IP addresses. This allowed the marking and routing of traffic within the network rather than at the application. The traffic from these IP addresses also used specific TCP/UDP ports based on an algorithm that incorporates the instance number. This was so that hosted systems with multiple customer instances would not clash.

Tip   Details of the port values can be found in the *Port Utilization Guide for Cisco ICM/IPCC/Enterprise and Hosted Editions*, which you can find at http://www.cisco.com/en/US/docs/voice_ip_comm/cust_contact/contact_center/icm_enter prise/icm_enterprise_7_2/configuration/guide/portutil72.pdf.

The IP addresses for the different interfaces (public/visible or private) and their priority (normal or high) were allocated to hostnames for easy configuration within the application. These names would also be detailed in the HOSTS file. Figure 6-5 shows a screen shot for a router setup that uses the visible, private, and high-priority private (termed *private high*) host names. Notice the *p* and *ph* at the end of the hostname to signify private and private high, respectively.

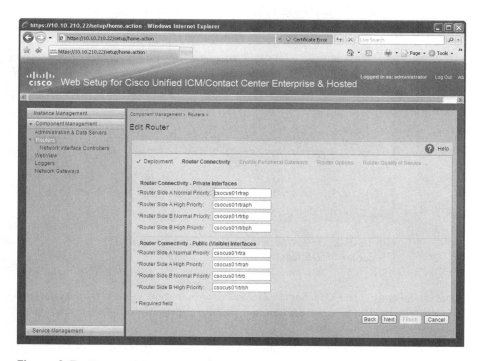

Figure 6-5   *Router A Hostnames for the Private and Public Networks*

Tip   For platforms that have their central controllers distributed over a WAN, it is common to find that the private IP addresses are in different subnets. A Windows server should have only a single default gateway defined; therefore, to route private network traffic out through the private interface, it is necessary to use the **route** command to add a series of static routes to the server.

Databases

An important aspect of designing a UCCE solution is to ensure that the databases are sized correctly. Database sizing has a direct impact on the amount of data that can be retained in all the databases.

The logger database is required to store all the configuration data and a limited amount of historical data. The HDS database stores all the long-term historical reporting data and call detail records. Many organizations want to retain at least 3 years worth of historical data so that they can analyze call trends over a long time period. Both the logger and the HDS databases are created by the installation engineer using the ICM Database Administrator (ICMDBA) tool, as shown in Figure 6-6.

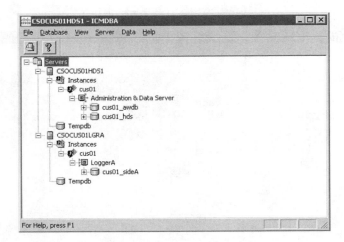

Figure 6-6   *The ICMDBA Tool Used for Creating the Logger and HDS Databases*

The Administration and Data Server also has a configuration and real-time database, but this is not created with ICMDBA during installation; instead, the installer program automatically creates this database.

The server specification detailed in the UCCE bill of materials document typically specifies disk sizes that can easily meet the requirements of all but the largest contact centers. However, it is the responsibility of the designer and installation engineer to correctly size the database during installation. Unfortunately, the UCCE Sizing Tool does not provide any guideline sizes. You can use an ICM System Sizing Estimator tool to give database sizing approximations.

Tip   You can find the ICM System Sizing Estimator tool at c:\icm\bin\icrdbcfg.exe.

Figure 6-7 shows a screen shot of the Sizing Estimator running on an Administration and Data Server.

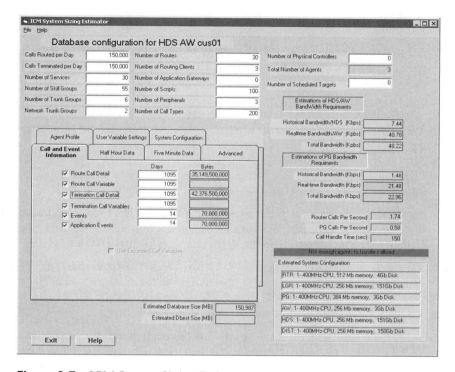

Figure 6-7   *ICM System Sizing Estimator*

The tool works by allowing the designer to enter approximate figures for the configuration data and the required retention periods. The tool then indicates an estimated required database size. As with all estimations, it is good practice to factor in an amount of anticipated growth.

Cisco A2Q Process

An important part of the design and ordering process is for the high-level solution to be approved by Cisco. Previously called Bid Assurance, the Assessment to Quality (A2Q) is a high-level design review of the proposed solution that takes place between the Cisco ATP partner responsible for deployment and the Cisco A2Q review team.

The A2Q process usually consists of the ATP partner submitting a series of documents to the review team. As the process is only a high-level review, the documents submitted include the following:

- The A2Q questionnaire, which comprises a series of questions to give the review team the necessary background and design overview.

- The bill of materials (BOM), which forms the kit list of the actual components to be ordered from Cisco to build the UCCE platform.

- A network design showing all the network connectivity, physical site locations, bandwidth, and QoS.

- A statement of work (SOW), which explains the deployment process and the teams, partners, and possibly Cisco professional service personal who can perform the deployment.

After the documents have been submitted, the review team schedules a conference call with the Cisco partner to discuss the design. The call typically lasts for approximately 30 minutes, and the conference participants include the following:

- Representatives from the ATP partner including the technical project manager and solutions architect responsible for the design.

- The A2Q review team composed of several Cisco engineers from the Contact Center Business Unit (CCBU) familiar with all technologies relevant to the design, including Unified Communications Manager, IVRs, and network infrastructure.

- The Cisco sales engineer assigned to work with the ATP partner, who typically has a detailed knowledge of the partner's capabilities and the customer's requirements.

The A2Q conference calls are not open to the end customer.

During the conference call, the review team works through the submitted documents to confirm and validate various design items and the rationale behind them. The review team also seeks clarification on who will actually perform the deployment and the methodology that will be followed. Although the ATP partner is the direct interface into Cisco, it is common for large partners to subcontract work to smaller companies. The accountability of the solution is that of the ATP partner and not the subcontractor.

The A2Q process can take place at any point during the sales cycle. Cisco recommends that A2Q takes place as early as possible because the process is not just a formality to receive approval. A2Q is an important step in the deployment process, and without A2Q approval, the ATP partner cannot purchase the UCCE software and licenses required for deployment.

As discussed, the A2Q process is a high-level design review performed during a brief conference call. A detailed design review could take days or weeks. Items discussed on the call typically involve the following:

- That the solution is sized correctly to meet the requirements, such as the number of Cisco Unified Communications Manager (Unified CM) servers to support a given number of agents, or the number of IVR ports to provide IVR resources for a defined number of busy-hour call attempts (BHCA).

- That the correct kit list is ordered. Often the wrong part codes are listed in the bill of materials, or some items are accidentally missed.

- That adequate and skilled resourcing has been scheduled to perform the deployment and that realistic time frames have been proposed.

The review team takes part in a large number of design reviews on a regular basis, so they have familiarity with a range of UCCE deployments. Because they see so many proposed designs, they can also offer comprehensive feedback and advice to the ATP partner on potential enhancements and ways to better the solution, perhaps even reducing the overall cost of deployment.

From the A2Q reviews I have taken part in, I would recommend the following points:

- Clearly document and detail the private and public network connectivity. The survivability of the UCCE platform during a failure depends on the correct deployment of a segregated private and public network. With complex deployments such as clustering over the WAN and split peripheral gateways, it is important to demonstrate to the review team that the platform can still transmit heartbeat and synchronization traffic during events of failure.

- Check the kit list thoroughly. Often the bill of materials (BOM) is produced early in the design process to provide the sales team with a figure to quote to the end customer. During the design process, the BOMs might change to suit new requirements. Be sure to include the correct agent license part codes, media kits, and the required support products such as Essential Operate Service (ESW) and the Unified Communications Software Subscription (UCSS).

- Ensure that the proposed solution is sized correctly to meet just slightly more than the minimum requirements, but is not overengineered. Many of the customers I have worked with have expanded their platforms over time to add more agents. Designing a solution to meet only the bare minimum is a false economy and can lead to performance issues.

The A2Q process is not a guarantee that the solution will be error-free when it is deployed, but it is a review that adds great value to all designs and has been proven to ensure that the end customer receives a solution that is fit for purpose.

Implementation

To achieve success in the operate and optimize phases of the lifecycle, it is necessary to have a successful implementation as this is the phase in which the foundation is laid. A misconfigured or badly performed software installation will continually cause problems later in the platform's lifecycle.

Server Builds

Before commencing with an installation of the UCCE application, it is worth ensuring that the underlying Microsoft Windows and third-party applications are installed correctly. All the server components for a UCCE solution must be compliant with the bill of materials document for the software version being deployed. The following list comprises the key items that should be checked:

- MS Windows version and correct service pack

- MS SQL Server version and correct service pack

- MS SQL Server binary sort order, Named Pipes enabled, and the correct client protocol order (1st Shared Memory, 2nd Named Pipes, 3rd TCP/IP)

- Network cards configured with the correct IP addresses and binding order

- Static routes defined on the servers to route private UCCE traffic out of the correct NICs

- Additional Windows components installed (SNMP, WMI Windows Installer Provider)

- Cisco third-party tools

Software Installation

UCCE versions prior to version 8.0 were installed and configured from a single setup.exe application from the installation media. The version 7.x installer would leave behind a version of the installer called icmsetup.exe in the c:\icm\bin directory so that this version of the installer could be run for future configuration changes or the addition/removal of other components.

With UCCE version 8.x, the UCCE software is still installed from a setup.exe application; however, the configuration of the UCCE nodes is now performed through a web-based setup process, making the installation and configuration a two-step process.

Not all the UCCE components currently use the new web setup. The ones that do are as follows:

- Loggers

- Routers (including NICs and network gateways for hosted or carrier-connected deployments)

- Administration and data servers

- Administration client

- WebView

The following components do not use the new web setup:

- Peripheral gateway

- CTI server

- CTI OS server

Figure 6-8 shows an example of configuration using the new web installer, whereas Figure 6-9 shows the installation/configuration of a PG, which in version 8.0 uses the traditional method.

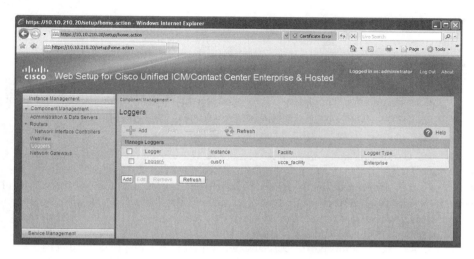

Figure 6-8   *New Web-Based Installer*

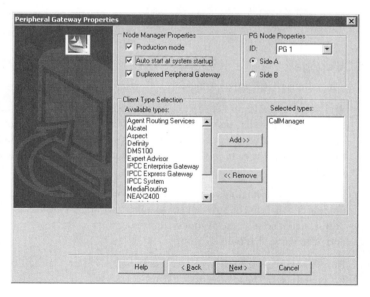

Figure 6-9   *Old-Style Installer Still Used for the PGs in UCCE 8.0*

Tip   A useful feature of version 8.0 is that you can specify a service release to be installed. The application of the service release is a two-step process because the server usually reboots after the initial phase of installation, but it does automatically resume with the service release after logging in.

Installation Order

Chapter 11, "Nodes and Processes," examines all the different processes that run on a UCCE server, and you can observe a preferred startup order to minimize the number of errors observed. A similar order also exists when performing an initial installation.

Note   The installation order detailed in this section is my preference based on the many UICM and UCCE installations I have performed over the years. Every experienced UCCE engineer is likely to have a slightly different way that he approaches an installation. When I perform an install, I like to check each node along the way so that if I have made an error, it can be quickly rectified rather than trying to troubleshoot several errors when all the nodes have been installed. This installation order assumes that the Windows OS, domain structure, SQL Server, third-party tools, and network infrastructure (including network services [DNS and HOSTS files]) are already in place. It is worth double-checking these before commencing with the installation, especially if they were installed by a different engineer. I recommend that you also perform a series of network *ping* tests to check connectivity for the public and private IP addresses.

Installing UCCE Logger A

The steps for installing UCCE Logger A are as follows:

Step 1.   **Run setup.exe and install the Logger A node.** The setup.exe installer performs a base installation of the UCCE application onto the server. The installer checks for third-party applications such as SQL Server and prompts the engineer if they are missing or configured incorrectly. Include a maintenance release if required.

Step 2.   **Run DomainManager.exe on Logger A.** This creates the customer instance credentials that all the subsequent installers will use. Within DomainManager, you should also allocate Windows user accounts to the Configuration, Setup, and WebView (if required) groups.

Step 3.   **Run ICMDBA.exe on Logger A.** Use ICMDBA to create the Logger Data and Log databases. These need to be sized correctly based on the required retention periods set in the purge cycles and the expected contact center size (agents, skill groups, and call volumes).

Step 4.   **Connect to the Web Setup page and configure Logger A.** Work through the configuration pages, entering the correct values that have been previously documented in the installation spreadsheets.

Step 5. **Start the Logger A service.** Start the service using ICM Service Control, and observe that each process starts correctly. The *csfs* process will complain that it is "Waiting for Link Enable," and the *histlogger* will be waiting for Message Delivery Service (MDS) messages. This is normal and nothing to be concerned about.

Installing UCCE Router A

The steps for installing UCCE Router A are as follows:

Step 1. **Run setup.exe and install the Router A node.** The setup.exe installer performs a base installation of the UCCE application onto the server. Include a maintenance release if required.

Step 2. **Connect to the Web Setup page and configure Router A.** Work through the configuration pages, entering the correct values that have been previously documented in the installation spreadsheets.

Step 3. **Start the Router A service.** Start the service using ICM Service Control, and observe that each process starts correctly. The router will not go active because it cannot see any PGs. MDS will also complain that Synchronizer operation is suspended as it cannot see the Side B router.

Tip If the newly installed node attempts to do an autoshutdown/restart, an example of which can be seen in Figure 6-10, a common cause of this is that the hostnames cannot be resolved. Check the hostnames in UCCE setup against the HOSTS file or DNS server. The autoshutdown can be stopped with the **stopshut** command. Alternatively, you can disable *Reboot Machine on Error* in web setup for the node.

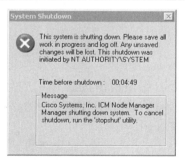

Figure 6-10 *Autoreboot Warning Message*

Installing UCCE Peripheral Gateway 1A

The steps for installing UCCE peripheral gateway 1A are as follows:

Step 1. **Browse to the Unified CM server to obtain JTAPI.** Download the JTAPI client from the Unified CM server and run the installation process on the PG.

Step 2.   **Run setup.exe and install the PG1A node.** The setup.exe installer performs the entire PG installation because web setup is not currently enabled for PGs.

Work through the configuration pages, entering the correct values that have been previously documented in the installation spreadsheets. To configure the Peripheral Interface Manager (PIM), you need to specify physical and logical controller IDs. These are integer values that are defined only when a PG is created in PG Explorer. The PG Explorer tool is not available until the administration workstation is configured. Many engineers specify dummy values at this point and then later return to setup after they have created the PG in PG Explorer. However, because this is the first PG, you could enter the value 5000 for both the physical and logical controller IDs because these are the default values created by PG Explorer. But be aware: How you configure subsequent peripherals determines which values are used. It is recommended that you double-check these values after you have used PG Explorer!

Step 3.   **Run setup.exe and install the CG1A node.** During the installation of the CTI Server, make a note of the client connection port number. This number will be required when configuring the CTI OS Server.

Step 4.   **Start the PG1A service.** Start the service using ICM Service Control, and observe that each process starts correctly. Observe that the PG connects to the central controller (Side A only). Error messages might appear in the process windows to say that the PG is not defined.

Step 5.   **Run setup.exe and install the CTI OS 1 Server.** This is a different setup.exe than the PG/CTI Server. As with the PG, for the CTI OS installation, you need to enter the peripheral ID of the Unified CM server. If you are not confident of what the ID is going to be, you should not perform this step until after you have installed the AW and created the PG with PG Explorer.

Installing UCCE AW HDS 1

The steps for installing UCCE AW HDS 1 are as follows:

Step 1.   **Run setup.exe and install the AW Distributor node.** The setup.exe installer performs a base installation of the UCCE application onto the server. Include a maintenance release if required.

Step 2.   **Run ICMDBA.exe on AW HDS1.** Use ICMDBA to create the HDS Data and Log databases. These need to be sized correctly based on the required retention periods set in the purge cycles and the expected contact center size. My preference during setup is to perform the full install of an AW and HDS; however, the minimum requirement is only for an AW so that the PG can be configured.

Step 3.   **Connect to the Web Setup page and configure the AW.** Work through the configuration pages, entering the correct values that have been previously documented in the installation spreadsheets.

Step 4.   **Start the AW Distributor service.** Start the service using ICM Service Control, and observe that each process starts correctly. Observe the UpdateAW process to see whether the Waiting for New Work prompt appears. At this point in the installation process, you can perform the basic configuration of the PGs. Before you configure a PG, however, you must also create a default agent desk setting because this is a required option for the Unified CM PG!

Step 5.   **Validate the system.** After the PG has been configured, check the PG and router processes. If the PGUser username and password are correct, the PG should be connected to the Unified CM server and its PIM and JTAPI processes should be ACTIVE. The CTI and CTI OS server processes should also be ACTIVE. The router MDS process should be In Service.

Note   With UCCE 8.0 and later, several different AW deployments are available depending on the Deployment Size option selected when working through web setup.

Small to Medium gives you the choice of

- AW-HDS-DDS
- AW
- Configuration Only

Large gives you the choice of

- AW-HDS
- HDS-DDS
- AW
- Configuration Only

Installing UCCE Logger B

The steps for installing UCCE Logger B are as follows:

Step 1.   **Run setup.exe and install the Logger B node.** The setup.exe installer performs a base installation of the UCCE application onto the server. The installer checks for third-party applications such as SQL Server and prompts the engineer if they are missing or configured incorrectly. Include a maintenance release if required.

Step 2.   **Run ICMDBA.exe on Logger B.** Use ICMDBA to create the Logger Data and Log databases. These need to be sized correctly based on the required retention periods set in the purge cycles and the expected contact center size (agents, skill groups, and call volumes).

Step 3.   **Connect to the Web Setup page and configure Logger B.** Work through the configuration pages, entering the correct values that have been previously documented in the installation spreadsheets.

Step 4.   **Start the Logger B service.** Start the service using ICM Service Control, and observe that each process starts correctly. The *csfs* process will complain that it is Waiting for Link Enable, and the *histlogger* will be waiting for MDS messages. This is normal and nothing to be concerned about.

Installing UCCE Router B

The steps for installing UCCE Router B are as follows:

Step 1.   **Run setup.exe and install the Router B node.** The setup.exe installer performs a base installation of the UCCE application onto the server. Include a maintenance release if required.

Step 2.   **Connect to the Web Setup page and configure Router B.** Work through the configuration pages, entering the correct values that have been previously documented in the installation spreadsheets.

Step 3.   **Start the Router B service.** Start the service using ICM Service Control, and observe that each process starts correctly. Routers A and B should now perform a state transfer and start running in duplex operation.

Tip   After Router B is started, the logger database should synchronize from Side A to Side B. This can be checked by looking for the Logger Sync (A->B) message in the *histlogger* process window. If the automatic database synchronization does not take place, it is possible to manually perform a synchronization using ICMDBA.

Installing UCCE Peripheral Gateway 1B

The steps for installing UCCE peripheral gateway 1B are as follows:

Step 1.   **Browse to the Unified CM server to obtain JTAPI.** Download the JTAPI client from the Unified CM server and run the installation process on the PG.

Step 2.   **Run setup.exe and install the PG1B node.** The setup.exe installer performs the entire PG installation as web setup is not currently enabled for PGs. Work through the configuration pages, entering the correct values that have been previously documented in the installation spreadsheets.

Step 3.   **Run setup.exe and install the CG1B node.** During installation of the CTI Server, make a note of the client connection port number. This number will be required when configuring the CTI OS Server; this number will also be different than the port number obtained for CTI Server A.

Step 4.   **Start the PG1B service.** Start the service using ICM Service Control, and observe that each process starts correctly. Observe that the PG connects to the central controller.

Step 5.   **Run setup.exe and install the CTI OS 1 Server.** This is a different setup.exe than the PG/CTI Server. Work through the configuration pages, entering the correct values that have been previously documented in the installation spreadsheets.

Installing UCCE AW HDS 2

The steps for installing UCCE AW HDS 2 are as follows:

Step 1.   **Run setup.exe and install the AW Distributor node.** The setup.exe installer performs a base installation of the UCCE application onto the server. Include a maintenance release if required.

Step 2.   **Run ICMDBA.exe on AW HDS2.** Use ICMDBA to create the HDS Data and Log databases. These need to be sized correctly based on the required retention periods set in the purge cycles and the expected contact center size.

Step 3.   **Connect to the Web Setup page and configure the AW.** Work through the configuration pages, entering the correct values that have been previously documented in the installation spreadsheets.

Step 4.   **Start the AW Distributor service.** Start the service using ICM Service Control, and observe that each process starts correctly. Observe the UpdateAW process to see whether the Waiting for New Work prompt appears.

After the final AW HDS has been installed, the remaining components can be installed in almost any order. I prefer to get the remaining PGs configured and then move on to installing the base software for the IVRs, followed by the Cisco Agent Desktop servers.

Tip   After Router B is started, the logger database should synchronize from Side A to Side B. If the automatic database synchronization does not take place, it is possible to manually perform a synchronization using ICMDBA.

Implementation Testing

The primary goal of UCCE implementation testing is to uncover problems with the application or its configuration that have occurred during the initial installation. Testing an entire UCCE solution can be complex because of the amount of customization that takes place with the call routing and reporting. Fortunately, testing the core installation is more focused on ensuring that the platform has been installed correctly and provides the required fault tolerance during failure scenarios.

Software testing is a formal engineering process that should be completed by an engineer who did not perform the installation. During testing, the test engineer works through a test specification composed of multiple prioritized test cases. Each test case details a series of scenarios or parameters. The results of the test case, as defined in the list that follows, are documented in the test results document:

■   **Pass:** The test case was executed per the test specification, and the result matched the expected result.

- **Fail:** The test case was executed per the test specification, and the result did not match the expected result.

- **Not run:** The test case was not executed. The reason should be documented.

- **Descoped:** The test case was not executed because the feature or function that it tests is unavailable and will not be available during the test period.

Prior to performing the testing, the test manager receives direction from the project manager and the end customer on what is an acceptable testing exit criteria. In an ideal world, you might expect a 100 percent pass rate; however, this is unusual for a large, complex software deployment. A typical customer might require that 100 percent of the priority 1 and 2 tests pass successfully and require at least an 80 percent pass rate for the priority 3 and 4 test cases. Other customers might request an overall 75 percent pass rate, with a documented action plan to resolve the remaining priority 1 and 2 issues before going live.

The test cases that will be created to test the core UCCE application installation comprise only a small subset of the overall UCCE solution test specification. Testing for the overall UCCE solution would need to cover all the routing, reporting, agent desktop, Unified CM, IVR, and third-party platforms. Comprehensive testing, even for a modestly sized deployment, can require a considerable effort and usually requires a dedicated testing team. However, performing a proper systems test is crucial to give the customer confidence that its solution is fit for purpose.

As previously mentioned, the focus for testing of the core UCCE application installation is to ensure that the software components have been configured correctly and that the nodes/processes fail over correctly should a problem occur. The areas under test can be summarized as follows:

- Configuration checking
- Router process redundancy
- Logger synchronization
- AW synchronization
- Peripheral connectivity
- PG process redundancy
- CTI Server process redundancy
- CTI OS Server process redundancy
- Router public network failure
- Router private network failure
- PG public network failure
- PG private network failure
- Individual server failures

> **Note**   A duplex deployment of the CTI OS Server process is not Active/Idle like the PG
> or CTI Server. When testing this process for redundancy, you are actually checking that
> one of the CTI OS Servers remains active when the other fails.

Table 6-4 gives an example test case for testing PG redundancy.

Table 6-4   *Example Test Case for Testing PG Redundancy*

Test Case ID	UCCE-CORE-PGR001	Test Engineer	B. Smith
Date	21st March 2011	Test Result	Pass
Test Category	UCCE Core Installation		
Test Title	Failover of Active Unified CM PM to Idle PG		
Test Purpose	To ensure that the duplex PG pair are in communication so that should the active PG fail, the idle PG will resume control		
Prerequisites	IP communication exists between both PGs and the Unified CM subscribers. • The chosen PG's PIM and JTAPIGW processes are both active. (the assumption is that the active PG is PG1A; if not, adjust the test procedure accordingly.) • The failover destination PG has its PG processes started and is currently in an idle state.		
Procedure	Establish a remote control session to both PG1A and PG1B. • Using ICM Service Control, select the Cisco ICM cus01 PG1A service and select Stop (or Cycle). • The PG1A processes begin a graceful shutdown. • PG1A notifies PG1B that it is shutting down. • Observe that the PG1B PIM and JTAPIGW processes activate. • PG1B should now be active and be in communication with the Unified CM.		
Notes			

> **Tip**   Cisco partners who have access to a partner login on Cisco.com should explore the
> Steps to Success pages available from the Partner Tools. These pages provide comprehen-
> sive Cisco guidelines and document templates (including test specifications) that can be
> used during all phases of the lifecycle methodology.

Summary

In this chapter, you worked through many of the important steps that should be covered before and during the installation of the core UCCE components. In particular, the key learning points from this chapter can be summarized as follows:

■ Cisco recommends a lifecycle approach to platform deployment.

■ Several design tools are available to ensure that the solution is designed and sized correctly to meet the needs of the enterprise.

■ UCCE solutions should be deployed only by a Cisco-approved ATP partner.

Chapter 7

UCCE Application Configuration

This chapter covers the following subjects:

- UCCE configuration spreadsheets
- Application configuration order
- Configuration tools used

Cisco Unified Contact Center Enterprise (UCCE) application configuration logically follows on from the core application installation detailed in Chapter 6, "UCCE Platform Deployment." The majority of the configuration tasks are performed during the implementation phase of the lifecycle methodology, but requirements capture and the scheduling of activities also take place in the prepare and plan phases.

After the core software installation is complete, it is necessary to configure the various different items such as skill groups, agents, teams, and dialed numbers specific to the customer. This chapter coverx a generic configuration order and look at the various best practices to follow during configuration.

Prepare

The prepare phase lays the foundation for a successful implementation phase. The key aim of this phase is the capturing of all the configuration requirements in a way that allows these details to be implemented in a logical manner with little or no revisiting of configuration tools.

Requirements Capture

Contact center projects usually fall into two categories: greenfield installations or the migration/upgrade of an existing platform.

Regardless of the type of project, the proposed configuration should be detailed in a requirements document. The types of data that this chapter focuses on are items such as agent names, teams, skill groups, and dialed numbers.

With a greenfield deployment for a new contact center, this configuration data is usually hypothetical. The business leaders have an understanding of how they want their contact center to be operated and have designed a solution based on these ideas. Depending on how far the project has progressed, the organization might not have even recruited all the agents, so it might not have all the required data at hand.

For a contact center migration, the organization typically already has a detailed list of all the required agent and call plan data. In many cases, this data can be exported from an existing Automatic Call Distributor (ACD) and reformatted using a spreadsheet ready for importing into UCCE.

Capture Spreadsheets

Spreadsheets are ideal tools for the storage and manipulation of large lists of contact center configuration. Call-routing flows should be captured as flowcharts or Microsoft Visio diagrams because it makes the conversion into UCCE scripting easier.

Both UCCE and Unified CM have bulk insert tools that can take formatted text documents and rapidly configure the data into the respective platform. Using these tools properly can rapidly increase the speed in which a platform is deployed.

When creating these spreadsheets, it is advisable to use the same layout and data format used by the bulk insert tools. When the data is to be provided by the end customer, it is often easiest to give the customer the blank templates of the correct format. Doing this minimizes any chance of errors by removing the need for the data to be reformatted before bulk entry.

Some of the fields required for UCCE bulk entry will not be available from the current ACD system, or they will be fields that the customer does not understand as they are specific UCCE terminology.

A key requirement of these spreadsheets is that they be as accurate and up to date as possible. Contact center environments are often dynamic, with agents and teams frequently changing. Because of this, there also needs to be a deadline or change freeze after which time no further changes to the spreadsheets should be made. Having this deadline in place allows the application engineers to set a date on which they will perform the data load. However, you should expect some degree of changes to be made after the bulk load has taken place. This rework time should be factored into the project plan.

Implementation

Many tools are used when installing and maintaining a UCCE platform. The majority of these tools can be found through a single application called the Configuration Manager.

Configuration Manager

The Configuration Manager tool, found in the UCCE Tools directory on the administrative workstation, is a starting point for all the configuration tools required for initial and ongoing configuration.

Figure 7-1 shows the Configuration Manager tool with some of its menu items expanded. With so many menus and applications, it can be daunting for a new user to understand where to start.

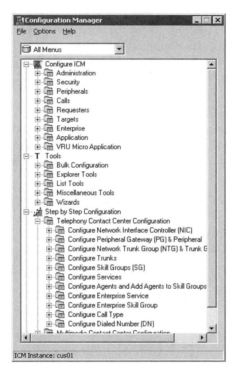

Figure 7-1 *Traditional and Modern Views of Available Configuration Tools*

The Configuration Manager has four main menus:

- Configure ICM

- Tools

- Step by Step Configuration

- Outbound Option

With the exception of the Outbound Option, the subapplications in the other three menus are identical, but just ordered differently. In early versions of Unified Intelligent Contact Manager (UICM), a Configure ICM application was used to perform application administration. Each of the menu items with this application opened various configuration pages. In the new Configuration Manager, the layout of the tools within the Configure ICM menu replicates the layout of Configure ICM. This allowed an easier migration for users upgrading from older versions as the menu location familiarity was retained.

The Tools menu provides a logical grouping of the tools based on their functionality. The most common groups of tools to use on a daily basis are the Explorer and List tools. The applications in the List Tools group could be described as being singularly defined items with no subconfiguration. For example, the Call Type list tool presents the administrator with an alphabetical list of all the Call Types defined for the system configuration, such as the ability to specify the service level but no subconfiguration items.

An Explorer tool is used for configuration items that have one or more layers of subconfiguration. Figure 7-2 shows an example of the Network Trunk Group Explorer. It is possible to see that a network trunk group has three levels of configuration. The top level is the Network Trunk Group, the second level is the Trunk Group, and the lower level is the actual Trunk. Each Explorer tool has a legend that illustrates the configuration mapping.

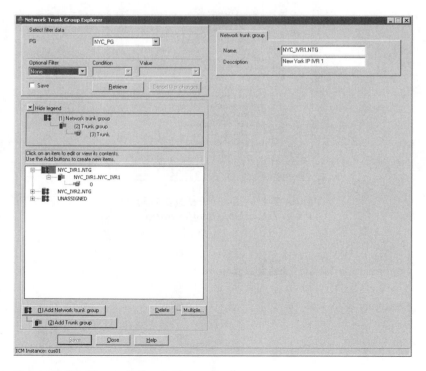

Figure 7-2   *Network Trunk Group Explorer*

> **Note**   Remember that the configuration tools for UCCE are identical to UICM. UICM supports many different ACD types. Configuration items for a legacy ACD might not be required for Unified CM. An example of this is the Agent Explorer tool. The Agent Explorer has four levels of configuration items: Agent, Route, Peripheral Target, and Label. For a Unified CM agent with UCCE, only the Agent configuration item needs to be defined. The other three levels can be ignored.

The third menu item in Configuration Manager is the Step by Step Configuration menu. As indicative of its name, the Step by Step Configuration menu attempts to present a logical flow for configuring a new installation.

Configuration Order

The UCCE configuration is stored in a relational database (discussed in more detail in Chapter 14, "UCCE Databases"). This means that many of the configuration items are linked to other items, often configured using different tools. This requires that the configuration process follows a logical order; otherwise, the administrator frequently returns to certain tools to complete the configuration. An example of this would be the creation of a new agent, agent desk setting, and skill group.

If you were to open Agent Explorer and start configuring a new agent, you cannot save the agent with the correct agent desk setting or skill group because they have not been created yet. You would need to configure the agent desk setting and skill group first, and then configure the agent in Agent Explorer and assign the correct agent desk setting and skill group. However, if you were configuring a skill group of ten agents, you might not want to assign the skill group to the agents while in Agent Explorer because this would require you to individually select the skill group for every agent. It would be quicker to configure only the agent and assign the agent desk setting in Agent Explorer, and then use Skill Group Explorer to select all ten agents and assign them in one action.

The sequence that follows details a configuration order that can be used for new UCCE installations to minimize the chance of having to revisit configuration items. Detailed configuration of each item varies depending on the version of UCCE administered. Information on using all these configuration tools can be found in the relevant version of the "Configuration Guide for Cisco Unified ICM/Contact Center Enterprise and Hosted," at http://www.cisco.com/en/US/products/sw/custcosw/ps1844/products_installation_ and_configuration_guides_list.html.

Step 1.   **Create a default agent desk setting (ADS).** Use the Agent Desk Settings list tool to create a default ADS. At this stage, you just assign a name and leave all the other settings at their default values.

Step 2.   **Create the Unified CM PG.** Use PG Explorer to create the peripheral gateway (PG) for the Unified CM. The peripheral client type for Unified CM is CallManager/SoftACD. You will also need to select an agent desk setting.

Caution Deployments using IP Interactive Voice Response (IVR) can be configured with a PG client type of "PG Generic." Then specify the Unified CM and IVR peripherals against a single PG. Doing this allows the IVR PGs and the Unified CM PGs to use the same logical and physical controller IDs. Although configuring the Unified CM PG, it is tempting to also configure the IP IVR PGs, but beware that when you click the Save button, PG Explorer sorts the peripherals into alphabetical order before it assigns the peripheral IDs and saves the configuration. Therefore, for a new installation, if you enter the following three peripherals

LDN_UCM (Unified CM cluster)

LDN_IPIVR1 (Unified IP IVR 1)

LDN_IPIVR2 (Unified IP IVR 2)

you would expect the logical and physical controller IDs to both be 5000, and the peripheral IDs to be 5000, 5001, and 5002 for peripherals LDN_UCM, LDN_IPIVR1, and LDN_IPIVR2, respectively. Ideally, your Unified CM would have a peripheral ID of 5000 because this is the default peripheral ID that you might have configured during UCCE software installation.

However, the PG Explorer sorts the peripheral names alphabetically before saving; therefore, in this example, the Unified CM PG is given the peripheral ID of 5002!

Even if the PG and its associated peripherals are deleted, the logical, physical, and peripheral IDs are not reused by PG Explorer. Therefore, it is not possible to regenerate an ID of 5000 if it is mistakenly assigned.

Step 3.   **Create the IVR PG.** Use PG Explorer to create the peripheral gateway for the Unified IVR or Customer Voice Portal (CVP) servers.

Note Now that the peripheral gateways have been created and the peripheral IDs confirmed, it is possible to activate the Unified CM PG. The IVR peripheral IDs can be given to the installation engineer responsible for the IVR deployment.

Step 4.   **Create the IVR trunks.** If you use Unified IP IVR, use the Network Trunk Group Explorer to create the network trunk groups, trunk groups, and trunks.

Step 5.   **Create the IVR.** Use the Network VRU Explorer to define the correct type of IVR that will be used.

Step 6.   **Create the skill groups and their associated routes.** For a small number of skill groups, the Skill Group Explorer tool is the easiest method for configuring the skill groups because it also enables you to specify a route. For a large number of skill groups, the Skill Group Bulk Insert tool could be used. However, the Skill Group Bulk Insert tool does not also create the routes for the skill group; these would also need to be bulk-inserted using the Route

Bulk Insert tool. Regardless of which method is chosen, each skill group also needs to have a unique peripheral number associated with it.

Step 7.   **Create the services and their associated routes.** Unlike legacy ACD deployments, services tend not be used with a UCCE deployment, except for translation routing to other peripherals such as the Unified IP IVR. Because only a single service and route are needed for each IP IVR, the Service Explorer tool should be used.

Step 8.   **Create the agent desk settings.** An initial default ADS was created as the first step to configure the Unified CM PG. The Agent Desk Settings List tool should be used to create the remaining agent desk settings.

Step 9.   **Create the agents.** Even small contact centers usually have a large number of agents. Individual agents can be added or modified using the Agent Explorer, but for the initial insertion of a long list of agents, it is best to use the Agent Bulk Insert tool. However, prior to doing this, you must create persons to associate the agents to. This is required only for Agent Bulk Insert and not if only Agent Explorer is used! Supervisor accounts should also be created as an agent as part of the same bulk insert for simplicity.

Note   The Agent Bulk Insert tool has a column entitled Supervisor Agent; however, it is not possible to set the agent to be a supervisor using the Agent Bulk Insert or the Agent Bulk Edit tools!

Step 10.   **Assign supervisors.** The Supervisor List tool lists only the supervisors and the teams that they supervise. To create a supervisor, the person first must exist as an agent. In Agent Explorer, the supervisor account can be selected and enabled as a supervisor. This process also creates a Windows domain account for the user.

Step 11.   **Create the agent teams.** The Agent Team List tool should be used to create the agent teams and assign the team members and team supervisors. Unfortunately, no Bulk Insert tool exists for agent teams.

Step 12.   **Configure device targets or agent targeting rules.** Modern UCCE installations will probably use agent targeting rules. These can be configured with the Agent Targeting Rule list. Older installations are likely to use device targets or a combination of device targets and agent targeting rules. Device targets are created using the Device Target Explorer and also require a label for each peripheral.

Note   In recent versions of UCCE, the requirement for device targets has been replaced by the use of agent targeting rules. Device targets are used when sending calls between peripherals. The device target has a label mapped to it for each peripheral that the call could potentially be delivered from. Therefore, an agent configured for a UCCE deployment that has one Unified CM cluster and two IP IVRs would need a single device target with three labels, one for each peripheral. This can result in a lot of configuration for a large contact center. Fortunately, after the device target is configured, it remains static and is unlikely to get changed. However, if the business expands and more peripherals are added, new device target labels need to be added to every device target. This is a considerable amount of administration and can be prone to error.

To reduce this administration for UCCE deployments, Cisco has introduced agent targeting rules. Rather than having a statically defined device target, the agent targeting rule allows the label to be dynamic.

Agent targeting rules are defined with the appropriately named tool in Configuration Manager. Three types of rule exist: Agent Extension, Substitute Agent Extension, and Translation Route. Three types of agent targeting modes for the peripheral gateway are possible (defined in PG Explorer): Device Target Preferred, Rule Preferred, and Rules Compare to Existing Device Target. The use of these modes allows an organization to continue using device targets, use the targeting rules, or use a mixture of device targets and targeting rules. The latter option is for organizations that are migrating from device targets to targeting rules.

The default mode for PG installation on new UCCE software versions is Rule Preferred.

Step 13. **Create the call types.** The customer's reporting requirements have an effect on how many call types need to be created. At an absolute minimum, there needs to be at least one call type for every dialed number, and a call type can map to only one call-routing script. To provide more detailed reporting, call types are often changed during the flow of a call script, which results in many different call types being created. The Call Type Bulk Insert tool can be used for the configuration of a large number of call types; otherwise, the Call Type List tool should be used.

Step 14. **Create the dialed numbers.** A long list of dialed numbers can be configured using the Dialed Number Bulk Insert tool. Individual dialed numbers can be configured using the Dialed Number / Script Selector List tool.

Step 15. **Create any translation routes.** Translation routes are a mechanism that allows a call and its associated Computer Telephony Integration (CTI) data to be transferred to another peripheral and retain call context. The Translation Route Explorer can be used to create translation routes; however, translation routes can be quite complex, so the easiest method is to use the Translation Route Wizard. As shown in Figure 7-3, the Translation Route Wizard works through a series of steps to define the translation route, select the number of peripherals and routing clients, associate the PG, and define and create the Dialed Number Information Service (DNIS) and labels for the call destination.

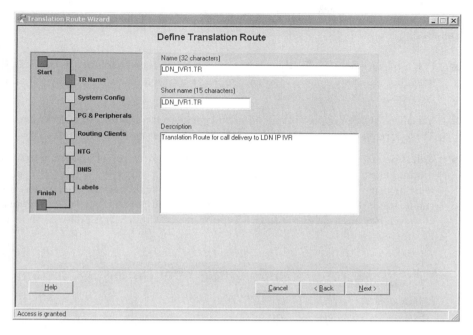

Figure 7-3   *Translation Route Wizard*

Step 16.   **Create reason codes.** Reason codes are used to record the reason why an agent changed into certain agent states. These can be created individually using the Reason Code List tool.

Note   In addition to reason codes, the majority of contact centers also use wrap-up codes to record the purpose of the call. Wrap-up codes are not defined using the Configuration Manager tools. For UCCE deployments using the Cisco Agent Desktop, the wrap-up codes are created using the CAD Administrator application and associated to the agents through the use of workflow groups.

Step 17.   **Create users.** Users accounts are required for several UCCE applications including WebView and the Internet Script Editor. They can be created using the User List tool.

Step 18.   **Complete the Unified CM PG configuration.** To complete the Unified CM PG setup, it is necessary to return to the PG Explorer tool and specify the network Voice Response Unit (VRU) and agent distribution. The network VRU is defined on the Advanced tab and represents the IVR that should be associated with the UCCE solution. Agent distribution is enabled on the Agent Distribution tab to allow agent reporting and also configure the administration and data server site names. The site names that should entered are the ones that were created during web setup for the administrative workstation nodes.

Several other configuration items are likely to be used during the creation of the UCCE call-routing scripts:

- **IVR applications:** These IVR applications are not the actual applications on the IVR itself, but rather are a named reference to the application. These are created with the Network VRU Script List tool.

- **Variables:** UCCE supports many different types of variables for use in scripting. These variables are created using the User Variable List tool.

- **Call type mapping:** For a call to a specific dialed number to invoke a certain call-routing script, the dialed number must be mapped to a call type and that call type must be mapped to a call-routing script. The Dialed Number/Script Selector List tool can be used to assign dialed numbers to call types (but not call types to call scripts). However, it is often easier to use Call Type Manager within Script Editor, as shown in Figure 7-4.

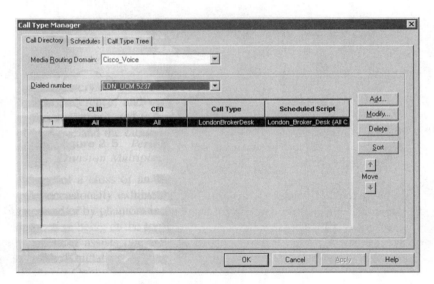

Figure 7-4 *Using Call Type Manager Within Script Editor for Dialed Number, Call Type, and Script Selection*

Securing Configuration Manager

The previous section illustrated that Configuration Manager is a powerful suite of tools that can be used to administer the contact center configuration. Giving every level of UCCE administrator full access to all the Configuration Manager tools could be potentially dangerous as an inexperienced administrator might accidentally delete or modify a vital piece of configuration that subsequently prevents the contact center from functioning correctly.

Fortunately, it is possible to use the Feature Control Sets function of UCCE to restrict the applications that a user sees in Configuration Manager. Feature control sets are implemented using the Feature Control Set List tool.

Figure 7-5 gives an example of a feature control set created for a user that should have access to only administer agents. This role gives the user access to the Agent Explorer, Person List, Agent Team List, Agent Desk Settings, and Skill Group Explorer so that the user has the administrative rights to perform basic user administration.

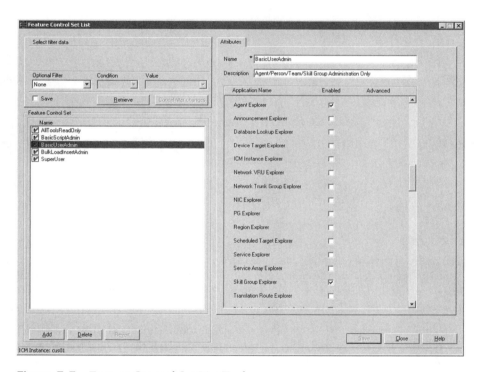

Figure 7-5 *Feature Control Set List Tool*

The feature control set is then assigned to a user account in the User List tool so that when the user logs in to an administrative workstation, only the allowed tools can be seen in the Configuration Manager application, as shown in Figure 7-6.

Figure 7-6   *Results of Using a Feature Control Set*

Deleted Items

The tools within Configuration Manager can also be used to delete configuration items. When an item is deleted, the configuration tool places a red cross next to the item and grays out any of the data entry fields. Figure 7-7 shows the Call Type List tool with the LondonBrokerDesk call type deleted.

In Figure 7-7, you can also see that an Undelete button has appeared in the lower-left corner of the Call Type List tool. Clicking this button undeletes the highlighted call type. However, after the Save button has been clicked, it is not possible to undelete the configuration item.

The deleted configuration appears in the Deleted Objects tool, which is found under the Miscellaneous Tools section in Configuration Manager. Figure 7-8 shows the deleted LondonBrokerDesk call type.

Even within the Deleted Objects tool, you can undelete the configuration item. Fortunately, because that many of the configuration items are referenced by other items, it can prove to be difficult to accidentally delete items. Cleanup of old configuration often takes many more hours than it took to actually create the configuration in the first place!

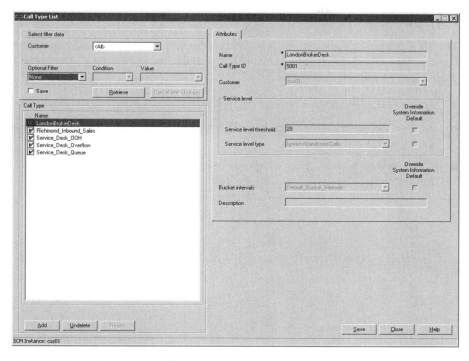

Figure 7-7 *Deleting a Configuration Item*

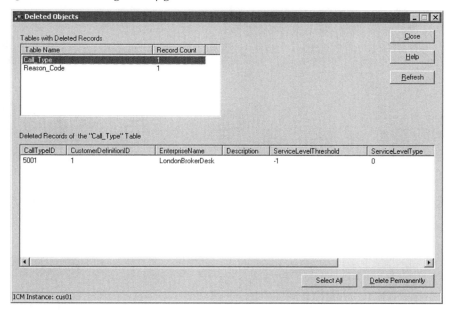

Figure 7-8 *Deleted Objects Tool*

Summary

This chapter examined the application-level configuration order and configuration items required for a UCCE solution to function. In particular, the key learning points from this chapter can be summarized as follows:

- For new deployments, following a defined configuration order reduces repetition.

- Several configuration items can be performed using bulk load tools and pre-prepared data spreadsheets.

- Configuration housekeeping is important because deleting old configuration can be difficult.

Chapter 8

Call Routing

This chapter covers the following subjects:

- Concepts of contact center call routing

- Details of enterprise and hosted call flows

- Introduction to next-generation contact centers

The efficient delivery of customer contacts to the appropriate resource is a fundamental requirement of any contact center. Depending on the nature of the business, the number of agents/skill groups, the different Automatic Call Distributor (ACD) types in use, and the number of sites, developing call flow scenarios to meet the differing business criteria can be a complex challenge.

Many of the traditional legacy ACD vendors originally provided difficult-to-use, command-line-driven interfaces for configuring call routing. This forced call flow modifications to be performed by trained switch engineers and often required lengthy change processes to be followed, even for simple call flow changes. Cisco Unified Contact Center Enterprise (UCCE) changed this approach by enabling the call flows to be designed and developed using an intuitive interface similar to creating a business flowchart.

This chapter explores the different ways that call routing can be achieved with both enterprise and hosted platforms. The chapter begins with an introduction to the difference between traditional carrier and private network routing using legacy time-division multiplexing (TDM) technology. The chapter then covers legacy call-routing techniques (many of which are still used today), current techniques that are available with IP networks, and the next generation of call delivery mechanisms that are being planned and deployed.

Call Routing Concepts

Multisite call contact centers are usually required to support different business functions and exist because of the large number of staff required to support an established customer base or often exist due to corporate acquisition. To ensure that business service-level agreements (SLA) are achieved, many contact center managers overstaff their operations at each location. Unfortunately, a downside to this occurs should the call distribution not be correct. One contact center agent's utilization and productivity decrease, whereas another contact center experiences a high call volume and an impact to its SLA. A contact center manager would find this frustrating because he has the resources to handle the call volume but no intelligent mechanism by which to distribute the calls evenly throughout the enterprise.

Before the common acceptance of Voice over IP (VoIP), the majority of private branch exchange (PBX) and ACD voice traffic was delivered over TDM technology. To support distributed call centers, major interexchange carriers and ACD vendors offered a variety of products and services that allowed the enterprise to route and distribute voice traffic to multiple sites. The two popular ways to achieve this call delivery are *carrier-based routing* and *private network routing*.

Carrier-Based Routing

Carrier-based routing typically relies on two factors: time/day and percentage allocation. For example, an enterprise with four contact center sites would create a call-routing plan depending on anticipated resources available at each site at certain times of the day. Figure 8-1 shows an example of call routing based on percentage distribution. The percentage values used would typically be representative of the anticipated number of resources available at each of the sites. You can see in Figure 8-1 that Sites C and D are smaller than A or B, so you would expect that they receive fewer calls.

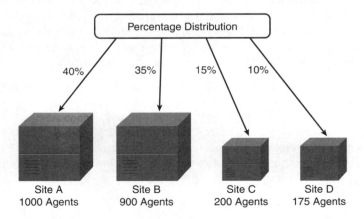

Figure 8-1   *Call-Routing Plan Based on Percentage Distribution*

Another easy-to-define metric for call routing is time of day. Similar to percentage distribution, time-of-day routing relies on a set of values that change infrequently. Typically, these values match the hours that agent resources are available at the contact center. Several contact centers in the same time zone might all be available during the same opening hours, but it is more common that slightly different hours are used. Popular reasons for this include the following:

■ Offices in different countries or time zones

■ An office that offers 24-hour support, weekend opening, or late-night opening

■ Groupwide training or meetings that all staff are required to attend

In these instances, it is common to route call traffic to different locations at different times of the same day. Figure 8-2 gives an example of time-of-day routing. Each of the sites receives calls based on the current time. This type of routing would typically be used by an organization that has a *follow-the-sun* 24/7 support desk, with each of the sites being in different time zones.

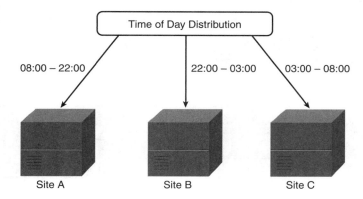

Figure 8-2 *Call Routing Based on Time of Day*

Combining time-of-day routing with percentage distribution gives greater control over call routing. Figure 8-3 gives examples to illustrate a more complex call flow scenario.

Unfortunately, the call-routing plans examined in the previous examples are statically defined based on historic and expected call volumes and resource availability at certain times and certain days of the week. If one of the contact centers were to unexpectedly be closed over a weekend, the contact center manager would need to ensure that the call-routing plan is modified to prevent call delivery to the closed site. Table 8-1 compares several of the common advantages and disadvantages of carrier-based routing.

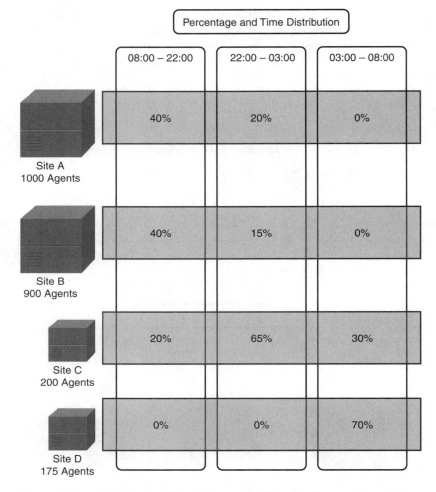

Figure 8-3   *Call Routing Using Percentage Distribution and Time of Day*

Table 8-1   *Carrier-Based Routing Advantages and Disadvantages*

Advantages	Disadvantages
Simple to understand and maintain call flow.	Call distribution is statically defined and not flexible to what is actually happening in the contact center at that moment in time.
Quick to initiate call diverts in the network should a disaster scenario occur.	Manual administration is required to adjust call percentage distribution.
The call routing occurs in the cloud, requiring no specialist hardware to be installed in the enterprise.	

What Is an IXC?   An *interexchange carrier (IXC)* is a regulatory term for a telecommunications company that provides Local Access and Transport Area (inter-LATA) communication.

An IXC carries voice traffic between telephone exchanges. In addition to the delivery of voice traffic, IXCs frequently offer the customer a range of enhanced telephony services. The services pertinent to contact centers include the following:

Nongeographic numbers, such as toll-free, reduced-cost, or premium-cost numbers.

Call distribution or diversion. This includes directing calls based on a call plan or Direct Inward Dial (DID) number range diverts during a disaster scenario.

Several organizations often use multiple IXCs for their outbound traffic. This enables the organization to select a carrier for different long-distance calls to get the most competitive call charges.

Private Network Routing

Private network routing using TDM equipment is achieved using various methods that are typically vendor-specific. The most common method is through the use of some type of intelligent overflow mechanism that is aware of the call volumes and resource availability at each ACD. The ACDs at each site are connected with TDM voice and data trunks, allowing the calls to be overflowed from one site to another.

This type of TDM *mesh* network can be expensive to implement because of the tie lines required between each ACD. It is also typically vendor-specific, so integrating switches from multiple vendors can prove to be difficult or even impossible.

Figure 8-4 demonstrates an example architecture of a five-site contact center. In this example, each site is connected through a TDM mesh network. It would be possible to implement a partial mesh. However, this would require some calls to pass through an intermediate switch at another site to reach their intended destination. Call transit through an intermediate device is termed *call tromboning*.

Figure 8-5 shows the call flow between two sites that are not fully meshed; therefore, the call needs to trombone through an intermediate switch to reach its destination. In this example, there is no direct connection from Site B to Site E, so the call must pass through an intermediary switch. For this particular call, Site D has been chosen; however, alternative paths (such as the route through Site C) might also be possible.

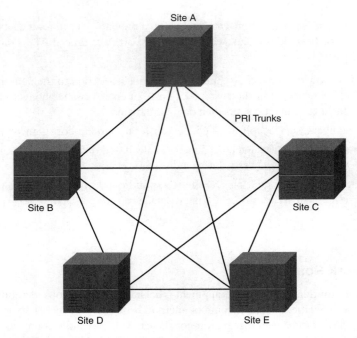

Figure 8-4   *TDM Mesh Network*

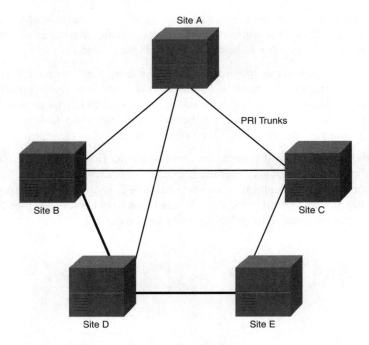

Figure 8-5   *TDM Partial Mesh Network*

Call overflow occurs when a call is delivered to a site but no agent resource is available at that particular site to answer the call, so the platform automatically routes the call over the private network to a different site that it believes has available resources. Figure 8-6 illustrates an example of call overflow. The inbound call has arrived on ACD A because the caller dialed a DID number that terminated at this site. From the DID number, the ACD is aware of the type of call and therefore the skilled resource that the caller should be connected to. Unfortunately, no resources are available at this site. However, because of the intelligent connection between the two sites, ACD A has visibility of available skilled resources at Site B, so it sends the call over the private telephony trunk between the sites.

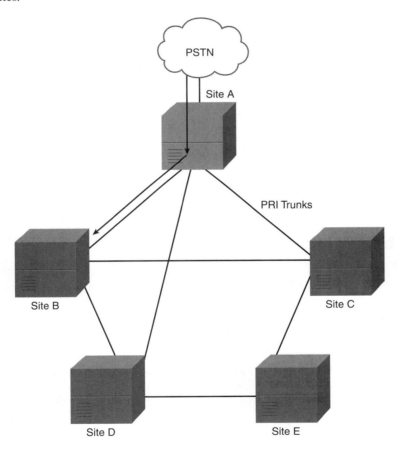

Figure 8-6 *TDM Call Overflow to a Second Site*

Even when implemented as a full mesh, this type of installation is an example of not treating the problem of inbound calls being received at the wrong site. Routing calls over a private network can prove to be expensive and also has physical limitations. For example, a T1 line between each ACD would allow a maximum of only 24 calls to be privately routed. Additional costs would be incurred through the purchase of multiple TDM voice cards for each ACD to support the private voice traffic. Operating costs are also increased as overflow calls require at least twice as many lines for each call. Table 8-2 compares several of the common advantages and disadvantages of private network routing.

Table 8-2   *Private Network Routing Advantages and Disadvantages*

Advantages	Disadvantages
Predictable inbound call volumes to the PSTN connection for each site.	The "tie lines" or telephony interconnects between ACDs are expensive to install and incur rental charges.
Call distribution between sites is handled internally and can usually be modified instantly.	Legacy ACD trunks have a physical limitation in the number of calls that can be sent over them.

Additional call-processing modules are required to enable all the ACDs to communicate and act as a single call center. Connecting ACD types from different vendors usually provide only basic telephony functions.

Traditional Call Routing

As you have learned from the preceding sections on carrier-based routing and private network routing, these traditional methods of delivering calls to distributed contact centers can cause capacity problems and have cost implications.

Even with many of the enhanced features available today, these two methods are still the most common form of call routing. This might be the case because many contact centers are still physically distributed based on the services they provide. For example, a large organization that provides different types of insurance products could have several contact center sites, each of which manages and provides a different insurance product. Each site or business unit is likely to have its own published number, so the need to transfer calls between each business unit is minimal.

With this type of business model, and the physical silos and segregation between sites, the carrier-based and private network call distribution solutions perform well and remain popular.

Current-Generation Call Routing

Although carrier-based and private network routing are still popular, many organizations can see the benefit of distributing their workforce over multiple contact center sites. Doing so provides a greater flexibility in resource allocation and is extremely useful when planning for disaster recovery as the loss of a single site does not necessarily mean the loss of a specific service.

The Cisco UCCE solution enables multiple sites to be logically brought together into a single virtualized contact center. Even though all the different skill groups, agents, and other resources are distributed, the UCCE platform has an overall view of each resource and its availability to process call or contact traffic.

UCCE supports two mechanisms to provide its intelligent contact routing:

■   Prerouting

■   Postrouting

Prerouting

Prerouting is the capability of the Unified Intelligent Contact Management (UICM) platform to instruct the service provider's network to deliver the call to a specific destination before the call is terminated on the customer's PBX equipment. UICM does this by having a signaling connection direct to the service provider's intelligent network, typically using a telephony protocol such as Signaling System 7 (SS7). The intelligent network does not have a static destination defined to deliver calls to; instead, when a call needs to be routed, it asks UICM for a destination. UICM can make real-time decisions because it is constantly receiving resource updates from all the contact center sites through its peripheral gateways (PG) that are connected to the ACD at each site. UICM can then return a destination label to the intelligent network, which then enables the public switched telephone network (PSTN) to route the call.

Figure 8-7 and the associated steps detailed in the list that follows explain a typical call flow using UICM prerouted calls.

Step 1. A caller dials a PSTN telephone number to speak with the required company.

Step 2. The carrier's intelligent network sends a route request to the UICM. The route request includes details about the caller's Automatic Number Identification (ANI) and the number dialed.

Step 3. The network interface controller (NIC) converts the SS7 signaling into a format that the UICM router can understand. Based on the dialed number, the router performs a route request to a specific UICM dialed number. This dialed number is mapped to a call type and associated routing script. The router is aware of resource availability for both Site A and Site B. It determines that the call should be routed to Site A and returns the appropriate label, or destination number, to the NIC.

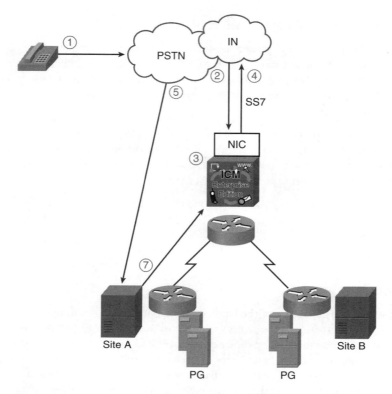

Figure 8-7   *Prerouting Call Flow with a Carrier and UICM*

Step 4.   The NIC sends the label back to the carrier.

Step 5.   The carrier routes the call over the PSTN to Site A.

Step 6.   Depending on the dialed number, its Dialed Number Information Service (DNIS), and the associated ACD logic associated with the DNIS, the ACD selects an agent. The ACD also informs the PG of this information and all the subsequent call-processing events.

Step 7.   The PG passes these event messages onto the UICM router.

Prerouting using a Cisco Unified Contact Center Hosted (UCCH) platform is similar to the previous example, except that all the UICM is contained within the service provider's "cloud." By doing this, the service provider can host several customers on the same platform. Sharing resources, including network Interactive Voice Response (IVR) facilities, reduces the costs needed to deploy this technology; it also gives the customer a fully managed service.

Postrouting

Postrouting uses the same intelligent routing engine as prerouting, but it is used purely in an enterprise network that does not have a connection to the service provider's network. Postrouting occurs after the call has already been delivered to an enterprise's ACD, so it is similar to private network routing, with the exception that the UCCE platform is aware of available resources around the enterprise. Therefore, it will route the call to the most appropriate destination using an intelligent algorithm, and not basic distribution rules.

Many UICM and UCCE deployments purely use postrouting for call delivery. The implementation of VoIP has removed many of the benefits available with prerouting as calls can now be sent around the customer's private IP network without incurring the previously large toll charges or sizing limitations enforced by TDM technology. Postrouting with VoIP also gives the enterprise flexibility on where it wants to locate its ACD equipment. Legacy TDM ACDs often required a physical ACD to be located on the same site as the agents. IP allows the enterprise to centrally locate much of the equipment while deploying only the minimum requirements at the remote sites.

Figure 8-8 and the associated steps detailed in the list that follows explain a typical call flow for a UCCE postrouted call.

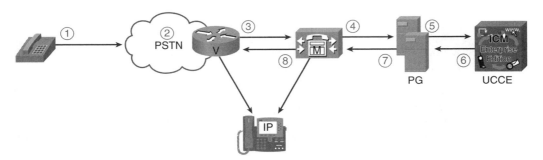

Figure 8-8   *Postrouting Call Flow with UCCE*

Step 1.   A caller dials a PSTN telephone number to speak with the required company.

Step 2.   The PSTN delivers the call to the terminating equipment, which in this case is a Cisco voice gateway.

Step 3.   The Cisco voice gateway notifies the Cisco Unified Communications Manager (Unified CM) server that a call has arrived with a specific dialed number.

Step 4.   The Unified CM has the dialed number configured as a Computer Telephony Integration (CTI) route point that is associated with the PG's Java Telephony Application Programming Interface (JTAPI) user account.

Step 5.   The PG performs a postroute request to the UCCE router.

Step 6.   The UCCE router executes a routing script based on the dialed number and associated call type. The router returns a label to the PG.

Step 7.   The PG returns a label to the Unified CM server.

Step 8.   The Unified CM server returns an IP address to the voice gateway and negotiates call setup between the voice gateway and the IP phone.

Next-Generation Call Routing

Telephony networks are changing. At the turn of the millennium, service providers realized that IP communications would vastly change the way they do business. As network technologies became more advanced, it is now possible to deliver a large number of simultaneous, high-quality audio streams over an IP connection. A large percentage of multisite enterprises connect their office using IP networks, so it is a natural progression for voice traffic to be sent over the IP WAN.

With the rentals on fixed-line telecommunications getting lower because of increased competition, service providers are using their vast infrastructure and data centers to provide network-based or hosted services that sit as an overlay to their networks. By implementing these services on scalable platforms, the service providers can partition or share the platform between multiple end customers. Multitenancy greatly reduces the cost of deploying similar services to different end customers and increases profits for the service provider.

Many analysts are predicting the end of the PSTN as you know it. Although realistically the death of the PSTN is many years away, the service providers realize that they needed to implement PSTN replacement projects to ensure that they remain in business.

As standards become ratified and approved by governing bodies such as the Internet Engineering Task Force (IETF), the service providers implement solutions based around these standards to ensure that they do not have interoperability issues with other service providers. One such standard is Session Initiation Protocol (SIP) and, in particular, the use of SIP trunks.

SIP Trunks

A SIP trunk connection is essentially an IP WAN link provisioned by a service provider that connects the enterprise's PBX to the PSTN or another PBX. Figure 8-9 illustrates a SIP trunk connecting a single PBX with the PSTN. This deployment appears to be similar to that of an ISDN trunk, but several fundamental differences exist:

- **The physical layer is a Layer 3 WAN technology.** With an ISDN line, the physical presentation is usually a copper or fiber cable connecting the building with the local exchange; the SIP trunk can use a multitude of different WAN technologies, including digital subscriber line (DSL), Frame Relay, and Multiprotocol Label Switching (MPLS). The physical cable is likely to connect between the building and the local exchange, but rather than connect directly to the PSTN, the link would typically route through a service provider's WAN backbone to a central office. The central office would house gateways to connect the IP stream to the PSTN. It is also likely to have

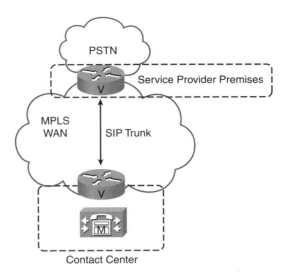

Figure 8-9 *Enterprise Contact Center Connected by a SIP Trunk*

IP interconnects to other service providers so that the call could remain as IP and still be onward-routed to other carriers if required.

■ **The trunk size is flexible.** In a similar way that ISDN Primary Rate Interface (PRI) lines can be fractionalized to provide smaller capacity than a full PRI trunk, SIP trunks have the flexibility to be sized up or down depending on the WAN circuit over which they are provisioned. This flexibility means that a contact center can quickly increase or decrease capacity based on expected call volumes.

■ **The trunk destination is flexible.** The service provider configures the SIP trunk to terminate at an IP address provided by the customer. Assuming that the WAN infrastructure is in place, the customer has the flexibility to move the SIP endpoint with relative ease to a different site if required. This flexibility makes SIP an ideal choice for use when disaster recovery planning, giving the contact center team the ability to move the trunk to a different IP PBX without impacting its call routing.

SIP trunks can also be used to replace tie lines interconnecting multisite PBXs. In the same way that the tie line provides a private network between sites, a SIP trunk can be used to the same effect but over an IP WAN link. Figure 8-10 illustrates a UCCE deployment using the distributed architecture with two Unified CM clusters connected with a SIP trunk.

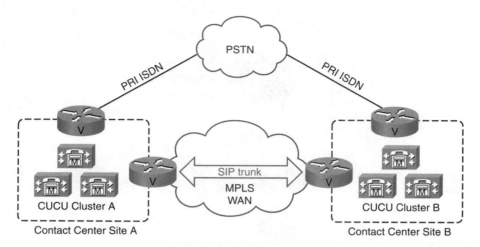

Figure 8-10 *Distributed UCCE Deployment Connected with a SIP Trunk*

Some of the benefits of using SIP in the contact center include the following:

- **Cost savings:** SIP trunks tend to be cheaper than ISDN and offer flexible pricing plans often per line and on a monthly basis.

- **Sizing:** SIP trunks provide the flexibility to ramp up or reduce capacity in line with expected call volumes.

- **Remote branch support:** With all telephony being encapsulated as IP, and all sites connecting back to a central WAN, it becomes relatively easy to implement home-working agents by extending the WAN to the agents' home with a DSL circuit.

- **The use of network services:** A problem with TDM-based private network trunks is that when routing calls around multiple sites, several voice lines remain in use for the duration of the call. Implementing VoIP provides the contact center with the capability to use network capabilities to tear a call down and deliver it to another destination without the need to keep additional valuable resources in use.

- **Centralized infrastructure:** Centralized or hosted services such as the actual ACD platform itself, or peripheral services such as voice recording and IVRs.

A typical architecture offered by service providers is to use the UCCH platform to provide a fully hosted contact center solution. All the services required by the contact center, including ACD, IP PBX, reporting, and voice recording, are hosted in the cloud by the service provider. The only equipment required on the end customer's site is a voice-enabled LAN with in-line power support for the IP phones and equipment to connect with the service provider's WAN.

Summary

This chapter covered the different call flow scenarios available with legacy ACDs, Cisco UCCE/UCCH, and multisite deployments connected with an IP WAN. In particular, the learning points from this chapter can be summarized as follows:

- The traditional methods of routing call traffic to distributed contact centers are still in use today.

- The UCCE platform supports both prerouting and postrouting.

- SIP trunks provide modern contact centers with flexible call delivery.

Chapter 9

Call Flow Scripting

This chapter covers the following subjects:

- An introduction to the role of call scripting
- The call script development lifecycle

At the heart of Cisco Unified Contact Center Enterprise (UCCE) is a routing engine that contains a real-time view of the entire enterprise. The UCCE router is aware of the real-time status of all agents, ports, and peripherals configured on the platform. For the router to deliver contacts to these resources, it needs to process route requests through a predefined set of logic rules. Within UCCE, these logic rules are defined through the use of call scripts.

Call scripts are created with the Script Editor application that is installed on an administrative workstation (AW). The call scripts are human-readable flowcharts of business logic that determine how the call is to be processed. The ultimate aim of a routing script is to return a destination to the router so that a call can be delivered to the most suitable resource.

This chapter examines the scripting development process and discusses several best practices that can be implemented to maintain good script administration.

> **Note**   You can find the UCCE Scripting and Media Routing Guide at
> http://www.cisco.com/en/US/docs/voice_ip_comm/cust_contact/contact_center/icm_
> enterprise/icm_enterprise_7_5/user/guide/ipce75sg.pdf.

Contact Center Call Flow

Companies have contact centers to provide their customers with a quality service when the customers want to make a purchase or has a query. When customers calls a contact center, they usually has a specific reason for the call and want to obtain a specific outcome. The purpose of the call might be the purchase of a product or obtaining a service.

To process the customer's call more effectively, the contact center typically tries to identify the purpose of the call before the call is delivered to an agent. This filtering process often takes the form of providing the caller with different telephone numbers to call or the selection of in-call menu options depending on the reason for the call.

To give the caller these options, it is essential that the contact center actually understands the majority of reasons why a caller makes those calls and then structures the business to process those calls efficiently.

Many contact centers assign their staff by products or business function. These units are further subdivided into skill groups and teams. Customer calls are then handled by the most appropriate resource as the contact center platform selects which skill group or specific agent is most suitable to assist that type of customer query.

The role of the contact center consultant or business analyst is to work with the contact center management team to create the business logic needed to efficiently deliver calls. In many cases, this business logic can be documented in the form of a flowchart. It is the responsibility of the contact center engineer to convert the business logic into a technical representation within the UCCE Script Editor application.

Contact Center Challenges

Creating a call script from a simple business logic flowchart is a relatively easy task. With the drag-and-drop user interface, even difficult call scripts can be created in a short period of time. The major challenge with call scripting can be found when performing the requirements captured from the business users and converting those business requirements into detailed logical call flows.

When calling a contact center, callers expects first-call resolution. They would like their call to be handled effectively, courteously, without having to repeat information, and without having to call back at a later time to go through the process again. Callers also do not want to have their call queued or to be left on hold for a period of time.

Contact center managers would also like the customers' calls to have first-contact resolution and minimal queue times as this improves customer satisfaction. The contact center, however, must balance the cost of resourcing and staffing overheads against that of customer satisfaction.

Many contact centers have service levels. A service level is a defined metric that is a measure of a contact center's effectiveness at handling customer contacts. The service level can vary depending on the type of contact being handled; for example, an inbound contact center might want 90 percent of all calls to be answered within 20 seconds. Staffing levels are the biggest factor in enabling a contact center to meet its service level. Without enough agents to handle the required call volumes, it would be impossible to achieve the desired service level; however, an overstaffed contact center would probably beat the target service level but have a high operational cost.

It is the role of the contact center manager to balance resourcing requirements so that the service level can be achieved without having the staff being underutilized. The contact center engineer can also assist by designing and developing call scripts that ensure that the call flow is error-free, efficient, and created in a manner that provides accurate reporting metrics.

Call Script Development Lifecycle

Although UCCE call scripts are created in a drag-and-drop GUI, the process that the engineer should follow is similar to that of software development. The high-level tasks detailed here represent the typical software development stages that should be followed to ensure a smooth transition from requirements capture through to operational support:

- **Business requirements capture:** A skilled business analyst knows how to "tease" requirements from the business users and management team. The aim of the requirements capture phase is to work with the various members of the business management team to understand how they want their contact center to behave. These requirements range from standard call routing to skill groups through to complex rules-based routing over several enterprise sites.

- **Conversion of business requirements into technical requirements:** It can also be the role of the business analyst, but usually the job of a solution designer or lead engineer, to convert the business requirements document into a technical requirements document that can be understood by the engineering team. The technical requirements need not detail the exact formula or script layouts as these tasks are left to the creativity of the scripting engineer.

- **Call scripting and configuration:** The actual creation of the call-routing scripts and associated configuration are the roles of the scripting engineer. The engineers use their skills to take the technical documentation created by the designer and create the call scripts and any relevant UCCE configuration, such as agents, skill groups, call types, call variables, and custom functions.

- **Call flow testing:** One of the golden rules of software development is that although a developer performs some degree of testing during the development process, the developer should not be responsible for performing detailed testing of his own code. The same rule applies with call scripting, especially for major script changes or a large service rollout. Having a second engineer perform a series of system tests greatly reduces the chance that any errors have crept into the development process. Another good testing practice is to get the end user (supervisor, team leader, and maybe a few key agents) involved in an acceptance test process. This gives the team who will be answering calls a visibility of how the new service will perform and also reassures them that the development process has been successful.

■   **Operational go-live and support:** After the acceptance test process has been success-fully completed, the call scripts will need to be scheduled to "go live" and into pro-duction to handle live customer calls. From a support point of view, it is good prac-tice to frequently monitor new scripts using the monitoring options in Script Editor. Doing so gives the support engineer a real-time view of call distribution through the scripts, allowing her to quickly spot any potential errors.

The end-to-end process detailed in the previous steps describes a single pass of the devel-opment process from requirements capture through to going live. The actual process of maintaining a UCCE platform is the repetition of these tasks. Figure 9-1 is a representa-tion of the development lifecycle. The initial scripting requirements capture begins at the center of the spiral. This is typically when the UCCE platform is actually being deployed for the contact center customer. As the spiral grows, it is clear to see the phases being repeated.

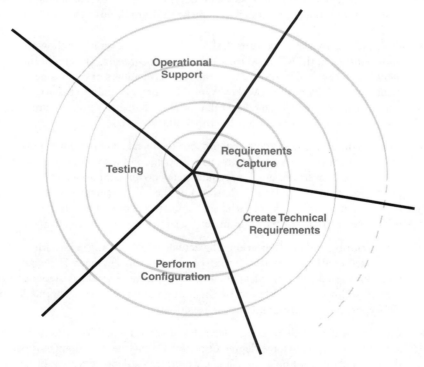

Figure 9-1   *Call Script Development Spiral*

Call Scripting Best Practices

Implementing and maintaining a set of UCCE call flow scripts can be a challenging and rewarding task. The following sections highlight many of the common approaches that should be used during call scripting administration.

Total Cost of Ownership

The total cost of ownership (TCO) is a key figure required by a company's management team when discussing the purchase and ongoing maintenance of a platform or service, especially when calculating yearly budgets. TCO tries to quantify the financial cost of maintaining a platform over a period of time.

After a UCCE platform has been purchased, the ongoing costs of maintaining the platform fall into three main areas:

- **IT hardware/software/licensing:** This includes tasks such as the replacement of faulty devices, applying the latest software updates, and the purchase of additional licenses as the platform expands.

- **Operational expenses:** Infrastructure costs include electricity for power and cooling, personnel costs including salaries and training, and the cost of downtime or outages.

- **Long-term expenses:** Examples of long-term expenses include major upgrades such as a technology refresh, platform replacement, or even decommissioning.

A large percentage of operational expense is taken by staff salaries. Badly configured platforms increase TCO because of the extra time needed for engineers to understand the current configuration and to make suitable modifications to achieve their current tasks. In a badly configured platform, changes made to one call script could have implications in another. Every addition or modification to the system potentially causes other call scripts to be changed, and over time, the system becomes an unmanageable mess.

As this mess builds, the productivity of the engineering team decreases, which in turn requires the management team to recruit more staff to manage the platform to increase productivity.

This section works through a series of best practices that apply to creating call-routing scripts in UCCE. At a high-level, call-routing scripts should adhere to several very simple rules:

- They should be clearly laid out and be efficient in their purpose.

- They should be easily understood by people other than the original engineer.

- They should be extensively tested and free from errors.

Expect the Unexpected

Although an important part of script development is associated with creating the scripts in a fashion that is easily readable by others so that they can be further enhanced in the future, another important factor is to create scripts and configuration that would cause minimum problems if modified incorrectly by another engineer.

Many years ago, I was working with a Cisco partner to implement CiscoWorks ITEM (IP Telephony Monitor) for an end customer. The customer had a Cisco Unified Communications platform and contact center, and my role was to implement the CiscoWorks configuration to perform several monitoring tasks called *synthetic transactions*. One of these tasks was the ability for the CiscoWorks platform to make IP telephony calls between endpoint devices. Should the call setup fail, a warning message would be sent to a monitoring console.

To perform the configuration, I required the customer to allocate me with two unused extension numbers. The customer's IP phone range was 6000 to 9999, and the customer had started allocating physical devices from 6000 upward, so it allocated me with extensions 9998 and 9999 as it was not expecting to require these numbers.

On the Unified CM server, I created a specific partition and calling search space for the particular automated task and configured CiscoWorks accordingly. For several months, this test performed successfully, and every 15 minutes, CiscoWorks would make a simulated call between the two extensions.

Then one day I received a call from one of the customer's engineers saying that he had received a call from the emergency services wanting to know why someone at the customer's site had been making emergency calls to these services every 15 minutes.

In the U.K., we use the number 999 to dial emergency services. After looking through the Unified CM configuration, I found that another engineer had added my monitoring partition to a general phone user calling search space. By doing this, my test phone with extension 9998 was no longer dialing test extension 9999. The Unified CM was interpreting this as dialing 9 for an outside line and then calling emergency services with the dialed number 999.

Needless to say, I quickly fixed the issues and then changed all the configurations to use different internal extensions that could not be overlapping with other dial plans. This real-life example highlights just one issue that can happen when multiple people or teams administer a platform. Care should be taken during the planning and design phases to minimize this type of error. A change management policy should be developed, used, and adhered to in any enterprise environment to avoid a wide range of issues from simple dial-plan errors to database corruption.

Change Is Good

Current thinking and good practice change frequently. Different ways of working usually happen as teams change or vendors/partners release information to enhance products either through product upgrades with new features or perhaps when documentation is released that details a preferred method or solution to a problem.

UCCE scripts should also be periodically updated to reflect these new ways of thinking. It is commonplace to discuss contact center scripting with a customer, only to find that it has a series of core-routing scripts developed years ago by someone who is no longer with the company. As none of the customer's contact center engineers understand the routing logic, no one has the courage to change the scripts because they are aware of the consequences if these scripts were to stop working.

Worse still are scripts that have received several minor modifications by different engineers over a long period of time. Each change is usually a "quick fix" to resolve a minor issue or to add a new feature, perhaps a new Interactive Voice Response (IVR) menu prompt or routing condition. As little care or thought was given to the script each time it was updated, the script has become a web of nodes and jumbled connecting lines.

Periodically refreshing call-routing scripts does not mean that each script needs to be redeveloped from the ground up. Many scripts require only a cleanup that involves the following:

- Running through the call flow logic to ensure that it is still relevant

- Removing any redundant script nodes, including erroneous comments

- Formatting the script so that the call flow is clear

- Checking to see whether new features can be implemented to simplify or improve the script

Tracking Change

Accountability and audit tracking are important. The UCCE platform administration must ensure that every user has his own dedicated user account. In Script Explorer, the history of the scripts are detailed with the username of the person who last changed it. This is a valuable tool to use when troubleshooting an issue after a script change as you can locate the actual engineer who performed the change.

Figure 9-2 shows the Script Explorer tool. By selecting a UCCE script in the left pane, information about the script's versions, author, and the date/time the script was modified can be easily obtained.

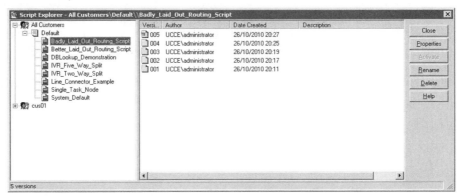

Figure 9-2 *UCCE Script Explorer*

It is possible to define how many previous versions of the script are retained. The default value is that all scripts are retained. Figure 9-3 shows where in System Information that script retention value is defined.

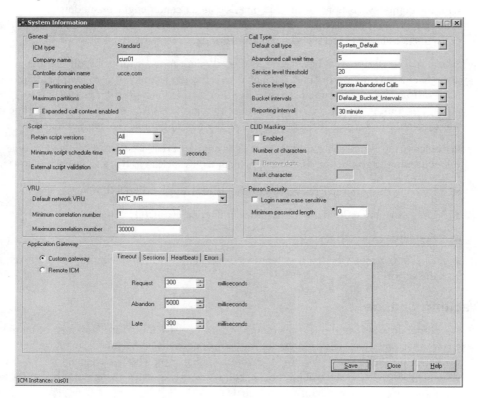

Figure 9-3   *Number of Retained Script Versions Shown in System Settings*

Script Explorer also allows a user to roll back to a previous version of the script if required. The current version of the script in use by the UCCE router is called the active version. Script Editor allows a user to modify scripts other than the active version. To display the available versions, you need to select the Show Script Versions check box in Script Editor. Figure 9-4 displays an example of a script called System_Default. When the Show Script Versions check box is selected, it is possible to see that three versions of the script exist. The blue star on version 003 indicates that this is the active script version.

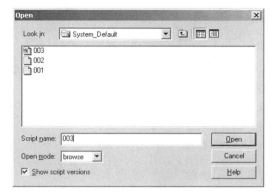

Figure 9-4 *Displaying the Available Versions of a Script to Edit*

Script Layout

Reading through a script should be performed in a logical fashion, similar to reading a book. Most pages in a book or magazine are read from the left side of the page to the right side and from top to bottom.

The layout of a call script should follow the same principle, with the call flow traveling from the Start node at the top of the page down the page and preferably across from left to right. Figure 9-5 gives an example of a poorly laid-out call script. In this script, you can see that the different sections of the call flow are not immediately obvious. The script has many connecting lines that cross over each other, and although sometimes this is unavoidable, in this particular case, it is poor practice by the engineer.

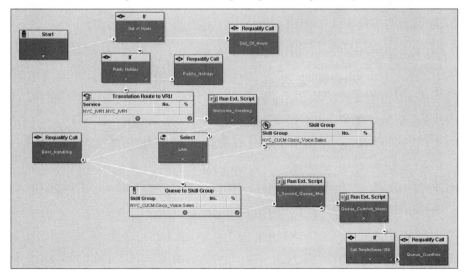

Figure 9-5 *Poorly Laid-Out Call Script*

The call flow in Figure 9-5 is also difficult to follow, which makes modifications and troubleshooting consuming and frustrating for engineers who are not familiar with the script.

In addition to creating a readable call flow, a common practice is to logically group associated script nodes into their respective functions. This is achieved through the use of horizontal and vertical spacing to separate the groupings.

Figure 9-6 demonstrates a typical call script, where the four key areas of the script have been grouped according to their function. The four areas are as follows:

1. Perform out-of-hours and public holiday checks.

2. Provide the caller with a welcome message from the IVR.

3. Attempt to deliver the caller to an available agent.

4. If no agents are available, put the caller into a queue loop.

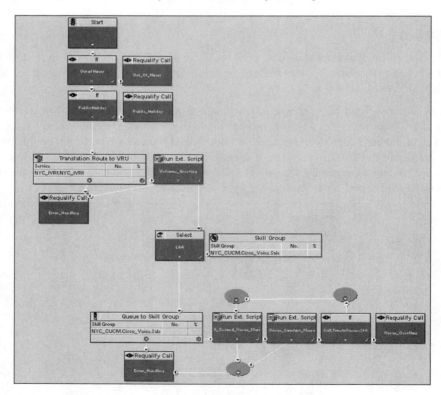

Figure 9-6   *Example of Call Script Grouping and Spacing*

Through the vertical spacing in Figure 9-6, these four areas are much easier to identify.

Although an ideal scenario is for a script to flow from top to bottom and left to right, this is not always possible. Sometimes scripts benefit from an alternative layout, but only if the resulting layout is still clear to follow. Figure 9-7 shows an example of a script that has two clear outcomes based on a caller's selection at the first IVR prompt. You could use the top-to-bottom and left-to-right layout for this script, but as this script is relatively simple and easily fits on a single page, I have decided to allow the script to fork left or right depending on the option chosen by the caller at the IVR. The resulting script layout is still clear.

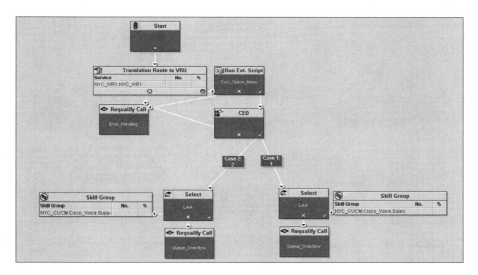

Figure 9-7 *Example of a Call Script with Two Outcomes*

Figure 9-8 details a script that requires the caller to select from a five-option IVR menu. Rather than try to fit the entire script into a single page much larger than possible to display clearly on a monitor screen, this script has been written so that a further script is chosen based on the IVR option selected by the caller. You can see that this script uses the Requalify Call Type node to change the call type based on the IVR selection and therefore invoke a new call script.

One of the most useful Script Editor nodes is the one that does not actually perform a specific function. The Line Connector node, when used properly, is fantastic for improving the layout of scripts and ensuring that they are more readable. Figure 9-9 gives an example of a call script with an improved layout from using the Line Connector node. Without the use of the Line Connector, the script in Figure 9-9 would have many joining lines crossing over each other and other nodes.

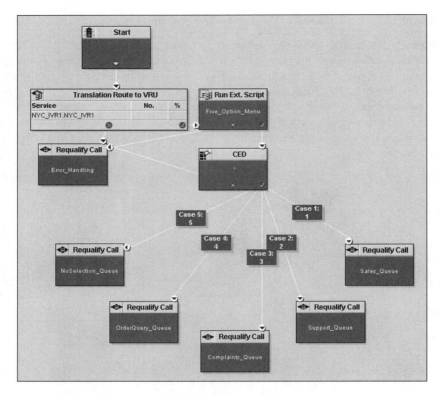

Figure 9-8   *Example of Call Script with Five Outcomes, Each of Which Invokes a New Script*

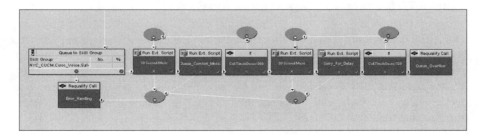

Figure 9-9   *Example of Using the Line Connector to Improve Script Layout*

Avoid Overoptimization

Highly optimized programming code usually improves execution efficiency by reducing the amount of computer processing power required to perform a task. Optimization is not the same as reducing several functions into a single function!

Within the UCCE Script Editor, it is possible to create custom functions. A custom function is an ordered list of logical statements that when executed, returns a result to influence contact routing. It is easily possible to create a custom function that contains several calculations that would actually be better implemented by splitting out the logic statements and creating several functions. Occasionally, these functions or formulas are required for the script to perform successfully, but in many instances, the readability of the script can be improved by splitting the logic over several nodes.

Figure 9-10 shows a single IF node (this is a logical function, that is, IF...THEN...ELSE) that contains several statements checking for multiple conditions. These conditions include checks for out-of-hours, public holiday, and emergency conditions. If any of these conditions are true, the caller is played a closed message by the IVR and the call is disconnected. By observing the real-time call monitoring in Script Editor, it is not possible to easily determine which logic condition (out-of-hours, public holiday, or emergency) is resulting in the callers being delivered to the closed announcement.

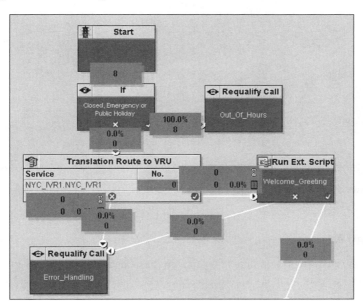

Figure 9-10 *Many Logical Conditions Within a Single Script Node*

Figure 9-11 implements the same logic, but it is configured using multiple IF nodes, one for each logic condition. The results to the caller are exactly the same as the script in Figure 9-10, but the tasks of troubleshooting and monitoring the script are made much easier.

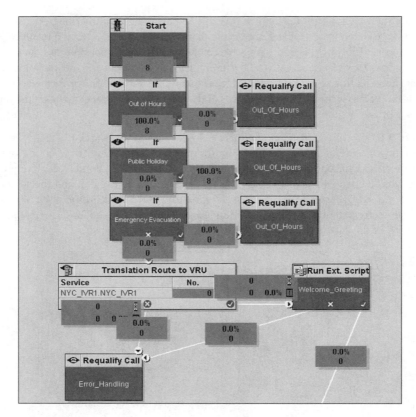

Figure 9-11   *Clearly Laid-Out Script Showing the Different Logical Conditions*

Meaningful Names

Almost every configuration item in UCCE requires a name. Names are everywhere in UCCE, and you are required to name many things including call types, call scripts, agent teams, skill groups, functions, and variables.

Prevent Misinformation

Many of the configuration items also have a description field so that the engineer can leave a meaningful comment for future reference.

Unfortunately, it can often be found that the description field is not used or just has text that replicates the name. For example, consider the following examples of poorly named items:

- **Call type name:** Team1_Inbound_Calls
- **Call type description:** Inbound Call Type for Team 1

The engineer who created this configuration did so with good intentions but failed to maximize the purpose of meaningful names. The Description field gives no more information than the detail in the Name field.

Even more frustrating than the Description field not being used is when the Description field is incorrect or misleading.

When completing the Description field, consider what information could be useful to someone when troubleshooting an issue. What information would that person need that might not necessarily be easy to find elsewhere in the UCCE platform.

One example could be the Description field for dialed numbers (DN) when a published DN is a nongeographic DN such as a toll-free number. A nongeographic number (NGN) is translated into a real E.164 number within a carrier's network and is transparent from the caller. The real E.164 number is used to deliver the call to a contact center site, and then the Dialed Number Information Service (DNIS) is used to map that call to a call type and call script. From a given call type or call script, the UCCE engineer would work through the configuration to find the DNIS, and from the DNIS, the engineer could probably work out the full DN. However, the engineer would not discover the NGN. Knowledge of this NGN might be required when speaking with the carrier, so it would be good practice to include this NGN in the Description field when configuring a dialed number.

Use Intention-Revealing Names

When choosing names for configuration items and scripts, try to use a name that describes the intention of the item. An item's intention refers to its purpose or function, and where possible that intention should be clearly described in the name, obviously without creating the name far too long or unwieldy. The UCCE Configuration Manager and Script Editor tools allow the administrator to create logical names for all configuration items; the concept of intention-revealing names applies to all configuration items.

An example of a good naming convention would be when using the System Default call type to name an error-handling script. The System Default call type is used when the UCCE router has experienced a routing problem and requires a default destination to deliver the call.

Naming the default call type and call script *System_Default_Error_Handling* gives a clear indicator of the purpose for both this call type and its associated call script.

Comment Node

UCCE Script Editor has a Comment node that allows the scripting engineer to leave one or more text strings at various positions on the script layout.

A valid argument exists that comments should be used only rarely within a programmer's code or a contact center engineer's scripts. This statement might be a shock, especially after reading the preceding sections about helpful naming and layout techniques.

The argument follows that if the scripting engineer has created all his configuration items with meaningful names and that his scripts are laid out in a clear manner, another engineer with similar experience would clearly understand the intent of the call script without having to refer to any comments.

It could be said that comments are used only when the engineer has failed to clearly express the intended actions of the script. Realistically, however, comments should be used when they provide worthwhile meaning about a function or section of the script.

The use of comments often causes the following problems:

- They rarely get updated when the actual functions or purpose of the script changes.

- They are used as a "to-do" list within the script. For example, the engineer might leave a comment that describes how she would change the script in the future to add a new feature.

- Sometimes they are used to track changes or as a poor audit log. These comments quickly become out of date with the actual changes made.

- Occasionally they are misleading and often incorrectly describe what the script is doing.

Use a Development Workstation

Creating call flow scripts is a similar process to developing software code. Modern software languages use specialized Integrated Development Environments (IDE) to provide the developer with all the tools required to make software development as trouble-free as possible. Although UCCE Script Editor does provide an intuitive GUI for developing scripts, often the same contact center engineer will also need to create IVR applications and custom reports and perform troubleshooting.

To facilitate these tasks, the user should create a development workstation that has all the software required to perform scripting and reporting development. So as not to violate the bill of materials, I would recommend that the development workstation is not a distributor AW, but rather a client AW.

Table 9-1 details all the recommended software to be installed on the development workstation.

Table 9-1   *Development Workstation Recommended Software*

Software Application	Description
UCCE Client AW	Using a client AW rather than a full distributor AW allows the development workstation to be created using a desktop operating system such as Windows XP.
Cisco Unified CCX Editor/CVP Studio	If you are using Cisco Unified IP IVR or Cisco Customer Voice Portal (CVP), an IVR application environment should be installed.
Microsoft SQL Server Tools	SQL Query Analyzer is an essential tool to query the configuration and reporting databases.
Cisco Agent Desktop Administrator	If the Cisco Agent Desktop (CAD) application is deployed, CAD Administrator is required.
Sybase Infomaker (or similar)	Sybase Infomaker is used purely for creating custom reports for WebView.

Custom Functions

To perform logical operations such as string manipulations, querying date/time, or mathematical functions, the Script Editor offers a series of built-in functions. It is possible, however, to use these existing functions to create additional functions. These additional functions are stored in UCCE and are called *custom functions*.

For example, the built-in Weekday function can be called in an IF node. Weekday returns the current day of the week as an integer value (Sunday = 1, Monday = 2, and so on). Based on the results of this built-in function, the IF node can then be set to route the call to its intended target or route path.

Alternatively, a custom function can be created that also uses the Weekday built-in function. Weekend returns a 1 to signify that it is currently a weekend; otherwise, a 0 is returned. This function does not exist in a regular deployment of UCCE and must be created by a scripting engineer; hence it is a custom function. The custom function can then be used in all routing scripts.

Custom functions should be specific to a task with well-tested inputs and outputs. The names of the functions should clearly indicate to the scripting engineer what the function does without the engineer having to understand the logic. Writing functions with clearly defined parameters and expected return values allows a junior engineer to write complex scripts by reusing previously created components.

Error Handling

Occasionally, problems occur with routing and administrative scripts. In programming terms, these problems are called *exceptions*, and they are handled by specific parts of the application designed to execute when the problem happens.

Exceptions can also occur during call script execution. There are many reasons why they happen, but it is usually because of the following:

- Faulty logic in the call script or IVR application

- An error in the UCCE configuration, such as a device target with a missing label

- A resource allocation issue, such as no free IVR ports to queue a call

Some of the UCCE components, such as Unified IP IVR, play a default announcement to the caller when an unrecoverable error occurs. However, it is generally considered to be unprofessional and poor customer service to play a default message and then disconnect the caller. It is even worse to just disconnect the caller without playing a message, for what appears to the caller to be no valid reason.

Several different error-handling scenarios exist:

- **Release the call:** To the caller, this just appears that he has been disconnected. As discussed, this type of error handling should be the last resort when all other attempts to retain the call have been exhausted.

- **Return a busy tone:** If the caller has not had any interaction with the contact center, (for example, she has not heard any welcome messages or IVR menus or has spoken with an agent), playing a busy tone and disconnecting the call is an acceptable method as the caller would just believe that the lines are busy and would likely call back later. If the caller had already interacted with the contact center before receiving a busy tone, this type of error handling would be on par with just releasing the call and would be frowned upon.

- **Return a default label:** The default label is defined with the dialed number and represents another destination that the router can attempt to deliver the call to. Many options exist using this method. The default label could be a standalone IVR application that then tries to invoke another UCCE script. It could be the pilot number for a hunt group, or perhaps the number for the switchboard.

Summary

This chapter provided an introduction to call scripting, including a detailed explanation of the call script development lifecycle. The chapter continued by offering a series of best practices to make the development process clearer and ensure that the ongoing operational process is smooth. The learning points from this chapter can be summarized as follows:

- Cisco UCCE call scripts are at the heart of the contact center platform.

- Following a structured development process and change management procedures produces systems and scripts of a high standard.

- Considerate development using informative names and clear layouts ensures that the scripts can be maintained by others.

Chapter 10

Reporting

This chapter covers the following subjects:

- An overview of the reporting methods and packages available for UCCE
- The reporting architecture and packages available in UCCE
- Things to observe when configuring reporting

The management information provided by reporting applications is arguably the most important feature of a contact center platform. Without this information, it would be almost impossible to determine the business efficiency of the contact center.

Reporting information is often considered to be only of use for the contact center manager, supervisor, or team leader who wants to keep an eye on his staff. However, the data available from many applications provides a holistic view of the entire contact center and is of great use to a wider audience, from the technical IT teams that maintain the infrastructure through to business leaders who might want only to understand the contact center's overall performance.

The term *business intelligence* is often used to represent the new reporting techniques employed by contact center analysts when examining business data, such as sales revenues or customer satisfaction metrics, with data available from the contact center platform. Business intelligence software often provides the analyst with historical, real-time, and predictive views of business operations. When performed in the context of contact centers, business intelligence can be used for the following functions:

- Examining historic contact center performance against current performance to determine resourcing required to meet certain service levels
- Benchmarking an individual agent's performance against their team or an average agent for individual performance reviews
- Comparing the sales with the corresponding after-sales support and repeat business to determine customer loyalty.

To implement a comprehensive business intelligence solution, it is imperative to obtain reporting metrics from multiple data sources rather than to generate multiple reports each from an independent source. Previously, multiple data sources also required multiple reporting interfaces, typically one for each business application in use. A single reporting interface is required regardless of Automatic Call Distributor (ACD) or media type. For example, multiple vendors, including Cisco, Avaya, and Aspect, produce contact center metrics that can be pushed into a business intelligence engine. This collated data is then presented to the analyst through various reporting interfaces. With the emergence of different media types, such as inbound/outbound calls, web collaboration, email delivery, and real-time chat, a single interface is also required to enable the analyst to understand the performance of multimedia agents.

Figure 10-1 details a generic reporting architecture with the real-time reporting information flowing from the peripherals on the right side of the diagram through the peripheral gateway (PG) and into the Unified Intelligent Contact Manager (UICM) databases. The reporting user has access to these databases through a selection of reporting tools.

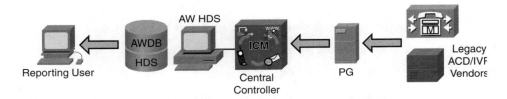

Figure 10-1   *Generic Reporting Architecture*

It is not purely a reporting analyst who should be interested in the reporting data available from the contact center. Table 10-1 details many of the business users that require access.

Reporting Packages

Reporting suites and applications are included with many telephony and contact center platforms. The Cisco Unified Contact Center Enterprise (UCCE) is no different, and Cisco offers two reporting packages—Cisco WebView and Cisco Unified Intelligence Center.

The Cisco UCCE platform databases store their data using Microsoft SQL Server in a comprehensive and well-documented database schema. Although this schema has evolved as the product has matured, it has retained much of its original structure. This has allowed several third-party developers to create extensive reporting suites for UCCE, providing enhancements and features not native to the UCCE product set.

Table 10-1 *Reporting Information Used by Different Business Users*

Target Audience	Potential Useful Reports
IT team responsible for platform maintenance and support	Various real-time and historic reports that focus on how calls are being handled by peripherals. For example, reports that generate statistics regarding the call load on a call-queuing platform would allow the IT team to make informed decisions on whether additional port capacity is required.
Contact center agent	Often, contact center agents will have access to simple call statistics, such as the ability to see how many contacts they have handled during their shift.
Team leader/supervisor	An important focus for the team leader is the productivity of their team as a whole, but with the ability to drill down into individual agent productivity when required. On a day-to-day basis, this information is used to ensure that the service level is being achieved and that abandoned calls and excessive queue times are kept to a minimum.
Contact center manager	The contact center manager has a duty to ensure that the various teams and business units within the contact center work toward a common goal of exceeding customer satisfaction while delivering value to the business.
Executive	A company executive is unlikely to hold much interest in day-to-day agent activities and probably has only a marginal interest in whether service-level agreements (SLA) have been met. The executive might want to know the headline figures perhaps by quarter or per annum, but he is more likely to be interested in that the contact center provides value for the money and whether its function is promoting the company's image in a positive light.

Ultimately, a reporting package is required to display the underlying contact center data in a human-readable manner so that the person observing the report can make an informed judgment as to the contact center's performance. In addition to this reporting fundamental, a modern reporting package should also provide the following:

- **Simplified report accessibility:** This enables a user with only general IT skills to access a report. Typically, the reporting access and management will be through a web interface.

- **A comprehensive set of standard reports:** A large percentage of management information metrics are common across the entire range of contact centers. ACD vendors are aware of the frequently-asked-for metrics and bundle standard reporting templates within the reporting package.

- **Report customization:** Despite a comprehensive set of standard reports, the majority of contact centers require even a small amount of customization to provide the metrics in a format commonly used within the enterprise. Customized reports can be tailored to be business-specific, making them more relevant to the analyst by delivering the specific required metrics, often in a single report rather than in multiple reports. Many customers who have migrated from a legacy ACD even ask for the new-world reports to be modified to have the same look and feel that they were familiar with from their old system.

- **A range of predefined and customizable time frames and periods:** Reports are often created in relative time frames, including Today, Yesterday, Last Week, and Last Month, in addition to specific periods banded by time and date. Many platforms provide real-time and historic reports. However, several modern platforms also enable the analyst to produce predictive reports based on historic trends.

- **Different display formats and exporting:** It is common practice for reports to be displayed on plasma screens and used as wallboards. Report analysts also enjoy using Microsoft Excel for manipulating and formatting data.

- **Data granularity:** Reports should be as granular or as generic as required by the report analyst. To accomplish this, the reporting package must display data for individual components such as agents, skill groups, or services, yet also group these components together to give a higher-level view of the data. The same is true for time and date intervals. The analyst could be interested in data on a monthly or yearly basis, but also require the ability to drill down to daily, hourly, or subhourly time intervals.

- **Hierarchical access and security:** Shared platforms, both internal to the enterprise and hosted platforms with multiple customers, require secure access to ensure that different business units or different companies cannot access each other's data. UCCE call-routing scripts frequently use call variables to store sensitive corporate data for screen popping and custom routing. These values are routinely written back into the database. Multitenant platforms typically share the underlying database structure and hence require secure logical partitions to ensure data integrity.

- **Automated report generation:** After a series of key performance indicators (KPI) have been defined, the contact center analyst regularly generates the same reports on the same reporting frequency. The creation of reports can often be time-consuming and repetitive, so the ability to schedule reports to be autogenerated and delivered to the analyst is an often-requested feature that minimizes the day-to-day administrative overhead.

Cisco WebView

WebView has been the integrated reporting platform for Cisco UCCE for many years since the early versions were released. Although WebView is still included in UCCE versions 7.5 and 8.0, version 8.0 is seen to be a transitional stage for WebView. Cisco will be removing WebView in version 8.5 to be fully replaced by the Cisco Unified Intelligence Center, which is covered in the next section.

Providing more than 200 standard reporting templates and the ability to create custom reports when required makes WebView more than just a standard reporting package. However, in comparison to more modern reporting tools that can accommodate multiple data sources and dashboard-style customized reporting, WebView could be considered to be slightly dated.

Figure 10-2 shows an example WebView historic call type report.

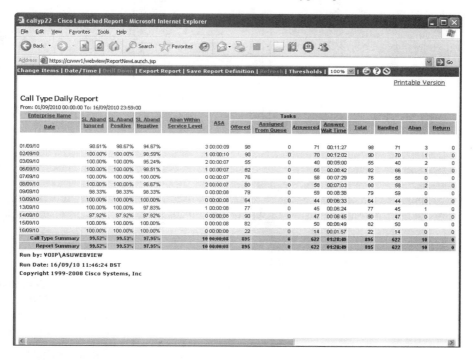

Figure 10-2 *Typical WebView Report*

WebView can be installed in a number of different configurations to support the size of the contact center and the anticipated performance load based on the likely number of simultaneous client connections. Figure 10-3 shows a general WebView application architecture, with the WebView server and database being coresident on the Distributor Administrative Workstation/Historical Database Server (AW/HDS).

All client access to WebView reports is through a web browser. After being logged in, a user can create both real-time and historic reports using the simple wizard that allows the user to select a reporting template, the items to be reported on, and the respective time period.

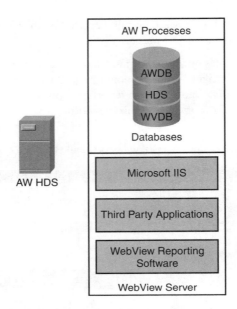

Figure 10-3   *WebView Architecture*

After they are created, reports can be saved to the user's favorites for easy retrieval, or they can be exported to a variety of supported formats.

Cisco Unified Intelligence Center

The Cisco Unified Intelligence Center (Unified IC or CUIC) is a relatively new addition to the UCCE product suite. Introduced in UCCE version 7.5 as Cisco Unified Intelligence Suite (CUIS), Unified IC has proven to be the comprehensive and scalable reporting solution required to ensure that UCCE retains a prominent place in the contact center market.

Designed as an end-to-end reporting solution, Unified IC is capable of interfacing to several disparate data sources and Cisco products to provide a single logical data view within a Web 2.0 framework.

Unlike Cisco WebView, the interface available with Unified IC enables an end user to create and manage both standard and custom reports without having to understand reporting development tools such as Sybase Infomaker. The capability to scale to a large deployment of clustered servers ensures that Unified IC will be the reporting platform that Cisco will promote in future versions of UCCE. Figure 10-4 shows an example of a dashboard in Unified IC that contains real-time agent status.

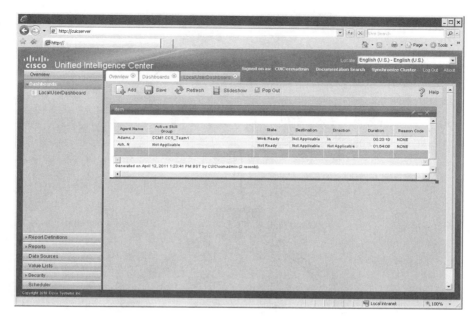

Figure 10-4   *Unified IC Dashboard*

Unified IC offers a scalable deployment model with a cluster of up to eight reporting nodes. These reporting nodes connect to the UCCE databases and serve reports to the reporting clients. For large deployments where several reporting nodes are used, Cisco recommends that an Application Control Engine (ACE) load balancer is deployed. This component provides load balancing across the multiple reporting nodes and acts as a single reference point for the reporting clients, therefore providing resiliency and eliminating the administrative overhead of manually configuring the reporting clients to distribute load. Figure 10-5 displays a high-level example of a Unified IC architecture using a load balancer.

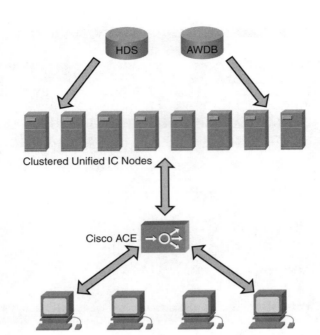

Figure 10-5   *High-Level Unified IC Architecture with a Load Balancer*

VIM Performance

Virtual Interaction Manager (VIM) Performance is an intuitive and easy-to-use integrated analytics package designed to drive higher productivity across all aspects of the contact center. Providing reporting, advanced OLAP-based analytics, and sophisticated management of contact center resources, VIM Performance enables business users to

- Make better business decisions at every level of management.

- Evaluate any customer contact asset based on quantitative, qualitative, or combined measures of performance.

- Manage all contact resources and services easily and safely in a robust business and security framework.

- Simply and quickly create intuitive business dashboards based on the KPIs that matter the most to them. These KPIs are based not just on real-time and historical call details but also on multiple concurrent sources, including real-time and historic contact center data, workforce management information, and customer databases.

- Rapidly identify, replicate, and scale best practices within their customer contact environments. Automate and streamline both business and IT processes within auditable commercial and IT structures, delivering more effective and timely actions.

- Improve productivity across the entire customer contact center, from agent performance to outsourcer SLA compliance and from IVR efficiency to manager effectiveness.

VIM Performance is a third-party reporting platform developed by Exony. VIM Performance can scale to meet a large number of reporting clients. The ability to scale combined with its native multitenancy and security have made VIM Performance the reporting platform of choice for many of the telephony carriers that host Cisco contact centers. VIM Performance is also a popular platform with large enterprise customers that require reporting information from many data sources or require the ability to perform real-time data manipulation and analytics.

Figures 10-6, 10-7, and 10-8 show just three of the many reports available with VIM Performance. Figure 10-6 and 10-7 are similar to the style of report available with WebView but have additional graphics, which provides the analyst with a clearer visualization of the metrics. Figure 10-8 is a dashboard-style report showing a combination of real-time and historic reporting metrics but presented in a modern and easy-to-read style rather than a traditional tabular display.

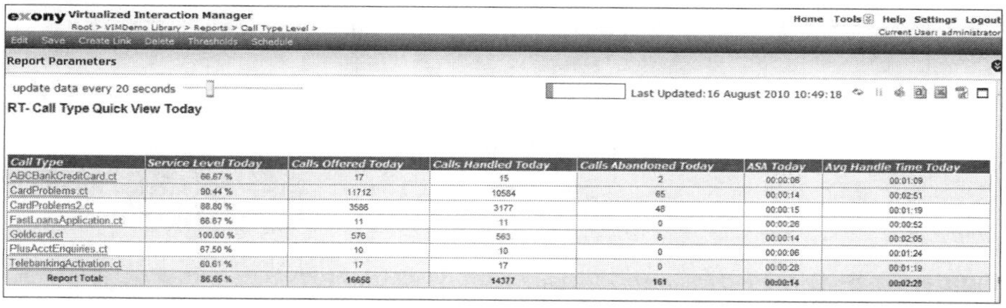

Figure 10-6 *VIM Performance Call Type Report*

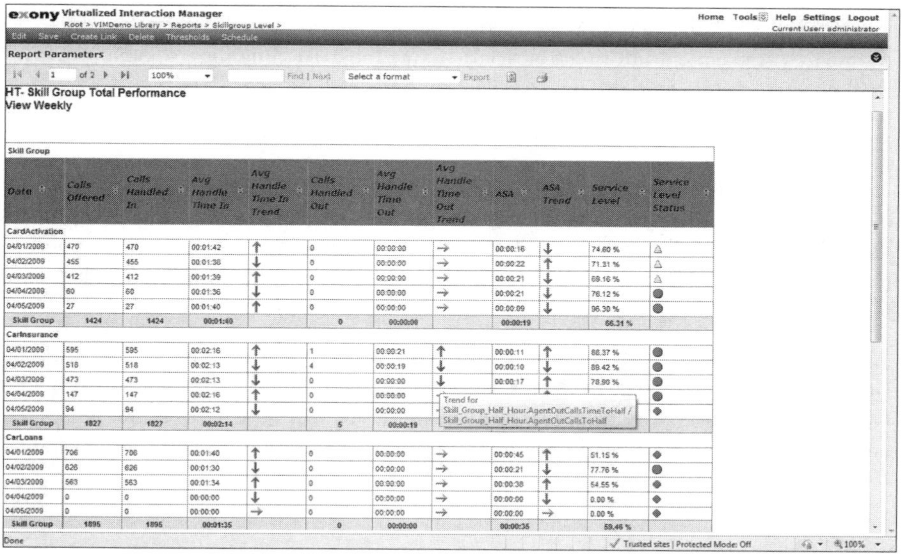

Figure 10-7 *VIM Performance Skill Group Report*

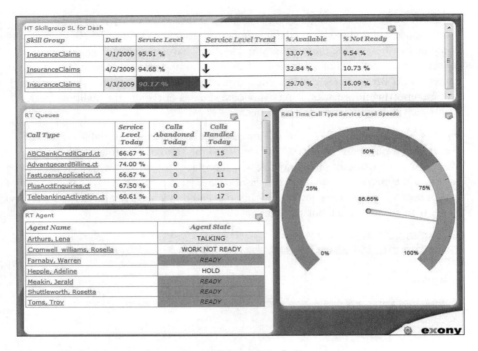

Figure 10-8   *VIM Performance Dashboard-Style Report*

Feature Comparison

Cisco WebView, UIC, and VIM Performance each provide a comprehensive toolset for obtaining management information from UCCE. Table 10-2 highlights some of the high-level product differences among each reporting package.

Wallboards

Real-time management information regarding the current state of the contact center is essential for contact centers to satisfy SLA requirements and meet customer expectations. Modern, CTI-enabled desktop applications provide both the agents and supervisors with access to this real-time data when sitting at their desks.

An active supervisor or team leader will spend a considerable amount of time walking the floor to ensure that her staff has all the assistance required. The time spent "on the floor" takes the supervisor away from her desk; however, a good supervisor still requires the ability to check the metrics to ensure that her team has enough agents ready or logged in to service the call volume.

Table 10-2 *Comparison Among Cisco WebView, CUIC, and VIM Performance*

Feature	WebView	CUIC	VIM Performance
Included out-of-the-box with UCCE	Yes	Yes (V8.0 onward)	—
Integration with data sources	ICM/UCCE	Definable, ICM/UCCE	Definable, ICM/UCCE
Report scheduling for email and printing	No email	No print	No print
Thresholds/drill down	Yes	Customizable	Customizable
Report Creation Wizard	Yes	Yes	Yes
Report development environment	No	No	Yes
Charting Wizard	No	Yes	—
Personal saved reports	Yes	Yes	Yes
Definable user groups	Supervisor only	Unlimited	Unlimited/hierarchical
Gauges and graphics	Simple	Yes	Yes
Trending/forecasting	No	No	Yes
Fully audited change control	No	No	Yes
Multitenancy support	No	No	Yes

Wallboards are used in many contact centers to give the agents and supervisors an easily readable display of important contact center metrics. Various configurations of wallboards are used depending on the business requirements, but the most popular choices are to have either a large plasma/LCD screen or a dedicated hardware wallboard solution.

When using one of the reporting solutions discussed in the previous section, it is possible to have a series of plasma/LCD screens connected to low-performance PCs that run a web browser. The web browser simply displays a report that is maximized on the screen. Although this solution can be cost-effective to implement, the reports that are displayed are often designed for use on a PC and can be difficult to read as the contents might not be clear enough to be used as a wallboard.

A popular alternative is to use a dedicated hardware solution such as the Inova OnTrack series of wallboards (see Figure 10-9). Driven by Inova Solutions' middleware server solution that connects to the UCCE database, Inova OnTrack M Series wallboards display key metrics and messages by collecting operational data from virtually any data source, including ACDs, workforce management systems, and internal databases. The Inova management software allows you to establish data thresholds that automatically trigger color changes and messages, immediately alerting teams within the call center to changing conditions. Information can be easily organized to appear anywhere on the display, with intuitive editing software and advanced scheduling capabilities. Inova also produces the OnTrack X Series wallboard. This series provides a low-power solution, requiring only 15 watts of power, which uses the same Power over Ethernet (PoE) technology as the Cisco IP Phones. One of the main advantages of using a dedicated wallboard rather than a plasma/LCD screen is that the wallboard uses ultra-bright, three-color LEDs that can be viewed from distances of 100 feet and beyond.

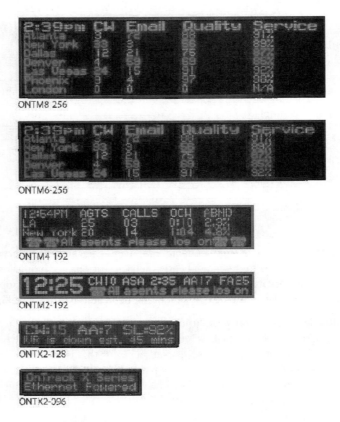

Figure 10-9 *Selection of the Available Inova M Series Displays*

UCCE Reporting

To understand reporting within a UCCE environment, it is important to understand where the reporting data comes from. Figure 10-10 demonstrates that real-time information is passed from the ACD/IVR to the peripheral gateways (PG). The PGs listen to the messages produced by the ACD/IVR and translate the vendor-specific messages into a common language that can be understood by the central controllers. This data gathered from each peripheral is logically separated and assigned by peripheral but is stored in a single database to enable enterprise reporting and also call routing. Reporting statistics are gathered as soon as the initial route request is performed. The data collection process is the same regardless of whether the platform is UICM or UCCE. Typically, queue statistics come from CVP/IP IVR PG, and the call-handling statistics are from the Cisco Unified Communications Manager (Unified CM) PG.

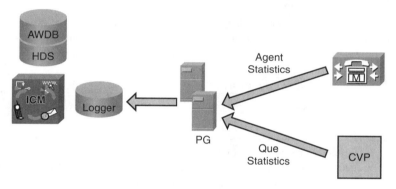

Figure 10-10 *Real-Time Data Collected from Peripherals and Transferred to the Database*

All call activity is written to the UCCE Logger database. Both Side A and Side B of the UCCE platform keep themselves in synchronization and are self-healing if one side is down for a period of time. The loggers replicate data to the Historical Data Servers (HDS). WebView and other reporting clients access the HDSs for reporting information. The loggers are not required to be used for long-term data storage; this is the role of the HDS. Therefore, the recommendation is to have data in the loggers for only a period of 7 to 10 days.

All agent, routing, and peripheral activity data is collected, including inbound/outbound calls, off-hook, and call transfers. Although the activity at the peripheral drives the reporting data received by the PG, it is the call flow resident in the UCCE router that determines the type and frequency of contacts received by the agents and associated peripherals. A great deal of thought and planning often go into the process of developing call scripts to optimize agent handling and maximize the use of available resources. What often happens is that the call scripts are developed and tested, and then as an afterthought, the call script is retrofitted with a series of nodes to try and achieve the desired reporting outcomes. This approach usually ends up with a compromise between call delivery functionality and only a subset of the reporting requirements.

When developing call flow scripts, it is therefore important to determine what reporting metrics are required before the final script is developed and tested. With call scripting, it is possible to achieve the same outcome using a variety of different call control methods; however, the different variations in the script can produce wildly different reporting metrics.

Reporting Notes

The following sections detail some of the best practices to be followed when implementing reporting for UCCE.

Reporting Terminology

The reporting and configuration elements of UCCE allow a wide range of reports to be created, even from the standard available templates. The most popular reports created are usually for agents, skill groups, or call types, as described in Table 10-3.

Table 10-3   *Popular Reporting Entities*

Reporting Entity	Description
Agent	This is the actual contact center agent who handles the customer contact. The agent is associated with a peripheral, is a member of a team, and is a member of at least one skill group. Agent-level reports are used to determine the individual agent's performance.
Skill group	A skill group is a logical container of one or more agents, typically with a similar set of competencies or skills. A high-level example could be to split the agents into two skill groups, one for sales and one for support. A more realistic example would be to subdivide the sales skill group into product areas. Therefore, an agent could be a member of multiple skill groups if he had knowledge of several different products.
Call type	Call types represent the category of the incoming contact. All incoming dialed numbers (and nonvoice contacts such as email) are allocated to one call type, on a many-to-one basis. Call types are considered to be the highest-level reporting entity within UCCE and as such are often used when headline figures are required.

General Reporting with Call Types

Generally call types and dialed numbers (DN) are assigned on a one-to-one mapping; however, it is possible to assign multiple DNs to a single call type if required. This typically happens if a contact center has several published numbers for the same service, for example, a toll-free number and a local area code number for the same service. Call types therefore allow the contact center to create a call treatment based on the number the caller dialed.

It is common practice to create *top-level* call types for all the inbound numbers. For example, if the contact center has two main inbound dialed numbers, sales and support, a call type would be created for each of these. A simple benefit of doing this is that it allows the contact center analyst to check the inbound call traffic statistics against the information provided to him by the carrier. The carrier would provide an itemized or summary statement detailing the metrics of how many calls it delivered to the inbound numbers for a particular date range. The analyst would then match these against the historic reports to ensure that they are the same. A common cause of differences between the number of calls delivered by the carrier and the number of handled calls at the contact center could be that the contact center was experiencing a high call volume during that period and was unable to answer all the simultaneous calls because of physical limitations such as the number of inbound call trunks. More often, call type reports are used by the analyst to understand the demand for the services offered by the contact center.

Figure 10-11 details how DNs are mapped to at least one call type, which is then assigned to call-routing scripts. When a call hits a call type, a call-routing script is executed and call treatment begins.

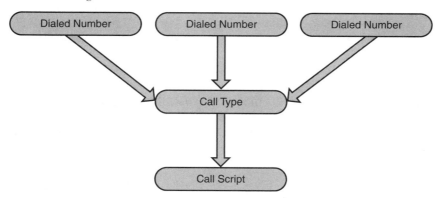

Figure 10-11   *Dialed Number-to-Call Type-to-Call Script Mapping*

Unlike skill group and agent statistics, which are affected only when a call is queued against or delivered to a skill group/agent, call type reporting counters have the flexibility of being set in almost all areas of call-routing scripts. This makes call types the most powerful reporting element in the UCCE platform. It is therefore possible to change the call type throughout the call-routing script to enable more granular reporting.

Figure 10-12 shows a simple call flow whereby the caller is presented with a voice menu that has three possible options. With UCCE call scripting, it is possible to set a call type before and after this IVR interaction. Doing so does not interrupt the caller experience as the technical aspect of setting these call types is transparent to the caller, but enabling this granularity of reporting can be extremely beneficial to the analyst examining call flow or the engineer troubleshooting a problem.

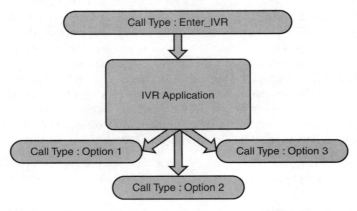

Figure 10-12   *Setting the Call Type Based on Caller Menu Decision*

With the example shown in Figure 10-12, you would expect that if ten calls entered the top-level call type, the sum total of the three lower-level call types should also equal 10. Should this not be the case, you would need to investigate whether a technical issue exists within the IVR script, or possibly whether calls are being abandoned at the IVR. A high level of abandoned calls at the IVR could signify a technical problem such as missing prompts or incorrectly configured IVR scripts, or perhaps the menu prompts are misleading and callers are failing to understand what they should do.

Using real-time reports with these top- and middle-level call types is an easy and quick way of getting a real-time view of what's currently happening inside the contact center. For example, it is possible to see whether particular areas of the business are receiving a higher-than-average call volume, possibly triggered by an external event, problem, or even a TV commercial promotion. With this visibility of the calls, the supervisors or contact center managers can dynamically reskill the agents if necessary to meet service levels.

Call Queuing

Many wallboard-style reports use call type information to display current calls in queue, historic call data such as the number of contacts handled, and the current SLA. Call types are typically used for these reports because the call type tables in the UCCE database have all this detail and are much more easily accessible without the need for the report developer to write database queries over multiple tables. Call handling and call flows vary greatly depending on the business requirements, but many modern call flows (especially for financial institutions) require that the caller listens to some form of disclaimer announcement and notification that her call might be recorded. Although this type of call flow might be necessary to appease industry regulators, it often does so at the expense of the caller by increasing the call duration.

With this type of call, a call type would have been set as soon as the contact was received on the UCCE platform, but because of the regulatory announcement, it might be several seconds or even minutes before the call reaches a part of the call flow script where an agent has the opportunity to answer and service the call. This poses an issue for the contact center team leader. If he were to perform reporting on the initial call type, it would show that all the calls had a long Average Speed of Answer (ASA) metric, which would reflect badly on the team when measured against company or industry-wide metrics. A common resolution to this problem is to change the call type just before the call hits a queue node in the call script. This ensures that the agents have a clean service level as the SLA timer is reset when the call type change occurs. This means that the queue statistics for the call type genuinely represent the actual time in queue, and not any accumulated time before the call went into queue.

Doing this ensures that the service level is affected only by the time taken for the agents to answer the call after all menu options and announcements have been heard by the caller. Changing the call type too early will reflect in a bad SLA for the skill group as answering calls that are still going through IVR menus is outside of their control.

Hiding Objects

With the ability to create a large number of call types for every call flow scenario, including top-level, medium-level, IVR options, Re-Route On No Answer (RONA), and any debugging or diagnostics, it is easy to accumulate a long list of call types that display in the reporting tools when generating new reports. Without a logical naming convention, it can quickly become overwhelming for the general analyst or contact center manager as to which call type she should use to generate the report she requires.

Cisco Unified Contact Center Hosted (UCCH) uses the concepts of customers and customer instances to enable a single platform to support a multitenant environment. Although not used in UCCE, the configuration elements to enable multiple instances still exists.

For reporting users to access reporting clients such as WebView, they need to have an account created for them. When this account is created, it is possible to assign the account to a customer instance. With UCCE, typically only one customer instance is defined. The instance is a five-alphanumeric string assigned by the installation engineer, usually an acronym of the customer's company name. When creating call types, it is also possible to assign the call type to the customer instance. It is therefore also possible to not assign some call types to the customer instance and leave them at the default.

When a reporting user is assigned to a customer instance and logs in to a reporting client such as WebView, he can see only the UCCE objects, such as call types, that have been assigned to the same customer instance. This is a simple and primitive way to "hide" many of the internal call types from the general reporting user.

Don't Mix and Match Reporting Entities

It is relatively straightforward to understand the concepts of skill group and agent-level reporting, especially if the analyst or contact center manager has existing skills developed from other ACD vendors. The concept of call types, however, often causes difficulty unless they are explained fully to the reporting user. Many users assume that call types are the number of calls delivered to a skill group or team. In many cases, when simple call-routing scripts are used, it is possible for the call type metrics to be similar or identical to the skill group metrics. This soon causes confusion if the call-routing scripts are modified to add further services or additional skill groups.

When working with users new to Cisco UCCE, it is important to fully explain the concept of call types and describe how they are different than other reporting entities. To further enforce the logical difference, when creating custom reports, do not mix and match different reporting entities. For example, do not use elements of call type data with a skill group report.

Wrap-Up Codes

A contact center platform can deliver calls to agent or IVR resources based on a variety of different indicators, including the number dialed, the caller's Automatic Number Identification (ANI), and menu options selected by the caller while the call is present at the IVR. Unfortunately, these indicators do not guarantee that the call presented to the agent can actually be handled by that agent. Occasionally, the caller might just select the first menu option in the hope that he will be answered by an agent quicker. Sometimes the agent might be multiskilled and the contact center manager is interested in the type of call that was handled, for example, a product inquiry, complaint call, or wrong number.

Through call types and skill group reports, it is possible for the analyst to observe the type of calls the platform is trying to deliver; however, wrap-up codes enable the analyst to see exactly the type of call handled by the agent.

A wrap-up code is usually in the form of a few words or short string of text that describes the type and handling of the call. The agent is presented with a static list of the most popular typical wrap-up codes when the call is complete. One of these codes is selected by the agent, and the code is stored in the database with the other call details.

Wrap-up codes are usually quite specific to the business or team handling the customer contacts. For example, a sales team might have a series of wrap-up codes for each product they sell. Generic wrap-up codes also exist that are often used for all teams. These generic codes often include terms such as "one and done" to signify that the contact was handled and processed and that no further follow-up is required. Or perhaps codes such as "Wrong number" can be used to signify that the caller made a mistake when dialing.

In UCCE, wrap-up code results are stored in the Termination_Call_Detail (TCD) table on the Historical Data Servers (HDS). None of the standard reporting templates access the TCD tables because of the potential amount of processing overhead required to service the report should a large amount of data be selected. This means that the UCCE platform does not provide any reporting templates to analyze wrap-up codes.

Note   Custom templates that include the same types of data provided by the standard reports, such as a custom call type report, are unlikely to impact database or reporting application performance. However, a resource-intensive customization that processes detailed data can decrease performance. For example, no standard Cisco reports contain call data that is stored in the Route_Call_Detail (RCD) and Termination_Call_Detail (TCD) tables. Custom reporting templates must be used to report on data from these tables. These custom reports will always have a performance impact on the database and on the reporting applications.

A popular solution used by many companies to achieve wrap-up code reports is to create a roll-up table in a database external to the native UCCE database tables. A stored procedure is created that extracts certain data from the TCD tables at a defined time when performance impact on the database is minimal. The stored procedure extracts the data and deposits it in a different database. Custom reports are then created to reference this external database to provide wrap-up code reporting.

Legacy Reports

When migrating from a legacy time-division multiplexing (TDM) environment to a new Cisco UCCE platform, many contact centers want to replicate their current call-routing and reporting environment within UCCE. For many customers, the reason for doing this is simple: Their business rules and approach to call handling has not changed, only the underlying technology.

Many humans in general are reluctant to change, and the same is true for many reporting analysts. The reports that they have cultivated and grown accustomed to over the years successfully provide them with the metrics they require to do their job and allow them to produce the reports needed for higher-level management.

With this in mind, many customers ask that their legacy ACD reports are replicated as custom reports in the Cisco UCCE platform. Unfortunately, many systems integration partners try to blindly deliver this request without educating the customer about the benefits possible even with the standard reports.

When comparing reports between different ACD vendors, the common problems that analysts face are the differences in terminology and the various formulas used to create the metrics. Table 10-4 details some of the common issues.

Although it is technically possible to create custom reports that give the look and feel of the old legacy ACD reports, it is often not advisable to do so. A wise approach would be to educate the customer that the reports will be different and go into great detail to explain why. As discussed in a previous section, the placement of certain call script nodes can have a great impact on the metrics observed in reports.

One instance where it might be useful to create reports that replicate the old reports is when migrating from WebView to Unified IC. Although Unified IC is an easy-to-use environment, it is possible to create new reports that are similar to the previous WebView reports. Doing this could minimize training requirements during the migration.

Table 10-4   *Common Reporting Metric Issues*

Issue	Description
Legacy and UCCE terminology identical.	Fortunately this is not an issue. This occurs when the terminology and formula used to calculate the metric are the same.
Legacy and UCCE terminology are the same but mean different things.	This occurs when the analyst observes the same terminology on the two different vendors' platforms but they mean different things. For example, two different vendors might use the term *Calls Offered*, but one vendor's meaning might be the number of calls offered while the other might refer to the number of calls answered.
Legacy and UCCE terminology are the same but the formulas used to calculate the metrics are different.	This is a common issue that occurs when comparing metrics. Both vendors use the same terminology, such as call duration. One vendor determines call duration to be the total time talking plus after-call work, whereas the other vendor's definition of call duration also includes the time the caller spent in queue.

Summary

This chapter provided an introduction to contact center reporting, the reporting tools available with Cisco UCCE, and several items to observe when performing reporting. In particular, the learning points from this chapter can be summarized as follows:

■ Reporting is an incredibly important feature of all contact centers. The information gathered and presented in the reports is useful to all business areas.

■ Several reporting packages are available with Cisco UCCE, with many more third-party applications also providing integration. Cisco Unified Intelligence Center is the preferred reporting package for UCCE version 8.0 and future releases.

■ The data displayed in the report has a great influence based on how the UCCE platform is configured. It is important to have reporting in mind when developing call-routing scripts.

Chapter 11

Nodes and Processes

This chapter covers the following subjects:

■ A detailed review of the nodes and processes within UCCE

■ A clean system startup sequence

■ A comprehensive run-through of the process communication and messages to observe

Cisco Unified Contact Center Enterprise (UCCE) is a highly resilient platform that provides layers of redundancy through distributed processes over a multiple-server architecture. Depending on the size of the deployment, usually based on the number of agents to be serviced and their complexity, the component parts of UCCE can each be distributed to achieve the performance and scalability requirements of the contact center.

A UCCE solution consists of several components. The minimum core components required for the solution to function are as follows:

■ Logger

■ Router

■ Administrative workstation (AW)

■ Peripheral gateway (PG)

■ Computer Telephony Integration (CTI) and CTI OS Server

Several additional, optional components include

■ WebView and/or Cisco Unified Intelligence Center (CUIC) Server

■ Outbound dialer

■ PGs for various multimedia options

■ Cisco Agent Desktop Server

In UCCE terminology, an individual component is often called a *node*. An example of a node would be the LoggerA service. Each node has a specific function to perform. In the case of the logger, its primary role is to manage database access to the underlying SQL database and to serve this data to other UCCE nodes when required.

For a node to perform its role successfully, the different functions of the node are divided into their respective areas, with each function usually having a dedicated software process. Each node has one or more processes for it to perform its task, with many nodes each having more than four processes.

Figure 11-1 details a logical view of a single server having two nodes installed, each node having multiple processes.

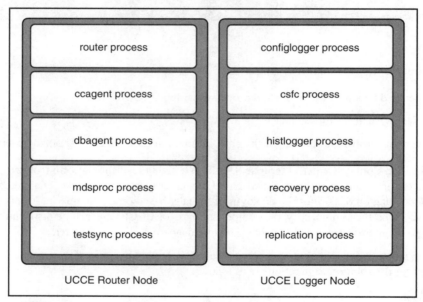

UCCE Rogger Server (Router and Logger)

Figure 11-1 *Logical Relationship of Servers to Nodes to Processes*

The majority of UCCE processes display their real-time output or logging in to a process window. These process windows are viewable when a user is logged in to the server. Figure 11-2 displays an example of an output from a UCCE process. This particular process is the logger process.

Successful and error-free communication among the servers, nodes, and processes is required for the correct functioning of a UCCE platform. Dedicated network links, network interface cards (NIC), IP addressing schemes, static IP routes, and IP quality of service (QoS) are all employed to ensure that this communication happens in a timely fashion.

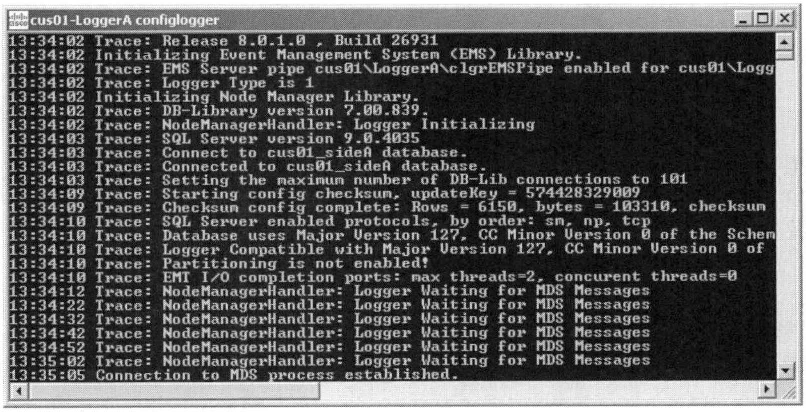

```
cus01-LoggerA configlogger                                      _|□|X|
13:34:02 Trace: Release 8.0.1.0 , Build 26931
13:34:02 Initializing Event Management System (EMS) Library.
13:34:02 Trace: EMS Server pipe cus01\LoggerA\clgrEMSPipe enabled for cus01\Logg
13:34:02 Trace: Logger Type is 1
13:34:02 Initializing Node Manager Library.
13:34:02 Trace: DB-Library version 7.00.839.
13:34:02 Trace: NodeManagerHandler: Logger Initializing
13:34:03 Trace: SQL Server version 9.0.4035
13:34:03 Trace: Connect to cus01_sideA database.
13:34:03 Trace: Connected to cus01_sideA database.
13:34:03 Trace: Setting the maximum number of DB-Lib connections to 101
13:34:09 Trace: Starting config checksum, updateKey = 574428329009
13:34:09 Trace: Checksum config complete. Rows = 6150, bytes = 103310, checksum
13:34:10 Trace: SQL Server enabled protocols, by order: sm, np, tcp
13:34:10 Trace: Database uses Major Version 127, CC Minor Version 0 of the Schem
13:34:10 Trace: Logger Compatible with Major Version 127, CC Minor Version 0 of
13:34:10 Trace: Partitioning is not enabled!
13:34:10 Trace: EMT I/O completion ports: max threads=2, concurrent threads=0
13:34:12 Trace: NodeManagerHandler: Logger Waiting for MDS Messages
13:34:22 Trace: NodeManagerHandler: Logger Waiting for MDS Messages
13:34:32 Trace: NodeManagerHandler: Logger Waiting for MDS Messages
13:34:42 Trace: NodeManagerHandler: Logger Waiting for MDS Messages
13:34:52 Trace: NodeManagerHandler: Logger Waiting for MDS Messages
13:35:02 Trace: NodeManagerHandler: Logger Waiting for MDS Messages
13:35:05 Connection to MDS process established.
```

Figure 11-2 *Output Window for the Logger Process*

This chapter covers each of the nodes and its associated processes and describes how those processes communicate within the node and with other nodes in the UCCE platform.

The UCCE distributed and redundant architecture enables the platform to suffer multiple node and process failures and yet still perform effectively. This style of redundancy also enables the nodes to be started in any order, perhaps after a system power-down. However, a more logical sequence exists, which this chapter covers with a detailed breakdown of what the processes are doing during startup.

UCCE Nodes

Although this chapter is UCCE-specific, the majority of the nodal and process communication also applies to Unified Intelligent Contact Manager (UICM) and Unified Contact Center Hosted (UCCH). Unified ICM is an almost identical architecture to UCCE but uses a different Peripheral Interface Manager (PIM) on the PG to connect to the different Automatic Call Distributors (ACD). UCCH has additional processes to connect to the service provider's Signaling System 7 (SS7) switch and the hosted customer instance.

The following sections detail the core services and their individual processes used in a UCCE, UICM, or UCCH solution.

Logger

An integral part of the UCCE platform is the series of SQL databases. These databases store the following various different types of data:

- All the UCCE platform configuration required for the platform to function, including items such as the call-routing scripts, agents, and skill groups

- Real-time and event data, including the status of peripherals and calls in queue

- Individual call leg details, including call variables and specific data associated with the call

- Historical data, typically summarized into time periods

As an important component within the central controllers, the logger node is deployed in a duplex configuration, with the first logger node called LoggerA and the second called LoggerB. These components are deployed on different server hardware, often in different physical locations:

- **configlogger:** The Configuration Logger process stores configuration data in the central controller database.

- **csfs:** The Customer Support Forwarding Service (CSFS) Synchronization process monitors the connection between the router and the logger through regular heartbeat traffic.

- **histlogger:** The Historical Logger process stores historical data in the central controller database.

- **recovery:** The Recovery process recovers historical data using recovery keys. After a process restart in a duplex environment, the recovery keys are used to determine which logger database has the most recent data. The recovery process then manages the synchronization of the data through a process called the *state transfer*.

- **replication:** The Replication process replicates historical data from the central controller to the Historical Data Server (HDS).

Note   In versions of UCCE prior to version 7.0, the configlogger and histlogger processes were combined into a single process called logger. Splitting the single logger process into two allows parallel processing of the two different data types, historical data, and configuration data.

Router

The router is the heart of the UCCE platform responsible for managing all the contact routing decisions. All the call-routing scripts and platform configuration are stored in the memory of the router. The router also receives real-time information from the PGs, therefore allowing it to have the full picture of what is happening in the contact center. This real-time data store coupled with the call-routing logic enables the router to receive and respond to routing requests from the routing clients. In the case of UCCE, the routing client is generally the Cisco Unified Communications Manager (Unified CM) PG, but Interactive Voice Response (IVR) PGs can also perform route requests.

The router nodes, like the logger nodes, are also deployed over two servers and called RouterA and RouterB, respectively.

The router consists of several processes:

- **router:** The router node also has a process called router. This process is used by UCCE to manage the route requests and provide a route response. This process also collects all the real-time platform information required to maintain a holistic view of the contact center.

- **ccagent:** The Central Controller Agent, or ccagent, is responsible for establishing a connection to all the PGs configured in the platform. The title bar of the ccagent process gives the engineer a easy way of determining how many PGs the router is in communication with. The number of PGs configured in a system is determined during router installation. Each PG is assigned an ID, typically starting with the number 1 and incrementing by 1 as additional PGs are configured. The title bar of ccagent displays the number of configured PGs and the number that are connected. For example, if the title bar displayed the text InSvc 1/2 PGs, it is clear to see that only one out of two configured PGs has registered with the router.

- **dbagent:** The Database Agent process controls the communications between the router and the logger by validating access to the central controller database.

- **mdsproc:** The Message Delivery Service (MDS) process manages the reliable message delivery between the UCCE processes.

- **testsync:** The Testsync process provides an application interface for the various test and debugging tools to connect to.

The router node also has several optional processes that appear when enabled during router setup:

- **AppGW:** The Application Gateway process allows the UCCE routing engine to connect to third-party applications through a published application programming interface (API). The API allows the passing of call variables and call data to the external application. The external application can then respond with additional data or a response to the client's request. This data is then typically used with the UCCE call-routing script to influence the call-routing decision. Connectivity for the Application Gateway node is defined in the Application Gateway List tool. This tool allows the process to connect to multiple gateways for resilience.

- **DBWorker:** The Database Worker process enables the router to connect to a simple SQL database. Typically containing only a single table with a small number of columns, the DBWorker process and its associated DBLookup script editor node are great for implementing simple database dips, such as checking the status of a caller based on his Automatic Number Identifier (ANI). Like the Application Gateway process, the DBWorker process can also connect to two databases simultaneously for resilience.

Although it is unlikely to be deployed with UCCE, the router can also have an additional processed called the network interface controller (NIC). Not to be confused with an

Ethernet NIC, this NIC provides an interface to the service provider's intelligent network, usually using SS7 signaling.

Peripheral Gateway

The PG provides an abstraction layer between the peripheral (usually an ACD or IVR) and the UCCE central controller. With UICM and UCCH, the supported peripherals can be from many vendors, but with UCCE, the peripheral that provides call control for the agent devices is the Unified CM, with Cisco Unified IP IVR or Cisco Customer Voice Portal (CVP) providing IVR and call queuing.

Similar to the router and logger nodes, the PGs are deployed in a duplex manner, but their physical location varies depending on the deployment architecture used. Typically, the duplex PG pair will be deployed at the same location as the ACD. For example, in a distributed call processing model using two or more independent Unified CM clusters, a duplex PG pair would be deployed at each of the sites coresident with the Unified CM cluster. This rule is true for all deployment models with the exception of the Clustering Over the WAN model. With this deployment model, the Unified CM cluster is typically split over two sites. Each site contains one side of the UCCE central controller, including a PG.

A single PG pair can service more than one peripheral. In typical UCCE deployments, the PGs usually service both the Unified CM cluster and the IVRs, but for larger deployments, dedicated PGs can be used.

ACD PGs, including Unified CM PGs, also have the CTI Server process and, if required, the CTI OS Server.

The type of ACD being deployed reflects directly on the different PIM process installed. UCCE uses the Enterprise Agent PIM (eagtpim) process, which is named after a remote agent component used in early versions of UCCE that allowed agents to work using analog cards installed in their PC rather than being connected to an ACD. This feature was withdrawn from UCCE a long time ago.

The PG node processes are as follows:

- **mdsproc:** The Message Delivery Service (MDS) process manages message delivery between the processes running on the PG.

- **opc-cce:** The Open Peripheral Controller is the heart of the PG. The OPC is responsible for synchronization with the other PG as part of the PG pair and prepares the call records for the UCCE database.

- **pgagent:** The Peripheral Gateway Agent (PGAgent) manages the session layer communication between the PG and the ccagent process running on the router. When deployed as a duplex pair, the pgagent process window displays with which side of the central controller router it maintains an active connection. If the process window displays **InSvc A:Active B:Idle**, you could determine that pgagent has an active connection with ccagent on Router A; therefore, only heartbeat traffic is being sent to

Router B. Router-side preference is configured during PG setup. The PG can be configured to have preference as Side A, Side B, or no preference. This preference is typically used to engineer traffic routing when the PGs are deployed remotely from the central controller but is also used during failure scenarios. Should the preferred side go offline, the nonpreferred side will take over. When the preferred side comes back online, the active side will switch back again. This switchback does not occur if the PGs are configured with no preferred sides.

- **testsync:** The Testsync process provides an application interface for the various test and debugging tools to connect to.

As previously discussed, the PG requires a different PIM process for the vendor-specific ACD to which it is connected. The UCCE PG requires a PIM process and a Java Telephony Application Programming Interface (JTAPI) process to facilitate communication with the Unified CM cluster. The following list details the processes typically found on a UCCE PG that combine both a Unified CM PIM and IVR PIM:

- **jtapigw:** Many third-party applications communicate with a Unified CM cluster using a Cisco-proprietary JTAPI. For the Jtapigw process to function, the Cisco JTAPI driver needs to be installed on the PG. Cisco JTAPI is available from the Plugins page on the Unified CM servers. You should ensure that the version of JTAPI installed on the PG is the same version of JTAPI available from the Unified CM server.

- **eagtpim:** This is the Enterprise Agent PIM process that connects to the jtapigw process required for connection to a Unified CM cluster.

- **ctisvr:** The Computer Telephony Integration (CTI) server process is installed on PGs, where the peripheral communicates real-time agent data to the PG and the agents use a CTI-enabled desktop application to inform the PG of agent state changes and information including CTI data (wrap-up codes, reason codes, and call data updates). The ctisvr process communicates with the OPC process running on the PG. Throughout early versions of UICM, the CTI Server provided the native connection to all agent desktop applications and third-party applications that required real-time data such as wallboards and call recording, where data tagging is used. To support developers and make the solution more scalable, Cisco developed the CTI Object Server (CTI OS) and requested that all CTI applications developed now be against CTI OS rather than the CTI Server.

- **ctios server:** The CTI OS Server process establishes a connection to the CTI Server process and provides an interface for desktop and third-party applications to develop against using the CTI OS Toolkit. The ctios server also establishes a connection to its duplex pair to provide resiliency. The title bar of the CTI OS process window displays the IP address and port of the active CTI Server it is connected to. It also displays the IP port that the process is listening on. An example of this display is **[ACTIVE, CG 192.168.15.30, CGPort 42027, Listen Port: 42028]**.

- **vrupim:** The Vrupim process is the PIM for IVRs connected through the GED125 specification. It is common for deployments with multiple IP IVRs to have several Vrupim processes running on the same PG.

Note   The type of PG configured in PG Explorer during initial configuration has a great influence over the processes running on the PG. When performing a UCCE install, it is possible to configure a single PG with multiple PIMs: one for the Unified CM cluster and one for the IP IVRs (vrupim). If you use this deployment method, a single PG with multiple PIM processes is present on the PG node.

However, it also possible to configure a PG for each peripheral, for example, a single PG1 for the Unified CM cluster and then an additional PG for each of the IP IVRs. If configured in this manner, the entire range of PG processes (including PIM, OPC, and MDS) are present for each configured PG.

Both methods are simple to configure and perform without issue. One benefit of performing the latter method is that it allows the individual PGs to be stopped or cycled without having an impact on the other PG processes, for example, if PG1 is configured for the Unified CM cluster and PG2 is configured for the IP IVR. The engineer could cycle PG2 without it impacting the connection to the Unified CM servers. If these were configured as a single PG, both the Unified CM connection and the IVR connection would be cycled.

Should this method be employed during configuration, the installation engineer must be aware that a different client type is specified in PG Explorer, and that the numbers used for logical controller and physical controller IDs between the peripherals will be different.

Administrative Workstation

The administrative workstation (AW) provides the systems administrator with an array of configuration tools to manage and maintain the UCCE platform. Within the UCCE architecture, several AW deployment models exist. The type of deployment chosen determines the actual processes running on the server.

The most popular AW deployment is the AW-HDS-DDS (prior to UCCE 8.0, this was called the AW/HDS server). Typically deployed in a redundant fashion with a Side A and a Side B, it is important to understand that these servers are not duplexed and have no process communication between them.

In many UCCE deployments, an AW-HDS-DDS will have three databases:

- **<instance name>_awdb:** Used for storing UCCE configuration and real-time data

- **<instance name>_hds:** Used by the HDS processes for long-term historical data storage

- **<instance name>_wv:** Used by WebView for storing WebView-specific configuration

The logger holds the database used by the central controllers, but rather than this database being modified by the client applications, the configuration tools actually modify a copy of the configuration data stored in the local database on the AW. When changes are made in this database, the AW processes communicate with the loggers to instruct them of the change.

As well as containing a copy of the configuration data, the AW database also contains data used for real-time reporting. Although this data is described as real-time, in practice it should actually be termed "near real-time" as the data is updated approximately every 10–12 seconds.

The AW consists of many software processes:

- **configlogger:** The Configuration Logger process stores configuration data in the AW database.

- **replication:** The Replication process receives historical data from the logger and inserts this data into the HDS database on the AW.

- **rtdist:** The Real-Time Distributor receives real-time data from the router and distributes this data to all the real-time clients that are connected to it. These clients can be other AWs, typically a client AW.

- **rtclient:** The Real-Time Client on the AW is responsible for updating the local AW database. The rtclient gets its data from the rtdist process.

- **updateaw:** The UpdateAW process ensures that the local AW configuration database remains current with configuration data from the central controller.

The AW node also has several optional processes that appear when enabled during setup:

- **webview:** The WebView process manages communication between reporting clients requesting pages from the Tomcat web server and the UCCE platform.

- **iseman:** Internet Script Editor provides quick management and configuration changes for UCCE call flow scripts.

Common Processes

Each of the nodes also has a common set of processes that run in the background and do not have visible process windows. Like the processes discussed in this chapter, these common processes also produce log files and can be used for troubleshooting if required. The common processes are as follows:

- **nm:** The Node Manager is a process that manages, restarts, and initializes each of the processes running on each node.

- **nmm:** The Node Manager Manager is a process that manages, restarts, and initializes the Node Manager process running on each node.

Note   The Node Manager also has the power to reboot the server if a critical process fails. This is usually observed when the Windows Shutdown box appears. The server restart can be halted by using the **stopshut** command. In new installations, the common cause of this shutdown is caused by the UCCE processes not being able to resolve the hostnames entered in UCCE setup into IP addresses.

Support Tools Node Agent

Cisco Support Tools is a suite of applications that allows the UCCE system administrator and Cisco partner to troubleshoot performance or configuration issues with the UCCE platform. Among other things, Cisco Support Tools enables the administrator to centrally collate process logs and manage the processes running on the remote nodes. This administration is performed through a web browser interface communicating with the Cisco Support Tools Server. This server in turn communicates with the remote nodes through the Support Tools Node Agent, which runs on all the UCCE nodes.

Unlike the majority of UCCE processes, the Support Tools Node Agent does not have a process window that displays the process output; however, the management of the Agent is through the ICM Service Control application.

UCCE Nodes Startup Sequence

As with all distributed systems, knowing which servers and services to start first and the order in which to start the remaining services is an important part of systems administration.

As discussed earlier in this chapter, the fault-resilient architecture allows the UCCE platform to automatically recover from several failure scenarios, and in many cases, this failover is seamless to the agents, supervisors, and customers. From a clean startup, perhaps after a power-down, this resiliency enables the UCCE nodes to be started in any order, and the processes will communicate with each other until the system is in an active state to process route requests.

Should an administrator start up the UCCE platform in a random order, he should expect to see lots of error messages in the process output windows. It is also possible that some of the servers might reboot if they detect serious errors.

Rather than experience the potential for error messages and multiple server reboots, it is possible to start the core UCCE platform in a clean and efficient manner that enables the administrator to monitor the node startup using a logical and planned process.

Table 11-1 details the startup sequence and gives a brief description of why the node was started in this order. The general objective of this startup sequence is to activate Side A of the platform; then start up Side B and allow the two sides to synchronize. For the purposes of this sequence, assume that any Unified CM servers and IVRs are already up and running.

Table 11-1 *Core UCCE Node Startup Sequence*

Node Sequence	Description
Logger A	The logger database contains all the system configuration required for the router process to service route requests. Without this data, the router process cannot function, so the logger is the first process to be initiated.
Router A	With Logger A active, when Router A is started, it connects to the logger to retrieve all the configuration data. This data is stored in the router's memory to allow immediate call processing; however, the router process will not go active until it is in communication with the configured PGs.
PG A	Router A will go active when it has established communication with half or more of the configured PGs. Assuming that only a single PG has been configured, but with multiple PIMs, by starting this PG, the UCCE platform will be in a state ready to process route requests. After this PG has been started, the CTI Server and CTI OS Server can be started too. These two processes do not need to be active before starting Side B of the platform, but starting them now saves the engineer time from having to return to this server later in the startup process.
Logger B	When Logger B starts, it checks the recovery keys in the databases to determine whether they are up to date. If any discrepancies exist, the logger will initiate a state transfer to synchronize both sides of the central controller.
Router B	The Router B processes establish a connection to the configured PGs and also request an updated copy of the configuration.
PG B	For UCCE, one side of the PG will be Active, whereas the other side remains in an Idle state. PG B will establish connections to both routers and PG A. CTI Server B and CTI OS Server can also be started.
AW/HDS servers	The AW servers are not required for the servicing of route requests. When started, the AW processes will establish connections to the databases and perform synchronization if required.
All other servers	All other servers can now be started, including Cisco Agent Desktop servers and WebView.

UCCE Detailed Startup

The trace output window for each process can be extremely helpful when observing a platform startup. The following sections break down each of the processes in order and highlight specific key outputs to observe.

No additional trace settings have been enabled in these outputs. The default settings are used. Because of the verbose nature of the processes, some superfluous output has been removed for clarity.

Note Some processes have debugging to the window disabled by default. It is possible to determine which ones have the display disabled as they have a trace message stating this in the process window. Tracing can be enabled through modification of a registry setting. Chapter 16, "Troubleshooting," details the setting of tracing.

Figure 11-3 shows the ICM Service Control application. Service Control can be used to start, stop, and restart all the UCCE services. ICM Service Control runs on all UCCE nodes. It is also possible to perform these tasks on remote UCCE nodes through this application.

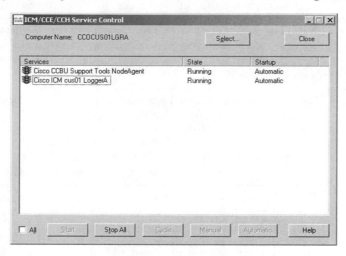

Figure 11-3 *Screen Shot of the ICM Service Control Application on Logger A*

Logger A

The output detailed in Example 11-1 displays the startup for the Configuration Logger process. Details to look for include

■ That the process has connected to the <instance name>_SideA database.

■ The binding order of the SQL Server protocols. This binding order is set when SQL Server is installed; the correct order is a) Shared Memory (SM), b) Named Pipes (NP), and c) TCP/IP.

- After it is initialized, the clgr process waits for a connection to MDS, which occurs when the router node is started.

Example 11-1   *Logger A Configuration Logger Process*

```
13:34:02 la-clgr Trace: Logger Type is 1
13:34:02 la-clgr Initializing Node Manager Library.
13:34:02 la-clgr Trace: DB-Library version 7.00.839.
13:34:02 la-clgr Trace: NodeManagerHandler: Logger Initializing
13:34:03 la-clgr Trace: SQL Server version 9.0.4035
13:34:03 la-clgr Trace: Connect to cus01_sideA database.
13:34:03 la-clgr Trace: Connected to cus01_sideA database.
13:34:03 la-clgr Trace: Setting the maximum number of DB-Lib connections to 101
13:34:09 la-clgr Trace: Starting config checksum, updateKey = 574428329009
13:34:09 la-clgr Trace: Checksum config complete: Rows = 6150, bytes = 103310,
checksum = 3810272, updateKey = 574428329009
13:34:10 la-clgr Trace: SQL Server enabled protocols, by order: sm, np, tcp
13:34:10 la-clgr Trace: Database uses Major Version 127, CC Minor Version 0 of
the Schema
13:34:10 la-clgr Trace: Logger Compatible with Major Version 127, CC Minor Version
0 of the Schema
13:34:10 la-clgr Trace: Partitioning is not enabled!
13:34:10 la-clgr Trace: EMT I/O completion ports: max threads=2, concurrent
threads=0
13:34:12 la-clgr Trace: NodeManagerHandler: Logger Waiting for MDS Messages
13:34:22 la-clgr Trace: NodeManagerHandler: Logger Waiting for MDS Messages
13:34:32 la-clgr Trace: NodeManagerHandler: Logger Waiting for MDS Messages
13:34:42 la-clgr Trace: NodeManagerHandler: Logger Waiting for MDS Messages
13:34:52 la-clgr Trace: NodeManagerHandler: Logger Waiting for MDS Messages
```

Example 11-2 details the initialization of the CSFS Synchronization process. The Waiting for Link Enable message is repeated until the first PG goes into an active state.

Example 11-2   *Logger A csfs Process*

```
13:34:02 la-csfs Initializing Node Manager Library.
13:34:02 la-csfs Trace: Version: Release 8.0.1.0, Build 26931
13:34:02 la-csfs Trace: EMT I/O completion ports: max threads=2, concurrent
threads=0
13:34:02 la-csfs Trace: Waiting for Monitor Thread to Complete Initialization
13:34:02 la-csfs Trace: Couldn't read registry value PreferredSNMPSide - Default
is SideA Preferred
13:34:03 la-csfs Trace: Attempting to initialize MDS...
13:34:03 la-csfs Trace: CSFSSyncThread : Waiting for Link Enable
13:34:04 la-csfs Trace: CSFSSyncThread : Waiting for Link Enable
13:34:05 la-csfs Trace: CSFSSyncThread : Waiting for Link Enable
13:34:06 la-csfs Trace: CSFSSyncThread : Waiting for Link Enable
```

Example 11-3 details the initialization of the Historical Logger process. It has a startup sequence similar to that of the Configuration Logger.

Example 11-3   *Logger A Historical Logger Process*

```
13:34:02 la-hlgr Trace: Logger Type is 1
13:34:02 la-hlgr Initializing Node Manager Library.
13:34:02 la-hlgr Trace: DB-Library version 7.00.839.
13:34:02 la-hlgr Trace: NodeManagerHandler: Logger Initializing
13:34:03 la-hlgr Trace: SQL Server version 9.0.4035
13:34:03 la-hlgr Trace: Connect to cus01_sideA database.
13:34:03 la-hlgr Trace: Connected to cus01_sideA database.
13:34:03 la-hlgr Trace: Setting the maximum number of DB-Lib connections to 101
13:34:09 la-hlgr Trace: SQL Server enabled protocols, by order: sm, np, tcp
13:34:09 la-hlgr Trace: Database uses Major Version 127, CC Minor Version 0 of
the Schema
13:34:09 la-hlgr Trace: Logger Compatible with Major Version 127, CC Minor Version
0 of the Schema
13:34:09 la-hlgr Trace: Partitioning is not enabled!
13:34:09 la-hlgr Trace: EMT I/O completion ports: max threads=2, concurrent
threads=0
13:34:12 la-hlgr Trace: NodeManagerHandler: Logger Waiting for MDS Messages
13:34:22 la-hlgr Trace: NodeManagerHandler: Logger Waiting for MDS Messages
13:34:32 la-hlgr Trace: NodeManagerHandler: Logger Waiting for MDS Messages
13:34:42 la-hlgr Trace: NodeManagerHandler: Logger Waiting for MDS Messages
```

Example 11-4 details the trace output from the Logger A Recovery process. The Recovery process obtains the recovery key used to check how current the database is. This process also gives an indication of the database utilization. In this example, you can see that only a fraction of the total database size is used. Database purge settings are configured so that the UCCE platform automatically maintains the database and prevents the database from filling.

Example 11-4   *Logger A Recovery Process*

```
13:34:02 la-rcv Initializing Node Manager Library.
13:34:02 la-rcv Trace: EMT I/O completion ports: max threads=2, concurrent
threads=0
13:34:02 la-rcv Trace: DB-Library version 7.00.839.
13:34:02 la-rcv Trace: Registry Watch Started for Subkey = SOFTWARE\Cisco Systems,
Inc.\ICM\cus01\LoggerA\Logger\CurrentVersion
13:34:02 la-rcv Trace: Registry Watch Started for Subkey = SOFTWARE\Cisco Systems,
Inc.\ICM\cus01\LoggerA\Recovery\CurrentVersion
13:34:03 la-rcv Trace: SQL Server version 9.0.4035
13:34:03 la-rcv Trace: Connect to cus01_sideA database.
13:34:03 la-rcv Trace: Connected to cus01_sideA database.
```

```
13:34:03 la-rcv Trace: Setting the maximum number of DB-Lib connections to 101
13:34:09 la-rcv Trace: Starting Recovery Key for Admin table is 574445249000.0

13:34:09 la-rcv Trace: MDS Connection Thread Started
13:34:09 la-rcv Trace: Copy History Thread Started
13:34:09 la-rcv Trace: Recover History Thread Started
13:34:09 la-rcv Trace: Purge History Thread Started
13:34:09 la-rcv Trace: Copy History Thread for t_Termination_Call_Detail Started
13:34:09 la-rcv Trace: Copy History Thread for t_Termination_Call_Variable Started
13:34:09 la-rcv Trace: Copy History Thread for t_Route_Call_Variable Started
13:34:09 la-rcv Trace: Copy History Thread for t_Route_Call_Detail Started
13:34:10 la-rcv Trace: Purge schedule is 00:30 M,T,W,Th,F,S,Su
13:34:10 la-rcv Trace: RecoveryServer is initialized.
13:34:10 la-rcv Trace: RecoveryClient client connection is initialized.
13:34:39 la-rcv Trace: 1% of the available free space is used in cus01_sideA
database.
13:34:39 la-rcv Trace: 6% of the available log space is used in cus01_sideA
database.
```

Example 11-5 details the trace output from the Logger A Replication process. The Replication process connects to the Logger A database and will update the HDS database with changes.

Example 11-5   *Logger A Replication Process*

```
13:34:03 la-rpl Initializing Node Manager Library.
13:34:03 la-rpl Trace: DB-Library version 7.00.839.
13:34:03 la-rpl Trace: Registry Watch Started for Subkey = SOFTWARE\Cisco Systems,
Inc.\ICM\cus01\LoggerA\Logger\CurrentVersion
13:34:03 la-rpl Trace: Registry Watch Started for Subkey = SOFTWARE\Cisco Systems,
Inc.\ICM\cus01\LoggerA\Recovery\CurrentVersion
13:34:04 la-rpl Trace: SQL Server version 9.0.4035
13:34:04 la-rpl Trace: Connect to cus01_sideA database.
13:34:04 la-rpl Trace: Connected to cus01_sideA database.
13:34:04 la-rpl Trace: Setting the maximum number of DB-Lib connections to 101
13:34:09 la-rpl Trace: SQL Server enabled protocols, by order: sm, np, tcp
13:34:09 la-rpl Trace: Database uses Major Version 127, CC Minor Version 0 of
the Schema
13:34:09 la-rpl Trace: Logger Compatible with Major Version 127, CC Minor Version
0 of the Schema
13:34:09 la-rpl Trace: Partitioning is not enabled!
13:34:09 la-rpl Trace: Starting Recovery Key for Admin table is 574445249000.0
13:34:09 la-rpl Trace: MDS Connection Thread Started
13:34:09 la-rpl Trace: Replicate History Thread Started
13:34:09 la-rpl Trace: Recover History Thread Started
13:34:09 la-rpl Trace: ReplicationServer client connection is initialized.
13:34:09 la-rpl Trace: RecoveryServer client connection is initialized.
```

Router A

Examples 11-6 through 11-11 display the startup traces for all the processes on the router node. Little happens with the router processes until a PG is started because the router has no need to go active until a PG exists that can perform route requests.

Example 11-6 *Router A Router Process*

```
13:35:01 ra-rtr Router Release 8.0.1.0 , Build 26931.
13:35:01 ra-rtr Trace: Perfmon enabled
13:35:02 ra-rtr Connection to MDS process established.
13:35:02 ra-rtr Trace: Synchronizing using version (build) 6931
13:35:02 ra-rtr Trace: GetInSync: Serialization Enabled.
13:35:02 ra-rtr Trace: GetInSync: Synchronization holdoff disabled.
```

Example 11-7 *Router A Database Agent Process*

```
13:35:01 ra-dba DBAgent Release 8.0.1.0 , Build 26931.
13:35:02 ra-dba Connection to MDS process established.
13:35:02 ra-dba DBAgent is registered with MDS; handle = 50.
```

Example 11-8 *Router A Real-Time Server Process*

```
13:35:01 ra-rts Initializing Node Manager Library.
13:35:02 ra-rts Connection to MDS process established.
13:35:02 ra-rts Trace: The rtsvr is registered with MDS; handle = 38
```

Example 11-9 *Router A TestSync Process*

```
13:35:03 ra-tsyr Trace: No time messages being generated for MDS configuration.
13:35:03 ra-tsyr Trace: Playback Mode Turned OFF
13:35:03 ra-tsyr Connection to MDS process established.
```

The MDS process captured in Example 11-10 is aware that the router is configured as part of a duplex pair. MDS establishes a connection with all the processes with which it requires communication. MDS cannot communicate with Router B because it is offline, so it suspends any attempt at synchronization.

Example 11-10 *Router A MDS Process*

```
13:35:01 ra-mds Initializing Node Manager Library.
13:35:01 ra-mds Trace: Monitor Server pipe cus01\RouterA\mdsCmdPipe enabled for
cus01\RouterA\mds
13:35:01 ra-mds MDS Process starting. Release 8.0.1.0 , Build 26931.
13:35:01 ra-mds Trace: AppRTT set in AGGRESSIVE mode
```

```
13:35:01 ra-mds Synchronizer initializing for duplex operation.
13:35:02 ra-mds Client ccag registered with handle 39.
13:35:02 ra-mds Client ccag started.
13:35:02 ra-mds Client rtr registered with handle 1.
13:35:02 ra-mds Client rtr started.
13:35:02 ra-mds Client dba registered with handle 50.
13:35:02 ra-mds Client dba started.
13:35:02 ra-mds Client rts registered with handle 38.
13:35:02 ra-mds Client rts started.
13:35:02 ra-mds Client nm registered with handle 37.
13:35:02 ra-mds Client nm started.
13:35:03 ra-mds Client tsyr registered with handle 48.
13:35:03 ra-mds Client tsyr started.
13:35:04 ra-mds Client rcv registered with handle 51.
13:35:04 ra-mds Client rcv started.
13:35:04 ra-mds Client hlgr registered with handle 132.
13:35:04 ra-mds Client hlgr started.
13:35:04 ra-mds Client rpl registered with handle 129.
13:35:04 ra-mds Client rpl started.
13:35:05 ra-mds Client clgr registered with handle 36.
13:35:05 ra-mds Client clgr started.
13:35:08 ra-mds Client nmlogger registered with handle 41.
13:35:08 ra-mds Client nmlogger started.
13:35:09 ra-mds Client csfs registered with handle 34.
13:35:09 ra-mds Client csfs started.
13:35:32 ra-mds Synchronizer suspending operation.
```

The Central Controller Agent process shown in Example 11-11 is aware that a single peripheral gateway has been configured in router setup.

Example 11-11 *Router A Central Controller Agent Process*

```
13:35:01 ra-ccag Initializing Node Manager Library.
13:35:01 ra-ccag Trace: Monitor Server pipe cus01\RouterA\ccagCmdPipe enabled for
cus01\RouterA\ccag
13:35:01 ra-ccag DMP Agent process starting.  Release 8.0.1.0 , Build 26931.
13:35:01 ra-ccag 1 Peripheral Gateways are configured.
13:35:02 ra-ccag Connection to MDS process established.
```

Peripheral Gateway A

On startup, the OPC process shown in Example 11-12 sets a large number of registry values.

Example 11-12 *PG1A OPC Process*

```
13:36:01 PG1A-opc Initializing Node Manager Library.
13:36:01 PG1A-opc Trace: Monitor Server pipe cus01\PG1A\opcCmdPipe enabled for
cus01\PG1A\opc
13:36:01 PG1A-opc OPC Software Version Release 8.0.1.0 , Build 26931.
13:36:02 PG1A-opc Connection to MDS process established.
13:36:02 PG1A-opc Trace: GetInSync: Serialization Disabled.
13:36:02 PG1A-opc Trace: GetInSync: Synchronization holdoff disabled.
13:36:32 PG1A-opc MDS is in service.
13:36:32 PG1A-opc Current time: 09/23/2010 12:36:32.330.
13:36:32 PG1A-opc Local time: 09/23/2010 13:36:32.330.
13:36:32 PG1A-opc Midnight: 09/22/2010 23:00:00.000.
13:36:32 PG1A-opc PG\\OPC Registry Value ActivationPDDelayTime set to 0.
13:36:32 PG1A-opc PG\\OPC Registry Value CallWrapupDataTimeout set to 0.
13:36:32 PG1A-opc PG\\OPC Registry Value ConfigurePDTimeout set to 30.
13:36:32 PG1A-opc PG\\OPC Registry Value ConfigurePGTimeout set to 10.
13:36:32 PG1A-opc PG\\OPC Registry Value ConfigureRCTimeout set to 10.
...
<The OPC Process sets a large number of settings here>

13:36:32 PG1A-opc Trace: Saved PG registry
```

Example 11-13 shows the PG's MDS initialization. After MDS has established connections to the other processes, it attempts to connect to the Side B PG. In this example, you can observe that the MDS process fails to connect to Side B and switches into simplex—or nonduplex—operation.

Example 11-13 *PG1A MDS Process*

```
13:36:01 PG1A-mds Initializing Node Manager Library.
13:36:01 PG1A-mds Trace: Monitor Server pipe cus01\PG1A\mdsCmdPipe enabled for
cus01\PG1A\mds
13:36:02 PG1A-mds MDS Process starting. Release 8.0.1.0 , Build 26931.
13:36:02 PG1A-mds Trace: AppRTT set in WATCHING mode
13:36:02 PG1A-mds Synchronizer initializing for duplex operation.
13:36:02 PG1A-mds Client opc registered with handle 1.
13:36:02 PG1A-mds Client opc started.
13:36:02 PG1A-mds Client pim1 registered with handle 33.
13:36:02 PG1A-mds Client pim1 started.
13:36:02 PG1A-mds Client pgag registered with handle 48.
```

```
13:36:02 PG1A-mds Client pgag started.
13:36:02 PG1A-mds Client pim2 registered with handle 34.
13:36:02 PG1A-mds Client pim2 started.
13:36:02 PG1A-mds Client nm registered with handle 41.
13:36:02 PG1A-mds Client nm started.
13:36:04 PG1A-mds Client tsyp registered with handle 65.
13:36:04 PG1A-mds Client tsyp started.
13:36:32 PG1A-mds Initiating test of peer Synchronizer.
13:36:32 PG1A-mds Trace: Sending TOS request: sequence = 1.
13:36:32 PG1A-mds Trace: Received TOS response: sequence=1 status=UNREACHABLE.
13:36:32 PG1A-mds Trace: Sending TOS request: sequence = 2.
13:36:32 PG1A-mds Trace: Received TOS response: sequence=2 status=UNREACHABLE.
13:36:32 PG1A-mds Peer Synchronizer was found to be unreachable.
13:36:32 PG1A-mds Synchronizer switching to non-duplex operation.
13:36:32 PG1A-mds MDS now in service.
```

PG Agent establishes several connections of different priority to the central controller.
Example 11-14 shows the pgag process connecting to the Side A central controller only
as Side B is offline. After the connection is established, the central controller goes into an
active state and can process route requests.

Example 11-14 *PG1A PG Agent Process*

```
13:36:01 PG1A-pgag Initializing Node Manager Library.
13:36:01 PG1A-pgag Trace: Monitor Server pipe cus01\PG1A\pgagCmdPipe enabled for
cus01\PG1A\pgag
13:36:02 PG1A-pgag DMP Agent process starting.  Release 8.0.1.0 , Build 26931.
13:36:02 PG1A-pgag Connection to MDS process established.
13:36:03 PG1A-pgag Connection to Central Controller side A established
(low priority).
13:36:03 PG1A-pgag Connection to Central Controller side A established
(medium priority).
13:36:03 PG1A-pgag Connection to Central Controller side A established
(high priority).
13:36:32 PG1A-pgag Trace: TOS requested but no TOS connection exists.
Assuming unreachable.
13:36:32 PG1A-pgag Trace: TOS requested but no TOS connection exists.
Assuming unreachable.
13:36:32 PG1A-pgag MDS is in service.
13:36:36 PG1A-pgag DMP Agent process activated.
13:36:36 PG1A-pgag Path to Central Controller side A established.
13:36:36 PG1A-pgag Trace: Received TOS request from side A: seq=1.
13:36:36 PG1A-pgag Trace: Can't forward TOS request (seq=1) to side B
(not connected).
13:36:36 PG1A-pgag Trace: Sending TOS response to side A: seq=1
status=UNREACHABLE.
```

```
13:36:36 PG1A-pgag Trace: Received TOS request from side A: seq=2.
13:36:36 PG1A-pgag Trace: Can't forward TOS request (seq=2) to side B (not con-
nected).
13:36:36 PG1A-pgag Trace: Sending TOS response to side A: seq=2  status=UNREACH-
ABLE.
13:36:39 PG1A-pgag Central Controller side A is in service.
13:36:39 PG1A-pgag Central Controller side A reports good response time.
13:36:39 PG1A-pgag Initializing message stream with side A of the Central
Controller.
13:36:39 PG1A-pgag Path to Central Controller side A is now active.
```

The JTAPI process connects the Cisco Unified Communications Manager (Unified CM) PIM process running on the PG with the CTI manager process running on the Unified CM cluster. The tracing output provides useful information, including the following:

■ The version of JTAPI installed on the PG. It is important to ensure that this is the same version of JTAPI running on the Unified CM cluster.

■ The username configured on the Unified CM cluster that JTAPI is using to connect with.

■ For each of the devices associated with the JTAPI user, the JTAPI process indicates when they come into service. In Example 11-15, it is possible to see that two CTI route points, 6000 and 6001, are configured.

Example 11-15 *PG1A JTAPI Gateway Process*

```
13:36:01 PG1A-jgw1 Initializing Event Management System (EMS) Library.
13:36:01 PG1A-jgw1 Trace: Release 8.0.1.0 , Build 26931
13:36:02 PG1A-jgw1 Trace: JGW arg 0, jgw1
13:36:02 PG1A-jgw1 Trace: JGW arg 1, CLEAN
13:36:02 PG1A-jgw1 Trace: JGW arg 2, DUPLEX
13:36:02 PG1A-jgw1 Trace: JGW arg 3, A
13:36:02 PG1A-jgw1 Trace: JGW arg 4, C:\icm\cus01\pg1a
13:36:02 PG1A-jgw1 Trace: JGW arg 5, 1
13:36:02 PG1A-jgw1 Trace: JGW arg 6, ICM\cus01\PG1A
13:36:04 PG1A-jgw1 Trace: Configuring JTAPI Object
13:36:04 PG1A-jgw1 Trace: CiscoJtapiVersion: Cisco Jtapi version 7.1(3.10000)-1
Release
13:36:04 PG1A-jgw1 Trace: disableAll() TraceManager for CTICLIENT
13:36:04 PG1A-jgw1 Trace: Calling getProvider() 192.168.15.11;login=pguser;pass-
wd=<***edited***>
13:36:10 PG1A-jgw1 Trace: Returned successfully from getProvider()
13:36:10 PG1A-jgw1 Trace: disableAll() TraceManager for CTICLIENT
13:36:10 PG1A-jgw1 Trace: Waiting for the provider to be in service
13:36:10 PG1A-jgw1 Trace: ProvOutOfServiceEv
```

```
13:36:10 PG1A-jgw1 Trace: ProvInServiceEv
13:36:10 PG1A-jgw1 Trace: Provider is in service

13:36:10 PG1A-jgw1 Trace: Creating Instruments for 2 addresses
13:36:10 PG1A-jgw1 Trace: JTapiServer: Wait for adding CallObservers to 2
addresses
13:36:10 PG1A-jgw1 Trace: ThreadAddressManager: Adding AddressObservers to 2
addresses
13:36:49 PG1A-jgw1 Trace: Initializing PIM Connection
13:36:49 PG1A-jgw1 Trace: Successfully initialized PIM Connection.
13:36:49 PG1A-jgw1 Trace: Adding Address Observers to all CTI Addresses
13:36:49 PG1A-jgw1 Trace: PIMConnection: Wait for adding CallObservers to CTI
addresses
13:36:49 PG1A-jgw1 Trace: PIMConnection: Complete waiting for adding CallObservers
to CTI addresses
13:36:49 PG1A-jgw1 Trace: JTAPIGW: Multi-line support is disabled
13:36:49 PG1A-jgw1 Trace:    MsgOpenConf:   InvID: 19878578
13:36:49 PG1A-jgw1 Trace:    MsgRouteCallbackInService:  Addr: 6000
13:36:49 PG1A-jgw1 Trace:    MsgRouteCallbackInService:  Addr: 6001
```

The PG PIM process detailed in Example 11-16 provides the following information:

- All the UCCE configuration items associated with the peripheral. In this example, the PIM is for a Unified CM cluster and details including the agents, team details, and dialed numbers.

- The PIM connects to the local JTAPI process running on the PG.

- After the PIM receives the PIM_SET_ACTIVE_REQ message from OPC, it goes into an active state.

Example 11-16 *PG1A PIM1 Process*

```
13:36:02 PG1A-pim1 Initializing Node Manager Library.
13:36:02 PG1A-pim1 EAGTPIM Release 8.0.1.0 , Build 26931
13:36:02 PG1A-pim1 Trace: DeskLinkDeviceTarget::SetNumExtensionDigits: Number of
extension digits set to 4
13:36:02 PG1A-pim1 Trace: Perfmon Initialization for the instanceName = cus01
PG1A pim1
13:36:02 PG1A-pim1 Trace: Entering init()
13:36:02 PG1A-pim1 Connection to MDS process established.
13:36:32 PG1A-pim1 MDS now in service.
13:36:46 PG1A-pim1 ProcessPIMSetIdleReq: Peripheral 5001 going idle.
13:36:48 PG1A-pim1 ADDED\UPDATED 3 AgentDeskSettings on Peripheral 5001.
13:36:48 PG1A-pim1 ADDED\UPDATED 5 DeviceTargets on Peripheral 5001.
13:36:48 PG1A-pim1 ADDED\UPDATED 10 ECCVariables on Peripheral 5001.
```

```
13:36:48 PG1A-pim1 ADDED\UPDATED 3 AgentGroups on Peripheral 5001.
13:36:48 PG1A-pim1 ADDED\UPDATED 4 Agents on Peripheral 5001.
13:36:48 PG1A-pim1 ADDED\UPDATED 2 AgentTeams on Peripheral 5001.
13:36:48 PG1A-pim1 ADDED\UPDATED 4 AgentTeamMembers on Peripheral 5001.
13:36:48 PG1A-pim1 ADDED\UPDATED 0 AgentTeamSupervisorMembers on Peripheral 5001
13:36:48 PG1A-pim1 ADDED\UPDATED 0 Services on Peripheral 5001.
13:36:48 PG1A-pim1 ADDED\UPDATED 0 TrunkGroups on Peripheral 5001.
13:36:48 PG1A-pim1 ADDED\UPDATED 0 Trunks on Peripheral 5001.
13:36:48 PG1A-pim1 ADDED\UPDATED 2 DialedNumbers on Peripheral 5001.
13:36:48 PG1A-pim1 ADDED\UPDATED 0 DialedNumberPlans on Peripheral 5001.
13:36:48 PG1A-pim1 ADDED\UPDATED 0 PeripheralTargets on Peripheral 5001.
13:36:48 PG1A-pim1 ADDED\UPDATED 0 PeripheralMonitors on Peripheral 5001.
13:36:48 PG1A-pim1 Trace: ConfigureMRDomains - (ADD) PID=5001 MRDomain=1
MediaClass=4
13:36:48 PG1A-pim1 ADDED\UPDATED 1 MediaRoutingDomain on Peripheral 5001.
13:36:48 PG1A-pim1 Peripheral 5001 sending OPC PIM_OK_ACK acknowledgment for com-
mand PIM_CONFIGURE_REQ (TransID=0).
13:36:48 PG1A-pim1 Trace: JTAPIClient::ActivateClientLayer: Attempting to activate
JTAPI Client Layer.
13:36:48 PG1A-pim1 Attempting to connect to JTAPIGW at IP address 127.0.0.1 port
40029.
13:36:48 PG1A-pim1 Connection to JTAPI Gateway established.
13:36:49 PG1A-pim1 Peripheral 5001 sending OPC PIM_OK_ACK acknowledgment for
command PIM_SET_ACTIVE_REQ (TransID=0).
13:36:49 PG1A-pim1 ProcessPIMSetActiveReq: Peripheral 5001 ACTIVATED.
13:36:49 PG1A-pim1 Attempting to ACTIVATE Peripheral's Routing Client.
13:36:49 PG1A-pim1 Peripheral's Routing Client successfully ACTIVATED.
```

Similar to the Unified CM PG, the VRU PIM detailed in Example 11-17 goes through the
same initialization process. The following list highlights three key areas to observe during
VRU PIM startup:

- The VRU PIM does not have any direct agent configuration but does have configuration relating to translation routing and postrouting.

- The IP address of the VRU and its connection port are shown.

- The VRU PIM also indicates when the peripheral goes into an active state.

Example 11-17   *PG1A PIM2 Process*

```
13:36:02 PG1A-pim2 Initializing Node Manager Library.
13:36:02 PG1A-pim2 VRUPIM Release 8.0.1.0 , Build 26931
13:36:02 PG1A-pim2 Trace: DSCP value used for QoS is 24
13:36:02 PG1A-pim2 Connection to MDS process established.
13:36:32 PG1A-pim2 MDS now in service.
```

```
13:36:46 PG1A-pim2 ProcessPIMSetIdleReq: Peripheral 5002 going idle.

13:36:46 PG1A-pim2 Peripheral 5002 sending OPC PIM_OK_ACK acknowledgment for com-
mand PIM_SET_IDLE_REQ (TransID=1).

13:36:46 PG1A-pim2 ADDED\UPDATED 3 AgentDeskSettings on Peripheral 5002.

13:36:46 PG1A-pim2 ADDED\UPDATED 5 DeviceTargets on Peripheral 5002.

13:36:46 PG1A-pim2 ADDED\UPDATED 10 ECCVariables on Peripheral 5002.

13:36:46 PG1A-pim2 ADDED\UPDATED 1 Services on Peripheral 5002.

13:36:46 PG1A-pim2 ADDED\UPDATED 1 TrunkGroups on Peripheral 5002.

13:36:46 PG1A-pim2 ADDED\UPDATED 1 Trunks on Peripheral 5002.

13:36:46 PG1A-pim2 ADDED\UPDATED 5 PeripheralTargets on Peripheral 5002.

13:36:46 PG1A-pim2 ADDED\UPDATED 1 MediaRoutingDomain on Peripheral 5002.

13:36:46 PG1A-pim2 Peripheral 5002 sending OPC PIM_OK_ACK acknowledgment for
command PIM_CONFIGURE_REQ (TransID=0).

13:36:46 PG1A-pim2 Attempting to connect to VRU at IP address 192.168.15.8 port
5000.

13:36:46 PG1A-pim2 Connection to VRU established.

13:36:46 PG1A-pim2 Trace: The VRU does not support the Time Synchronization

13:36:46 PG1A-pim2 ProcessPIMSetActiveReq: Peripheral 5002 ACTIVATED.

13:36:46 PG1A-pim2 Attempting to ACTIVATE Peripheral's Routing Client.

13:36:46 PG1A-pim2 Failed an attempt to ACTIVATE the Peripheral's Routing Client.
Will retry.

13:36:48 PG1A-pim2 Peripheral's Routing Client successfully ACTIVATED.

13:36:48 PG1A-pim2 Peripheral's Routing Client successfully ACTIVATED.
```

Router A will go active only when it is in communication with half or more of the configured PGs. In Example 11-18, only one PG is configured but with two peripherals; one is
the Unified CM PIM and the other is the VRU PIM.

Example 11-18 *Router A Going Active*

```
13:36:38 ra-rtr The router has completed loading the initial configuration from
the logger.

13:36:38 ra-rtr Configuration delivery from the logger is complete.

13:36:38 ra-rtr Router preparing to verify the config sequence number from the
logger.

13:36:38 ra-rtr All configuration operations complete.

13:36:39 ra-rtr Physical controller NYC_PG (ID 5001) is on-line.

13:36:39 ra-rtr Physical controller NYC_PG (ID 5001) configured to MDS 39, DMP 1.

13:36:39 ra-rtr Configured peripheral gateway NYC_PG (ID 5001) with 2
peripheral(s).

13:36:39 ra-rtr Peripheral NYC_CUCM (ID 5001) configured to MDS 39, DMP 1.

13:36:39 ra-rtr Peripheral NYC_IVR1 (ID 5002) configured to MDS 39, DMP 1.

13:36:48 ra-rtr PG has reported that peripheral NYC_IVR1 (ID 5002) is
operational.

13:36:48 ra-rtr Peripheral NYC_IVR1 (ID 5002) is on-line.
```

```
13:36:51 ra-rtr PG has reported that peripheral NYC_CUCM (ID 5001) is
operational.
13:36:51 ra-rtr Peripheral NYC_CUCM (ID 5001) is on-line.
13:37:02 ra-rtr Trace: CTI Server reported online for NYC_PG.
```

The Central Controller Agent shown in Example 11-19 displays that it is now connected to 1 out of 1 configured PG.

Example 11-19   *Router A Central Controller Agent*

```
13:35:01 ra-ccag DMP Agent process starting.  Release 8.0.1.0 , Build 26931.
13:35:01 ra-ccag 1 Peripheral Gateways are configured.
13:35:02 ra-ccag Connection to MDS process established.
13:36:36 ra-ccag Device PG01 path established with DMP ID 1 from address
192.168.15.20.
13:36:36 ra-ccag Now connected to 1 of 1 configured Peripheral Gateways.
13:36:36 ra-ccag Trace: Sending TOS request to device PG01 (seq=1).
13:36:36 ra-ccag Trace: Received TOS response from device PG01: seq=1,
status=UNREACHABLE.
13:36:36 ra-ccag Trace: No more connected PG's for TOS (seq=1).
Assuming unreachable.
13:36:36 ra-ccag Trace: Sending TOS request to device PG01 (seq=2).
13:36:36 ra-ccag Trace: Received TOS response from device PG01: seq=2,
status=UNREACHABLE.
13:36:36 ra-ccag Trace: No more connected PG's for TOS (seq=2).
Assuming unreachable.
13:36:36 ra-ccag MDS is in service.
13:36:39 ra-ccag Central Controller service is available.
13:36:39 ra-ccag Device PG01 initializing message stream.
13:36:39 ra-ccag Device PG01 path changing to active state.
```

The CTI Server process shown in Example 11-20 establishes a connection to MDS and OPC. When the Unified CM PG PIM goes active, the CTI Server can also go into an active state.

Example 11-20   *CTI Server*

```
13:37:02 cg1A-ctisvr Initializing Node Manager Library.
13:37:02 cg1A-ctisvr CTIServer Release 8.0.1.0 , Build 26931, Built 03/08/10
12:15:12
13:37:02 cg1A-ctisvr Trace: Perfmon Initialization for the instanceName = cus01
CG1A
13:37:02 cg1A-ctisvr Connection to MDS process established.
13:37:02 cg1A-ctisvr MDS now in service.
13:37:02 cg1A-ctisvr ProcessSetIdleReq: Enterprise CTI Server going idle.
13:37:02 cg1A-ctisvr PG System Event: IdleCTIServer, PG Status: NORMAL
```

```
13:37:02 cg1A-ctisvr Enterprise CTI Server sending OPC CTI_OK_ACK acknowledgment
for command CTI_SET_IDLE_REQ (TransID=1).
13:37:02 cg1A-ctisvr Added 2 AgentTeams.
13:37:02 cg1A-ctisvr Added 4 AgentTeamMembers.
13:37:02 cg1A-ctisvr Added 10 ExpandedCallVariables.
13:37:02 cg1A-ctisvr Added 4 Agents.
13:37:02 cg1A-ctisvr Added 3 SkillGroups.
13:37:02 cg1A-ctisvr Added 1 Services.
13:37:02 cg1A-ctisvr Added 7 Devices.
13:37:02 cg1A-ctisvr Added 1 ConfigKeys.
13:37:02 cg1A-ctisvr Enterprise CTI Server configuration complete.
13:37:02 cg1A-ctisvr Enterprise CTI Server sending OPC CTI_OK_ACK acknowledgment
for command CTI_SET_ACTIVE_REQ (TransID=0).
13:37:02 cg1A-ctisvr ProcessSetActiveReq: Enterprise CTI Server ACTIVATED.
13:37:02 cg1A-ctisvr Enterprise CTI Server is now listening for client connections
to hostname:ccocus01pg1a port:42027.
13:37:02 cg1A-ctisvr PG System Event: Peripheral Online (PeripheralID 5001), PG
Status: NORMAL
13:37:02 cg1A-ctisvr PG System Event: Peripheral Online (PeripheralID 5002), PG
Status: NORMAL
```

Logger B

Example 11-21 shows the Logger B process being activated. From the trace output, you can see a difference between Side A's and Side B's update keys. This was caused by additional configuration work taking place when Logger B was offline. Further down the trace, you can see that the Network Target, Device Target, and Label tables were updated with new configurations. To complete the synchronization, the Configuration Logger process restarts.

Example 11-21   *Logger B Process*

```
13:40:12 lb-clgr Initiating state transfer RECEIVE operation.
13:40:13 lb-clgr Trace: Objects transferred = 10375, total bytes 421381.
13:40:13 lb-clgr Trace: Expanded 76047 bytes into 421381.
13:40:13 lb-clgr Trace: Synchronizing Configuration Data
13:40:13 lb-clgr Trace: LastUpdateKey for B Configuration is 574370171091.0
13:40:13 lb-clgr Trace: LastUpdateKey for A Configuration is 574428329009.0
13:40:13 lb-clgr Requesting normal MDS termination.
13:40:13 lb-clgr Connection to MDS process closed.
13:40:13 lb-clgr Trace: Thread[1160]: Start Config Transaction 15376
13:40:14 lb-clgr Trace: Thread[1160]: Logger update by process Launcher(upcc) on
machine CCOCUS01HDSA.  User is UCCE:administrator.  SQL Server user is DBO
13:40:14 lb-clgr Trace: Thread[1160]: Update for table Cfg_Mngr_Globals completed
13:40:14 lb-clgr Trace: Thread[1160]: Commit Config Transaction 15376, new
LastUpdateKey is 574428329003.0
```

```
13:40:14 lb-clgr Trace: Thread[1160]: Start Config Transaction 15380
13:40:14 lb-clgr Trace: Thread[1160]: Logger update by process conicrex(upcc) on
machine CCOCUS01HDSA.  User is UCCE:administrator.  SQL Server user is DBO
13:40:14 lb-clgr Trace: Thread[1160]: Add for table Network_Target completed
13:40:14 lb-clgr Trace: Thread[1160]: Add for table t_Device_Target completed
13:40:14 lb-clgr Trace: Thread[1160]: Add for table t_Label completed
13:40:14 lb-clgr Trace: Thread[1160]: Commit Config Transaction 15380, new
LastUpdateKey is 574428329009.0
13:40:14 lb-clgr The Logger has completed Database Synchronization, 11 Config
Message Log Entries Received and Added.
13:40:14 lb-clgr Trace: Synchronization of Configuration Data Complete
13:40:14 lb-clgr Trace: Logger will now Restart and Complete State Transfer
```

Example 11-22 shows the state transfer taking place from Side A to Side B. The identical update key values determine that the databases are now synchronized.

Example 11-22   *Logger B Process*

```
13:40:27 lb-clgr Initiating state transfer RECEIVE operation.
13:40:28 lb-clgr Trace: Start message received. Class count = 38.
13:40:28 lb-clgr Trace: Objects transferred = 10374, total bytes 419647.
13:40:28 lb-clgr Trace: Expanded 75402 bytes into 419647.
13:40:28 lb-clgr Trace: Synchronizing Configuration Data
13:40:28 lb-clgr Trace: LastUpdateKey for B Configuration is 574428329009.0
13:40:28 lb-clgr Trace: LastUpdateKey for A Configuration is 574428329009.0
13:40:28 lb-clgr The Logger has completed Database Synchronization, 0 Config
Message Log Entries Received and Added.
13:40:28 lb-clgr State transfer operation completed successfully.
13:40:28 lb-clgr Logger Sync: 20100923 13:40:27:894 (A->B).
```

The router process in Example 11-23 indicates that the router processes have also synchronized their configuration data and are now operating in a duplex state.

Example 11-23   *Router B Process*

```
13:40:11 rb-rtr MDS is in service.
13:40:11 rb-rtr Initiating state transfer RECEIVE operation.
13:40:12 rb-rtr Trace: Start message received. Class count = 429.
13:40:12 rb-rtr Trace: Objects transferred = 17682, total bytes 1983153.
13:40:12 rb-rtr Trace: Expanded 398897 bytes into 1983153.
13:40:12 rb-rtr State transfer operation completed successfully.
13:40:12 rb-rtr Duplexed initialization complete.
```

Peripheral Gateway B

The MDS process in Example 11-24 shows the client processes registering with MDS, and both sides of the PG are now in communication, so the PG moves into a passive duplex state.

Example 11-24 *PG B MDS Process*

```
13:41:02 PG1B-mds Initializing Node Manager Library.
13:41:02 PG1B-mds Trace: Monitor Server pipe cus01\PG1B\mdsCmdPipe enabled for
cus01\PG1B\mds
13:41:02 PG1B-mds MDS Process starting. Release 8.0.1.0 , Build 26931.
13:41:02 PG1B-mds Trace: AppRTT set in WATCHING mode
13:41:02 PG1B-mds Synchronizer initializing for duplex operation.
13:41:03 PG1B-mds Client opc registered with handle 1.
13:41:03 PG1B-mds Client opc started.
13:41:03 PG1B-mds Client pim1 registered with handle 33.
13:41:03 PG1B-mds Client pim1 started.
13:41:03 PG1B-mds Client pim2 registered with handle 34.
13:41:03 PG1B-mds Client pim2 started.
13:41:03 PG1B-mds Client pgag registered with handle 48.
13:41:03 PG1B-mds Client pgag started.
13:41:04 PG1B-mds Client tsyp registered with handle 65.
13:41:04 PG1B-mds Client tsyp started.
13:41:04 PG1B-mds Client nm registered with handle 41.
13:41:04 PG1B-mds Client nm started.
13:41:12 PG1B-mds Communication with peer Synchronizer established.
13:41:12 PG1B-mds Synchronizer switching to passive duplex operation.
13:41:12 PG1B-mds MDS now in service
```

With both sides of the router now active, PG B establishes communication with both routers. PG A was already connected to Side A but is also now connected to Side B. See Example 11-25.

Example 11-25 *PG B PG Agent Process*

```
13:41:02 PG1B-pgag Initializing Node Manager Library.
13:41:02 PG1B-pgag DMP Agent process starting.  Release 8.0.1.0 , Build 26931.
13:41:03 PG1B-pgag Connection to MDS process established.
13:41:04 PG1B-pgag Connection to Central Controller side A established
(medium priority).
13:41:04 PG1B-pgag Connection to Central Controller side B established
(low priority).
13:41:04 PG1B-pgag Connection to Central Controller side B established
(medium priority).
13:41:04 PG1B-pgag Connection to Central Controller side B established
(high priority).
```

```
13:41:06 PG1B-pgag Connection to Central Controller side A established
(low priority).
13:41:06 PG1B-pgag Connection to Central Controller side A established
(high priority).
13:41:10 PG1B-pgag Test connection to other side of Peripheral Gateway
established.
13:41:12 PG1B-pgag MDS is in service.
```

Administrative Workstation

The Update AW process shown in Example 11-26 connects to the local awdb and remote Side A logger databases. The process determines that its local database is already up to date and therefore does not require any further database synchronization.

Example 11-26   *Administrative Workstation Update AW Process*

```
13:44:07 dis-uaw Trace: Release 8.0.1.0 , Build 26931
13:44:07 dis-uaw Initializing Node Manager Library.
13:44:09 dis-uaw Trace: Creating worker threads.
13:44:09 dis-uaw Trace: Real-time feed not active - Sleeping for 5 seconds
before retry...


13:44:14 dis-uaw Trace: Real-time feed not active - Sleeping for 5 seconds
before retry...
13:44:19 dis-uaw Trace: Real-time feed not active - Sleeping for 5 seconds
before retry...
13:44:24 dis-uaw Trace: Attempting to connect to local database "cus01_awdb"
13:44:24 dis-uaw Trace: Connected to SQL Server 9.0.255 on server CCOCUS01HDSA.
13:44:24 dis-uaw Trace: Attempting to connect to central controller database
"cus01_sideA" on server "ccocus01lgra"
13:44:28 dis-uaw EMS message forwarding has started.
13:44:28 dis-uaw Trace: Connected to SQL Server 9.0.255 on server CCOCUS01LGRA.
13:44:28 dis-uaw Trace: Starting incremental copy operation.
13:44:28 dis-uaw Trace: Recovery keys: 0.0 (in memory), 574428329009.0 (local
AWControl), 574428329009.0 (router AWControl).
13:44:29 dis-uaw Trace: Nothing to do.
13:44:29 dis-uaw Trace: Waiting for new work...
13:44:29 dis-uaw Trace: Starting incremental copy operation.
13:44:29 dis-uaw Trace: Recovery keys: 574428329009.0 (in memory),
574428329009.0 (local AWControl), 574428329009.0 (router AWControl).
13:44:29 dis-uaw Trace: Nothing to do.
13:44:29 dis-uaw Trace: Waiting for new work...
```

Summary

This chapter covered in detailed analysis all the nodes and processes that function together to provide a redundant and resilient architecture. The learning points from this chapter can be summarized as follows:

- The UCCE architecture is deployed in a duplex, resilient manner using multiple nodes consisting of several processes.

- From a clean power-on, starting the processes in a specific sequence ensures an orderly and error-free startup.

- Even with the default trace settings, all the UCCE processes provide a detailed output that can be used for general troubleshooting. For specific troubleshooting, the trace settings can be modified to provide a detailed output.

Chapter 12

Unified CM and IVR

This chapter covers the following subjects:

■ Integrating Cisco Unified Communications Manager (Unified CM), IP Interactive Voice Response (IVR), and Customer Voice Portal (CVP) with Unified Contact Center Enterprise (UCCE)

■ Unified CM configuration specifics for UCCE

■ IVR configuration and routing

The Cisco UCCE solution consists of four distinct components:

■ Contact center routing engine, or central controller

■ Unified Communications infrastructure

■ Queuing and self-service platform

■ Agent and supervisor desktop software

The focus of this chapter is to detail how the Unified Communications infrastructure and the queuing/self-service platforms integrate with the UCCE central controllers.

In a legacy environment, Unified Intelligent Contact Center (UICM) integrates with time-division multiplexing (TDM) Automatic Call Distributors (ACD) and IVRs to provide call control and reporting. In a pure Cisco IP environment, the private branch exchange (PBX) and IVR functionality is provided by products within the Cisco Unified Communications suite, in particular the Cisco Unified Communications Manager, Cisco Unified IP IVR, and Cisco Unified CVP.

Cisco Unified Communications Manager

Cisco Unified Communications Manager (Unified CM) is the software application that provides the PBX functionality for the UCCE solution by controlling many of the telephony devices including the IP phones and voice gateways. The Unified CM software runs on a Cisco Media Convergence Server (MCS). Multiple MCSs are typically deployed as a cluster that is architected to support the required number of agents and provide fault tolerance in the event of a failure.

The Unified CM server provides the agents and back-office staff with everyday telephony functionality, including the ability to answer and make calls, put users on hold, and transfer calls. The Unified CM application has the capability to perform some intelligent routing, such as the handling of calls based on the time of day; however, it is common practice to leave all the intelligent routing for the contact center agents to the UCCE platform.

Cisco Unified IP Interactive Voice Response

Cisco Unified IP Interactive Voice Response (IP IVR) is a software application that provides self-service and call-queuing functionality for the UCCE solution. The self-service functionality ranges from simple dual-tone multifrequency (DTMF) voice menus to speech recognition and text-to-speech capability with the required third-party components installed.

IP IVR only uses the Service Control Interface (SCI) for communication with UCCE; therefore, IP IVR is under the control of the UCCE software and sits behind the Unified CM. This means that calls are directed to IP IVR, rather than having it control where calls are sent.

Note   Initially only IP IVR was offered as an IVR solution for UCCE. It came in two versions: IP Queue Manager (QM) and IP IVR. Both were identical platforms, but IP QM had a reduced feature set and hence a lower price per port. IP QM has since been removed from the Cisco price list, and many customers have either upgraded to IP IVR or CVP. It is also important to note that IP IVR uses the same installation media as Cisco Unified Contact Center Express (UCCX). It is the license key that determines whether UCCX or IP IVR is installed.

Cisco Unified Customer Voice Portal

Like IP IVR, Cisco Unified Customer Voice Portal (CVP) is also a software application that provides self-service and call-queuing functionality for the UCCE solution. CVP, however, is a more distributed solution that allows greater flexibility in the placement of its components and provides a more scalable and fault-tolerant IVR solution.

CVP uses the Voice Response Unit (VRU) peripheral gateway interface for communication with UCCE; therefore, it is able to sit in front of or behind the Unified CM depending on the chosen deployment model. Typically for UCCE deployments, the Comprehensive Call Flow model will be used. This call flow is detailed in the CVP section later in this chapter.

CVP supports many features not possible with IP IVR, including the use of VoiceXML applications, Session Initiation Protocol (SIP) voice traffic, and video calls.

The majority of new UCCE deployments use CVP, and many older UCCE deployments that traditionally used IP IVR are planning migrations to CVP.

Tip When installing and upgrading components such as Unified CM, IP IVR, and CVP, ensure that they are compatible with your version of UCCE. To ensure full compatibility and Cisco support, refer to the Cisco UCCE Compatibility Matrix.

Integration with UCCE

Chapter 3, "Deployment Models," looked at the various high-level architecture deployment models for UCCE, including distributed and centralized call processing as well as Clustering over the WAN. The following sections examine how Unified CM, IP IVR, and CVP interface to UCCE. In each of the Figures 12-1, 12-2, and 12-3, the Unified CM or IVR is considered as a peripheral. For these peripherals to connect to UCCE, they must connect through a peripheral gateway (PG).

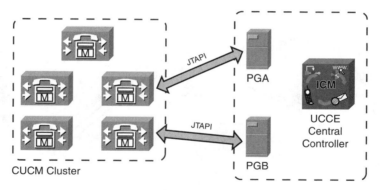

Figure 12-1 *Interfacing a Unified CM Cluster with a UCCE PG*

Unified Communications Manager

The Unified CM cluster maintains a redundant Java Telephony Application Programming Interface (JTAPI) connection with two UCCE PGs. It is good practice to configure each PG in the PG pair to connect with a different subscriber. The PG connects to the CTI Manager service running on the subscriber. Only one PG is active at any one time. The other PG remains in an idle state unless the connection from the subscriber with the currently active PG fails. Figure 12-1 shows a Unified CM cluster connected to a redundant pair of PGs.

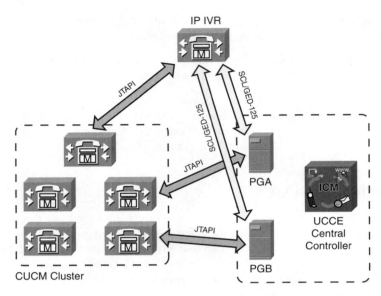

Figure 12-2   *Interfacing an IP IVR with Unified CM and a UCCE PG*

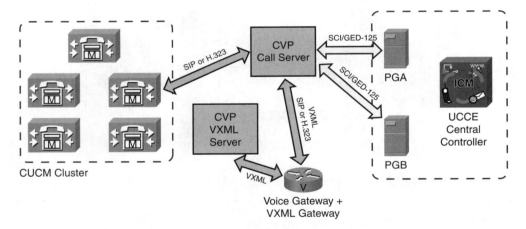

Figure 12-3   *CVP Architecture Using the Comprehensive Model*

UCCE with IP IVR

The IP IVR maintains several connections for proper functioning:

■   A JTAPI connection with at least one subscriber. Several subscribers can be specified in an ordered list. The IVR connects with the Computer Telephony Integration (CTI) Manager service.

- A Simple Object Access Protocol (SOAP) / Administrative XML (AXL) connection to an ordered list of AXL service providers on the Unified CM cluster. This connection performs configuration changes.

- A Service Control Interface (SCI) connection to the UCCE PGs. Typically, the PGs are deployed as a redundant pair. The PG is either in an active or idle state.

Figure 12-2 shows a single IP IVR connected to both a Unified CM cluster and a pair of PGs.

UCCE with CVP

Figure 12-3 shows a CVP deployment using the Comprehensive Call Flow model, which is the popular model deployed for UCCE when agents are required rather than pure standalone IVR functionality. The CVP Call Server maintains an active/idle connection to a redundant pair of PGs.

Cisco Unified Communications Manager

The following sections introduce several Unified CM configuration items that directly affect the integration of Unified CM with UCCE.

Cisco JTAPI

The Java Telephony Application Programming Interface (JTAPI) is used for communication between the Unified CM cluster and the JTAPI Gateway (JTAPIGW) process running on the PGs. The JTAPIGW process uses the configuration entered during PG setup to establish an authenticated connection to the CTI Manager process running on the subscribers. Both the JTAPIGW and the PIM processes need to be active on at least one PG before the UCCE can process route requests from the Unified CM cluster.

When installing the Unified CM PGs, the JTAPI client should be installed. The client is available for download as a plugin from the Unified CM. It is recommended that the version of JTAPI on the PGs be the same version as that running on the Unified CM. To determine the current installed JTAPI version, enter the following command from the command-line prompt:

```
C:\ java CiscoJtapiVersion
```

Alternatively, a graphical interface can be used to determine the version in addition to several configuration options, including trace levels and the timeout values used during failover. This tool is available from **Start > All Programs > CiscoJTAPI > Cisco Unified Communications Manager JTAPI Preferences**. Figure 12-4 shows a screen shot of the tool. The JTAPI version is listed in the window title bar.

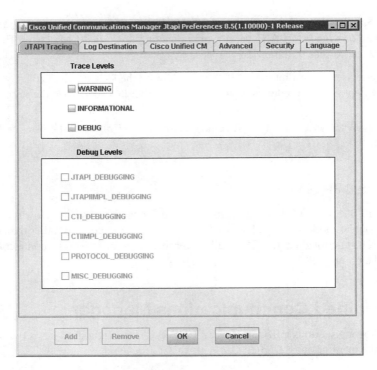

Figure 12-4   *Cisco JTAPI Preferences Application on the Unified CM PGs*

CTI Route Points

A CTI route point configured on the Unified CM cluster designates a virtual device that can receive multiple simultaneous calls for an application. For UCCE, CTI route points represent dialed numbers configured on the UCCE system. For a Unified CM—controlled endpoint to make a route request to UCCE, the CTI route point number must be configured on Unified CM and associated with the JTAPI user configured on the PG. If the corresponding number has also been configured as a dialed number in UCCE, the CTI route point will register with the PG.

The JTAPI user used for Unified CM—to—UCCE communication is often called PGUser. To configure PGUser, an application account must be created on the Unified CM cluster. The username and password for the account are entered into the PG configuration during setup. This allows the PG to establish an authenticated connection to the CTI Manager service running on the Unified CM cluster.

All CTI route points and IP phones (for agent login) that require UCCE control must be associated with the PGUser.

Figure 12-5 shows the relationship between CTI route points and dialed numbers. It also shows the relationship between IP phones and device targets. Traditionally, a device target was created for each IP phone extension that an agent would log in to. Recent versions of UCCE have removed the explicit requirement to configure device targets through the use of agent targeting rules. However, the IP phones in use by UCCE agents must still be associated with the PGUser; otherwise, the agent login process will fail.

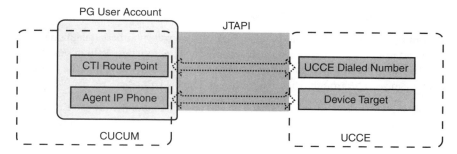

Figure 12-5 *Mapping of CTI Route Points and UCCE DNs*

Agent Phone Settings

When configuring Cisco IP Phones for agents, there are several settings that the administrator should be aware of that have an impact within a contact center environment. The following settings are configured per directory number (line/extension):

- **Auto Answer:** Many contact center agents that handle high call volumes prefer to wear headsets rather than use the IP phone's handset. This allows the agent freedom to type using both hands. Within the Agent Desk Settings tool in UCCE Configuration Manager it is possible to set specific agents to have Auto Answer enabled. It is also possible to specify Auto Answer within Unified CM on a per-phone basis. The benefit of configuring Auto Answer on the Unified CM is that the agent will hear a tone just before a call is delivered to him or her. Within Unified CM, it is also possible to specify that the call is auto-answered with the headset.

- **Call Waiting:** The majority of Cisco IP Phones support two or more lines. The default call waiting setting for a new phone is to allow a maximum of four calls and a busy trigger of two calls. UCCE will not send a second call to an agent who is already handling a UCCE-delivered call; however, if the IP phone is configured with a busy trigger greater than 1, it is possible that the agent might receive a second call direct to his extension. Many contact centers prefer for this not to happen, so the busy trigger setting must be set to 1.

- **Busy Timer:** If implementing Ring On No Answer (RONA), make sure that this value is larger than the RONA setting; otherwise, you'll get conflicts. It is possible to implement RONA in UCCE and use the busy timer in Unified CM in case a caller dials the agent's extension directly, but it is best to standardize on a single approach for the entire business rather than have different approaches within the enterprise.

■ **No Answer Ring Duration:** This setting allows the Unified CM to divert the call if it is not answered within a specified number of seconds. The UCCE Agent Desk Settings tool also has the capability to configure this as an RONA. Both options can be used to divert the call to another service or back into the queue if the agent fails to answer the call. However, only one should be configured, not both; otherwise, they will conflict. For contact center agents, the preference is to use RONA in UCCE.

Partitions and Calling Search Spaces

Partitions are comprised of logical groupings of directory numbers (telephone extensions) and route patterns with similar reachability characteristics. Calling search spaces comprise an ordered list of partitions and determine the partitions that the calling devices can search through when attempting to make a call.

Combining partitions and calling search spaces allow an administrator to segregate the organization's dial plan. Controlling the dial plan enables a telephony security model to restrict call access to certain devices and directory numbers.

When configuring Unified CM for UCCE, it is common practice to create partitions to logically group the directory numbers for the additional components:

■ **IVR:** A partition for the CTI route points and CTI ports associated with IP IVR to prevent staff from calling the CTI ports directly.

■ **UCCE external dialed numbers:** A partition for all the inbound dialed numbers from the public switched telephone network (PSTN).

■ **UCCE internal transfer dialed numbers (DN):** A partition for all the internal dialed numbers that can be used for agents dialing or transferring to other contact center teams within the organization. A separate partition for internal DNs is created so that the agents cannot dial or transfer calls to the primary inbound DNs. While transferring calls to the external DNs is unlikely to cause a problem, many organizations prefer for this not to happen so that they have an accurate record of external inbound call traffic that is separate from call transfers for reporting purposes.

■ **UCCE administrative dialed numbers:** A partition for numbers that the general employees should not be able to access. This partition could contain numbers for administrative services such as setting announcements, emergency evacuation scripts, or RONA dialed numbers.

Queuing and Self-Service

All voice interaction that is not human to human is likely to be serviced by an Interactive Voice Response (IVR) platform. IVRs allow the caller to interact with the business without needing an agent resource for that part of the call. IVRs are generally used for the following reasons:

■ **Simple, high-volume queries:** Such queries include repetitive transactions such as requesting a bank balance or telephone voting for TV shows. These types of queries typically attract a high volume of calls. As the call format and flow are relatively simple, it makes sense for these calls to be serviced by an IVR rather than an agent. Staffing a contact center to handle high-volume, short-duration, repetitive calls could be expensive, and handling these types of calls would be demoralizing for the agents.

■ **Security-conscious transactions:** Fraud can occur when humans obtain personal financial information such as credit card details. Many contact centers consist of sales teams that handle financial transactions. Fraud can potentially occur as the agents are required to process the credit card details when accepting payment. Many organizations have implemented IVRs to handle credit card payments, therefore removing the human element from the credit card transactions. Another benefit of doing this is that the voice-recording platforms used to record the agent calls are usually not configured to record IVR interactions, so no spoken credit card details will be stored in the voice recordings.

■ **Reducing agent handling times:** The formulas often used to size agent resources for contact centers take into account the call volume over a certain time period and record the average duration of those calls. If a contact center is able to reduce its average handling time, it can also reduce the amount of agent resources, or retain the existing agent resources and handle a higher call volume. Call-handling times can be reduced by offloading repetitive operations to an IVR before the call is handled by the agent. Such operations include prompting the caller to enter her account details or automatically giving her frequently requested information. This minimizes the amount of work the agent needs to perform when the call arrives, which in turn reduces the handling time.

■ **Identifying the caller:** Although many organizations publicly say that all their customers are equal, the reality is that some customers can have a much higher or lower ranking than the average. The ability to identify the caller can be extremely useful in deciding where to deliver the call. Platinum customers can be delivered to their preferred sales advisor or a sales team that handles high-net-worth customers. Customers that perhaps have outstanding debt can be automatically directed to the debt recovery team rather than through the sales service they have selected.

■ **Out-of-hours service:** Not many organizations are fortunate to have a global presence and implement a follow-the-sun contact center model, whereby the caller can be answered by a contact center agent somewhere in the world depending on the time of day. Most organizations have a core set of working hours and choose not to handle calls during out-of-hours times such as overnight or during a weekend. IVRs do not require days off, so they can be used to provide a 24/7 presence, perhaps with a smaller feature set than that which is available with an agent.

■ **Call queuing:** For the times when no agent resources are available, the caller must be delivered somewhere. Call queuing is the simplest of IVR functions and typically involves the caller hearing an annoying looped music track interspersed with frequent announcements reminding the caller how important he is. When an agent resource becomes available, the caller is removed from the queue and connected to the agent.

Many IVR systems that require input from the caller, such as the selection of an option from a voice menu, use DTMF signaling to indicate to the IVR the chosen option. However, many modern IVR platforms support speech recognition, and the use of this technology is gradually gaining acceptance by the public.

The voice menus used to greet the caller and request for input are usually professionally prerecorded messages. These messages are stored as files on the IVR and played to the caller as needed. This often results in hundreds of different, static announcements being recorded during the development of the IVR application. Unfortunately, this results in a lack of flexibility as changes in the business or IVR requirements often require that the announcements are rerecorded. Many IVR vendors also support the use of text-to-speech (TTS). TTS engines allow the IVR developer to pass a text string to the engine, which is then converted into an audio stream and played to the caller. Long gone are the days of robotic-sounding voices. Today's TTS platforms can produce very clear, human-quality voices with different languages, sex, and dialect. Using a TTS engine with your IVR has the benefits that all your announcements use the same voice and that prompts can be changed without needing any rerecording. The use of TTS does, however, impact on performance and cost, so many IVRs that implement TTS actually use a combination of TTS and static announcements.

It is not possible to queue calls on the Unified CM cluster or UCCE, so a deployment must have an IVR to provide queuing facilities for when no agents are available. A typical UCCE solution with utilize either IP IVR or CVP, not both. Technically any IVR (including TDM-based IVRs) could be used as long as it has a compatible interface that will communicate with UCCE. This is great news for organizations that already have an existing IVR in which they have realized significant investment as it gives the organization the opportunity to leverage the current IVR solution while potentially planning a migration to an IP-based solution.

The IVR interface specification compatible with UCCE is detailed in an engineering document often referred to as GED-125. The interface specification is not specific to any particular IVR vendor. While it is a proprietary protocol, the protocol details are published to allow any manufacturer to implement the interface for its IVR. By doing this, the vendor enables its IVR to interface through a peripheral gateway (PG) to use the IVR for call routing, routing target selection, real-time monitoring, and reporting purposes.

The communication between the IVR and the PG takes place through an exchange of messages using a message set that is based on Computer-Supported Telecommunications Applications (CSTA) client/server messaging conventions. All the signaling takes place over a TCP/IP connection. With this interface, the IVR takes on the role of the server while the PG performs the role of the client issuing requests to the IVR and also originating unsolicited event messages.

The IVR interface specification is divided into two major sections:

- The communications interfaces define the low-level conventions and protocols required to establish and maintain data connections between the IVR and the PG.

■ The applications interfaces define the high-level messages that allow the IVR and PG to exchange call-processing information. Four different application-level interfaces exist; these are detailed in Table 12-1. It is important that the correct interface is chosen when configuring IVR integration.

Table 12-1 *IVR Application Interfaces*

Interface	Description
Event Data Feed	The Event Data Feed provides a means for the IVR to pass current status information to UCCE in real time on an event-by-event basis for reporting purposes.
Call Routing Interface	The Call Routing Interface is used by the IVR to ask UCCE for instructions on how to route a call, either to a destination label or to an application.
Time Synchronization Interface	The Time Synchronization Interface is used by both UCCE and the IVR to ensure that their clocks are synchronized for reporting purposes.
Service Control Interface	The Service Control Interface enables a UCCE call script to control the call when it has arrived at the IVR. This enables the call to be terminated at the IVR, yet the UCCE router determines the treatment that the call should receive.

When configuring an IVR using the Network VRU Explorer tool within UCCE Configuration Manager, it is also necessary to define the type of IVR. The type does not relate to the vendor, but it is determined by the deployment architecture and the application interface used. Figure 12-6 displays where the IVR type is defined during configuration, and Table 12-2 details some of the different types of IVRs used with UCCE. Several of the IVR types, such as Type 3 and Type 7, are specific to hosted environments and are not relevant to enterprise deployments.

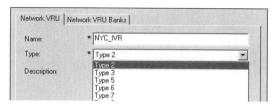

Figure 12-6 *Available IVR Types in Network VRU Explorer*

Table 12-2   *Types of IVR*

Type	Description
Type 2	Used for IVRs at the customer premises that require a translation route to a VRU script node to deliver the call to the IVR. IP IVR uses Type 2
Type 9	Used by UCCE system PG deployments
Type 10	Used by CVP deployments configured using the Comprehensive Call Flow model

Note   UCCE versions prior to 7.1 used several different VRU types depending on the deployment model, including Type 2, 3, 5, 7, and 8. These are still supported for existing deployments, but Cisco recommends that all new CVP installations use Type 10.

CVP Versus IP IVR

IP-based IVRs have no physical telephony trunks or interfaces like a traditional IVR. The telephony trunks are terminated at the voice gateway. Some IVR solutions, including the IP IVR, terminate an IP RTP stream on the IVR server, whereas for CVP, the voice call remains on the voice gateway and only becomes an RTP stream when connected to an IP phone.

Many early adopters of UCCE chose IP IVR as their IVR solution as this was the only IP-based IVR available at the time. There still remains a large deployment base of IP IVR, but the majority of new deployments use CVP as the chosen IVR solution. For those customers with IP IVR who want to migrate to CVP, Cisco offers a license upgrade facility.

Table 12-3 compares the functionality of CVP and IP IVR.

Tip   Table 12-3 details that using CVP allows twice as many agents to be deployed per Unified CM cluster than the same deployment with IP IVR. This is because the use of the JTAPI connection between the IP IVRs and the Unified CM subscribers puts a higher performance load on the subscribers. For large deployments, it is recommended that CVP is used.

Note   Both CVP and IP IVR support Media Resource Control Protocol (MRCP)—based Automatic Speech Recognition (ASR) and Text-to-Speech (TTS). Cisco does not supply ASR and TTS engines, but they are compatible with all vendors who support MRCP.

Table 12-3 *Comparisons of CVP with IP IVR*

Feature	CVP	IP IVR
Cost	Lower port cost than IP IVR, but can require additional servers, server licenses, and networking hardware	Higher port cost than CVP, but a relatively self-contained solution
Port capacity per server	500 ports using H.323 1200 ports using SIP	300 ports
Maximum agents per Unified CM cluster	4000	2000
Deployment model	Centralized or distributed	Centralized only
Call termination	On the voice gateway	On the actual IP IVR server
Call control	H.323 or SIP	JTAPI
Codec support	G.711 and G.729 simultaneously	G.711 or G.729

Cisco Unified IP IVR

The following sections examine the UCCE call flow and configuration when using Unified IP IVR.

IP IVR Call Flow

Unified CM provides the call processing and switching to set up a G.711 or G.729 Real-Time Transport Protocol (RTP) stream from the voice gateway to the IP IVR. The IP IVR communicates with Unified CM through the JTAPI protocol and communicates with UCCE through the Service Control Interface (SCI) through a VRU PG. Figure 12-7 shows a call flow diagram for call delivery to an IP IVR, the individual call steps for which are detailed in the list that follows.

Step 1. The caller dials the contact center, and his PSTN call is terminated on a voice gateway.

Step 2. The voice gateway is under the control of the Unified CM. It sends a message to the Unified CM with details of the dialed number and asks for a destination to deliver the call.

Step 3. The Dialed Number Information Service (DNIS) of the call is a CTI route point on the Unified CM, which is under the control of a JTAPI user registered with the UCCE Unified CM PG. The PG performs a postroute request to the UCCE central controller to find a destination for the call.

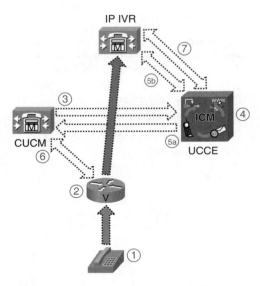

Figure 12-7   *Cisco Unified IP IVR Call Flow*

Step 4.   UCCE runs a call-routing script. In the call-routing script is a translation to a VRU node that performs a translation route.

Step 5a.   The UCCE Unified CM PG returns a label to the Unified CM. This label is a CTI route point configured as a JTAPI trigger on the IVR.

Step 5b.   The UCCE IVR PG sends a message to the IP IVR to tell it to expect to receive a call on a specific port.

Step 6.   The Unified CM instructs the voice gateway to deliver the call to the IP address of the IP IVR. The voice gateway establishes an RTP stream between it and the IP IVR.

Step 7.   By using the Service Control Interface, UCCE is able to control the call at the IP IVR and send run script requests to play specific IP IVR applications using the Run External Script node in the UCCE call-routing script.

For a call-routing script to use an IP IVR resource to interact with the caller, the UCCE platform must first request that the call is delivered to the IP IVR. Figure 12-8 shows a very basic script that uses the translation route to VRU node to perform a translation route request and establish a call connection with the IVR. When the call has arrived at the IVR, it also needs instructions on what actions it should perform. This is achieved with the Run External Script node. The UCCE script in Figure 12-8 requests that the IVR executes the application called Welcome_Greeting.

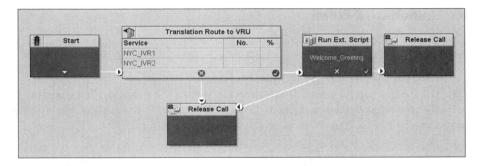

Figure 12-8   *Basic IP IVR Call-Routing Script*

Tip   All IVRs have a finite number of ports, which results in a maximum number of simultaneous calls that can be present at the IVR. It is recommended that you only send a call to the IVR if it is expected to receive IVR treatment. I have previously seen many customers' UCCE scripts that send calls to the IVR in preparation for call queuing regardless of whether an agent is available. This just results in a temporary waste of IVR resources.

Tip   Translation routing was originally designed for use in TDM ACDs so that the UICM platform could retain an association between a specific call and its CTI data for calls that were being prerouted by a carrier or postrouted to another peripheral.

For a TDM or plain old telephone service (POTS) call, no data is sent with the actual call as this is not possible. This means that it if a call was handled by an agent or an IVR and was then required to be transferred elsewhere, any CTI data associated with that call would be lost when the transfer took place. If all call-tracking data is lost, the reporting platform would see both call legs as two separate calls rather than a single call.

A translation route is a temporary destination for a call to give the peripheral the opportunity to tie up the call with its associated CTI data before delivering the call to its final destination.

The temporary destination is a single DNIS number taken from a pool of (usually sequential) DNISs. The DNIS pool is sufficiently large enough so that the numbers in it are not used up too quickly. This allows the translation-routing process enough time to match the call with its data and deliver the call to its destination.

When the peripheral (ACD or IVR) sees the call arrive at the specified DNIS, it performs an adjunct route request to the PG with the DNIS details. The PG then combines this with the data it received from the UCCE central controller and sends the call to the correct destination. As the PG now knows the current location of the call, it is able to maintain its associated CTI data.

Cisco Unified CCX Editor

The Unified CCX Editor is a graphical programming environment used for creating and validating telephony applications for the Unified Contact Center Express and IP IVR platforms.

The CCX Editor is a plugin available to download from the administration pages of IP IVR. When the application is opened, it connects to the IP IVR and allows the developer to access the IP IVR applications stored in the IVR's repository.

IP IVR applications are constructed using Java-based steps available within the editor. No knowledge of Java is required to create reasonably complex IVR applications; however, with a knowledge of Java, it is also possible to create custom Java steps.

Figure 12-9 shows a simple application created with the CCX Editor that takes a string stored in Call Variable 10 from the UCCE call script and attempts to play the .wav file with the same name as the string.

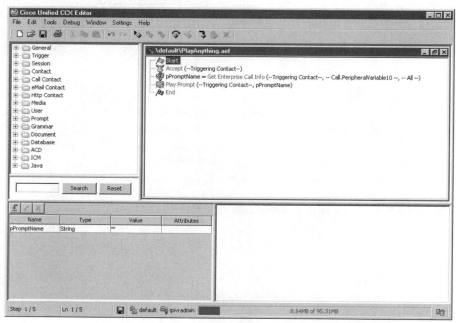

Figure 12-9   *Simple IP IVR Application Developed with the UCCX Editor*

Tip   The CCX Editor is a full development suite for IP IVR applications and contains various validation and debugging features to ensure that the applications perform correctly. After creating or modifying an application, it is recommended that the Validate feature from the Tools menu is selected to ensure that the script is valid before saving the script in the repository. The CCX Editor will allow you to save an invalid script, but the IP IVR will not execute invalid scripts, which results in errors being generated in the UCCE call-routing script.

IP IVR Configuration

The following sections examine the UCCE-specific configuration for IP IVR.

> **Tip**   When configuring a new installation of IP IVR, it is important that the peripheral number defined for the IVR in the Network Trunk Group Explorer matches the group ID of the Telephony Call Control Group (the group that lists all the CTI ports). If these values do not match, any call that is translation-routed to the IVR will fail. An error message is generated on the router process that explains that the translation route timed out.

IP IVR Load Balancing

Unlike CVP, which has the capability to use content-switching devices to load-balance traffic, the IP IVRs have no built-in load-balancing ability to automatically distribute calls evenly over the IVRs. To achieve this, the load-balancing logic needs to developed within the UCCE call-routing script. Figure 12-10 shows a translation route to a VRU node that is used to select an IVR destination for the call. The purpose of this node is to list all the available destination options for the call and allow the router process to determine the preferred final destination. To select the preferred destination, the translation route to a VRU node in our example has two columns: Consider If and Select Minimum Value. These are both evaluated for each of the two IVRs.

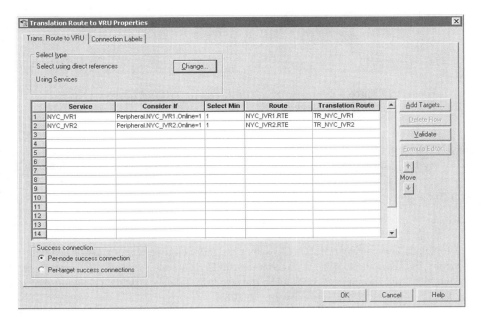

Figure 12-10 *Translation Route to VRU Node Settings*

The Consider If column has a formula that checks whether the IVR is online. The formula also evaluates whether there are any free ports on the IVR, but this cannot be seen in the screen shot.

The Select Minimum Value column contains a static value. In this example, both destinations have the integer value of 1.

Each service listed is evaluated based on the defined logic, and a preferred service is chosen. In this particular example, both IVRs are online and both have free ports available, as both also have the minimum value set to 1; the result is that either service could be selected. The final decision on which service to choose is defined under the Select Type heading. Clicking the Change button displays the window shown in Figure 12-11.

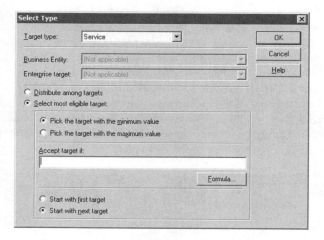

Figure 12-11 *Translation Route to VRU Settings with Select Next Target*

Tip   If you prefer to have the IVRs configured so that one is a primary and the other is secondary for backup purposes, just change the value in the minimum value column to 2 for the second IVR. The router will then select only the second IVR if the first one is offline or if all the ports are busy.

The Select Type dialog box is set to **select the most eligible target** starting with the *next target*. In this example, this means that if both IVRs are eligible and IVR1 was chosen last time, this time the translation route to the VRU should select IVR2. This configuration allows an even call distribution over both IVRs.

Cisco Unified CVP

Unlike Unified IP IVR, which is quite self-containing and can run on a single server, a CVP solution comprises several different products. This also allows CVP to be highly scalable as it is possible to distribute its software components over multiple servers to handle a higher call volume or even introduce content services switches to provide load balancing.

Originally, the CVP platform was based on the H.323 protocol; however, SIP is now the main protocol for CVP. H.323 is still supported, but new orders placed for CVP are only shipped with SIP.

CVP is a powerful IVR solution for organizations that have multiple distributed branch sites as CVP allows calls to receive IVR treatment and queuing at the network edge. In a branch solution, this means that while the call is participating in IVR treatment, it would remain on the ingress voice gateway in the branch and voice streams would not need to traverse the WAN.

CVP has five different deployment models:

- **Comprehensive Call Flow:** The Comprehensive Call Flow model is the most popular CVP deployment model and the model that is used with UCCE. It offers a pure IP-based contact center with IVR for call control and queuing.

- **Basic Video Service:** The Basic Video Service model is an extension of the Comprehensive model to allow video callers to interact with video agents. This model does not support video IVR.

- **Standalone VXML Server:** The Standalone VXML Server model is used for purely automated self-service IVR. This model has the ability to deliver calls to a contact center agent if required, but no call queuing is possible as CVP only has limited call control.

- **Call Director:** The Call Director model enables CVP to act as a voice switch to route calls over IP throughout the enterprise. This model is often used as a precursor to migrating TDM ACDs to IP. In Chapter 8, "Call Routing," we discuss the use of tie lines to connect an organization's distributed ACDs and perform private network routing. Using the Call Director model allows the organization to route those calls as IP to the legacy ACD over an existing IP WAN rather than requiring TDM trunks. Often Unified ICM is used to route these calls.

- **VRU-only:** The VRU-only model allows an organization to connect its CVP platform to a carrier through a Signaling System 7 (SS7) link for prerouting and queuing.

Figure 12-12 details the CVP architecture for the Comprehensive Call Flow model.

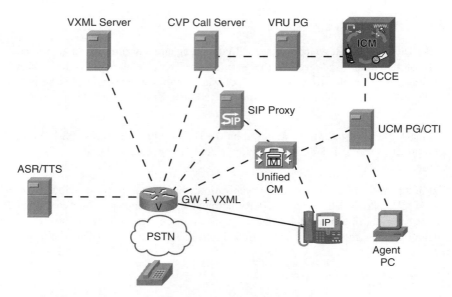

Figure 12-12   *CVP Architecture of the Comprehensive Call Flow Deployment Model*

The main components that comprise this architecture are as follows:

■ **CVP Call Server:** The SIP Service, ICM Service, IVR Service, and H.323 Service all run on the CVP Call Server. Together they provide the IVR and queuing functionality.

■ **SIP Proxy:** Forwards SIP requests and responds with destinations to the requesting device.

■ **Ingress Voice Gateway:** Typically provides inbound connectivity from the PSTN; however, it could also be used at the end of a SIP trunk, so it is not exclusively used for TDM connectivity.

■ **VXML Gateway:** Acts as the client requesting VXML pages from the VXML Server.

■ **VXML Server:** Serves VXML pages to the VXML client. The VXML Server usually has an interface to back-end customer applications or databases.

■ **ASR/TTS:** The Automated Speech Recognition and Text-to-Speech server used for recognizing and producing voice and media streams, respectively.

■ **Unified CM:** Provides call control functionality for Unified Communications endpoints.

■ **Unified CCE:** An advanced contact routing engine.

Figure 12-13 details a call flow scenario using SIP, the steps for which are described in the list that follows.

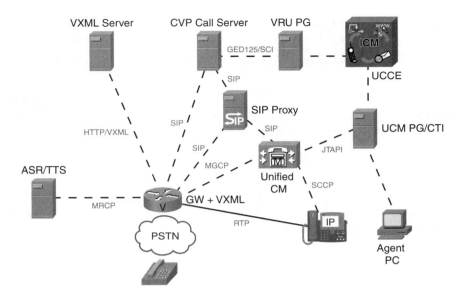

Figure 12-13 *High-Level CVP SIP Call Flow*

Step 1. An inbound PSTN call arrives at the ingress gateway. The gateway is configured to send a SIP invite message to the SIP proxy server. (If CVP was using H.323, the gateway would send a Register, Admission, Status (RAS) request to the H.323 gatekeeper.)

Step 2. The SIP proxy server forwards the invite message to the SIP service running on the CVP call control server.

Step 3. The CVP call control server performs a route request to the CVP VRU PG using the GED125/Service Control Interface protocol.

Step 4. The PG performs a postroute request to the UCCE router that executes a call-routing script based on the dialed number in the request.

Step 5. Assuming that the UCCE call-routing script requires the caller to receive IVR treatment, the routing script uses a Send To VRU node to return a destination label of the VXML gateway to the CVP call control server. The SIP proxy server translates the destination label into the IP address of the VXML gateway. In this example, the voice gateway and VXML gateway are coresident.

Step 6. The VXML gateway sends an HTTP new call message to the CVP call server with the label originally provided by UCCE. The CVP call server then informs UCCE that the caller is able to receive IVR treatment and that UCCE should continue processing the logic in the call-routing script following the Send To VRU node. Each time the call-routing script reaches a Run Script node, it will instruct CVP to play the required IVR application.

Step 7.   If the UCCE call-routing script requires the call to be delivered to an agent, UCCE will provide a destination label to the CVP call server.

Step 8.   The CVP call server sends a SIP invite message to the SIP proxy server, which finds the IP address of the SIP trunk connected to the Unified CM cluster and forwards the SIP invite message.

Step 9.   Unified CM then routes the RTP stream to the agent's IP phone, and UCCE signals the agent's desktop application to expect an inbound call.

Summary

This chapter covered the three most popular Unified Communications products that integrate with UCCE to form an overall UCCE solution. In particular, the key learning points from this chapter can be summarized as follows:

- The Unified CM cluster provides the telephony control for endpoints.

- IP IVR and CVP provide self-service and queuing functions.

Chapter 13

Data-Driven Routing

This chapter covers the following subjects:

- Why data-driven routing is used

- The different database lookup options available

- Detailed example using UCCE DB Lookup

With the wealth of features available in modern contact center technology, including multiskilled and multimedia agents, outbound dialing campaigns, and intelligent prerouting in the carrier's network, the ability to influence call routing based on a simple database search is often overlooked.

The complexity that can be achieved through the standard call-scripting tools in Cisco Unified Contact Center Enterprise (UCCE) Script Editor using tools from the script palette, such as the Route Select node or custom functions, often removes the requirement to perform additional computation or data retrieval. However, several methods exist to give the contact center engineer extra control over contact routing and agent screen pop based on an external data source.

The majority of data-driven routing involves a request being made to an external database. The values provided in response to the request are then used by the call-routing logic, perhaps to influence the call delivery or provide a detailed screen pop to the agent; however, not all data-driven routing requires a database. The external data provided in the response could be values provided as part of an HTML/XML request or real-time data from a third-party application.

An important item to consider when implementing data lookups is the time taken for the external data source to provide the data to the UCCE routing engine. When a route request arrives at a UCCE peripheral gateway (PG), the UCCE router has a predefined timeout value for it to deliver a route response to the PG or network interface controller (NIC). If the UCCE router also has to make a data request to an additional device, such as an external database, the response from this database needs to be delivered quickly.

Should the external source fail to provide a response within the timeout, the router will attempt to deliver the contact to a default destination. If the contact engineer expects that this data request will take longer than the timeout, the call will need to be queued before a request is made. This approach of call queuing will work in UCCE when the contact is being handled in an enterprise environment as the call has already been delivered to a contact center site and can be queued at an Interactive Voice Response (IVR) resource. However, a route request from a carrier's NIC in a hosted or prerouting environment has to be serviced within the timeout parameters; otherwise, the intelligent call routing will fail and the default route will be selected.

This chapter explores the various methods available to enable database routing within the UCCE environment.

What Can Be Achieved with Data-Driven Routing

Basic contact centers provide simplistic contact routing and delivery using straightforward logic. Calls are usually distributed based on the dialed number and are delivered to the longest available agent in the most appropriate skill group. Quite often the caller is presented with some form of welcome announcement or disclaimer advising him that his call might be recorded and a simple IVR menu prompting him to select the department he wants to speak with.

This basic form of contact routing has been available on the majority of call center platforms for the last decade, and many organizations use this technology to provide the caller with in-call options. Implementing IVR-based voice menus enables the contact center to publish fewer public dialed numbers because the caller can now dial a single number and then choose which business unit or team she wants to speak with through the correct menu selection.

One of the complaints that customers voice is that they do not want to listen to an IVR and then select from a list of services, many of which are not applicable to them. For example, a caller with an insurance policy from XYZ Co. might call his contact center and be prompted by an IVR to select from three options:

> For home insurance, press 1; for car insurance, press 2; and for health insurance, press 3.

After selecting a menu option, the caller might be prompted to enter her account number and a PIN to clear security; the call could then be delivered to an agent.

Modern contact center platforms have the capability to provide the caller with a more immersed experience tailored to the caller's needs.

In the preceding example, the contact center has asked the caller to select from all the available options. However, it is likely that the caller might have only one insurance policy with the company, so the other two menu options are irrelevant.

In this scenario, it would make sense to identify the call first from his account number and PIN. After the caller is identified, data-driven routing could be employed to deliver only relevant information to the caller. In the case of the IVR menu, if the caller has only one type of insurance policy, say home insurance, the menu option need not be played; the call could be delivered directly to the home insurance team. Alternatively, the caller might be interested in purchasing a policy for his car or health, so the following menu option could be presented to the caller:

> If you want to talk to us about your existing home insurance policy, press 1, or hold for all other services.

Adaptive menu options such as the preceding example serve to ensure that the customer has a positive experience and removes much of the monotony from a call.

Having access to an external data source provides an endless amount of opportunities and customization that can take place in the routing engine and provide a high degree of intelligence for call delivery. Some of the popular uses for external data lookup are as follows:

- **Agent screen pop:** The duties of a contact center agent should be made as easy as possible through the use of technology. Significant agent satisfaction gains can be achieved through to the use of screen popping call and caller data to an agent's screen before she answers the call. Simple information, such as the service the caller had dialed and the duration the caller spent in queue, is useful to the agent to determine how to handle the call. Enhanced information, including the caller's name, account details, and call history, provide the foundation for a high customer and agent satisfaction through reduced manual processing by the agent and less detail repetition from the caller.

- **Specific queue music or in-queue announcements:** Contact centers should be careful when targeting callers with advertising campaigns while the caller is in queue. It would be a disaster for the company to advertise about its great customer service if the caller has been in a queue for a long period of time, or has actually called the complaints line! However, in-call advertising can be successful if the caller has been identified and a potential up-sell opportunity exists for a product or service that complements an existing product used by the caller. Tailored IVR announcements should not just be limited to sales opportunities. If you happen to know that the caller has a preference for classical music, why not play various classical tracks to the caller while in queue?

- **Call delivery to preferred agents:** When an existing customer or potential customer calls a contact center, business (the act of selling, purchasing, or querying) takes place between two human parties. Repeat business is possible when relationships are formed. In contact centers, typically with a large number of staff, callers infrequently speak with the same agent twice. Sometimes this can be of benefit to the caller, especially if on a previous occasion the caller was unhappy with the level of service provided by the agent. However, many calls to a contact center actually resolve issues, and it is human nature to want to speak with an agent with whom you have had a previous positive experience. This is especially helpful if the problem resolution has taken several phone calls and the agent is familiar with the problem history. Using data stored in an external database, it would be possible to identify the agent that the caller previously spoke with and, if that agent is available, deliver the call to this preferred agent.

- **IVR self-service:** Performing database lookup at the highest level, IVR self-service applications have a complex integration between the routing engine and their corresponding back-end interfaces. Many telephone banking and payment gateways are implemented using IVR self-service.

An overwhelming benefit of using data-driven routing is the provision of a tailored service for the caller that results in a greater customer satisfaction. As you have seen in the preceding examples, customer service can be improved simply by identifying the caller and answering the caller by name.

Data-driven routing also provides benefits beyond customer satisfaction. Reducing agent handling time by screen-popping the caller's account details and also creating an easier-to-use system for the agent by not making her repeat tasks for every call, such as asking the caller for his account details and manually entering those details into the customer relationship management (CRM) system, also improves agent satisfaction and can reduce agent churn. Reducing agent handle time also decreases the number of agents required to manage the call load.

Data Lookup Options

At this point, you know that data lookups can occur for various reasons. It is also important to understand that these lookups can take place at different phases of the call, such as the following:

- **Phase 1:** Identifying the caller. To provide the caller with any preferential routing or intelligent menu options, it is first necessary to identify the caller. Typically, this takes place during the first phase of the call and can be combined with a security check.

- **Phase 2:** Custom IVR menus or self-service applications usually happen as a second phase of the call, giving the caller the option to decide which team or business unit he wants to speak to. For some self-service applications such as telephone banking, the call can also end in this phase because the caller many have no need to be connected to an agent.

- **Phase 3:** Delivery to an agent, perhaps with an amount of Computer Telephony Integration (CTI) screen-pop data also being delivered with the call. This data might be enough for the agent to successfully handle the call, or alternatively this data could be used to trigger another data request to a CRM application. Integration with a CRM solution would typically result in a greater amount of detail being returned to the agent.

For many calls, Phase 3 would be the last part of the caller's experience; however, sometimes the caller is required to be transferred to another team or back to an IVR.

Transferring data with a call prevents the need for the new agent to request any details from the caller. Callers find the experience of repeating themselves to every agent frustrating.

Several methods exist within the UCCE platform for performing data lookups:

- **Static lookup:** Although not technically a database lookup, it is common to assign values to the call variables within a UCCE script.

- **Database (DB) Lookup node:** Specifically designed for performing pure database lookups, the DB Lookup node within Script Editor is a simple-to-use feature for data retrieval.

- **Application Gateway:** The Application Gateway node opens an extensive application programming interface (API), allowing application developers to use the UCCE call flow scripts to interface to third-party applications during real-time call processing.

- **Within an IVR application:** The GED-125 interface enables UCCE to communicate with IP IVR, Customer Voice Portal (CVP), and any GED-125-compliant third-party IVR. GED-125 allows the UCCE and the IVR to pass values stored in call variables. The data stored in these variables can be obtained by the IVR application while the call is in progress at the IVR.

- **Agent desktop/CRM integration:** CRM integration, keystroke macros, and web-driven applications are all popular forms of data retrieval for when the call has arrived at the agent's desktop.

The sections that follow examine these different methods for performing data lookups in greater detail.

Static Lookup

For small data structures, such as matching a caller's Automatic Number Identification (ANI) against a list of ten possible candidates, it is possible to achieve this using a list of IF statements within the call script. Other frequent occurrences of using formulas to check for conditions include the use of administrative scripts to set global values. An example of this could be an administrative script that runs on a daily basis and checks the current date. Depending on whether the date matches a series of IF statements, the script could set a global userPublicHoliday variable to be true if the day is a public holiday.

DB Lookup Node

The DB Lookup node is a script node available from the Script Editor palette capable of retrieving data from an external database. When invoked in a script, the DB Lookup node returns a single row of data from the database based on a key value that is passed to it in a call variable. The values returned by the DB Lookup are also stored in variables that can be accessed by the remaining call script.

No detailed development skills are required to use the DB Lookup node. The DB Worker process needs to be enabled on the UCCE router, a database needs to be created, and the associated database configuration must be entered into the Database Lookup Explorer tool in Configuration Manager. The process required to develop a database lookup using the DB Lookup Node is detailed later in this chapter.

The DB Worker process runs on both routers and can connect to several databases. Typically, the customer database will have a replicated copy on another database server, and the UCCE platform will connect to both databases.

Application Gateway

The UCCE Application Gateway interface, detailed in GED-145, provides an API to allow developers to interface the UCCE call router into third-party applications. It is important to understand that the Application Gateway interface is not a prepacked application, but rather a development interface that requires a programmer to write code against for it to function in a call-routing scenario.

Application gateways are configured using the UCCE configuration tools, selected from the Script Editor palette and placed into the required call script. When the call script is executed and the Application Gateway Script node reached, the application gateway performs a query to the third-party application. Assuming that the application gateway is functioning correctly, a response will be returned to the UCCE router. This response can then be used to influence further routing or CTI call data.

The application gateway can be configured using several fault tolerance methods to provide a higher degree of resilience. The Application Gateway process runs on both UCCE routers.

Within an IVR Application

The common IVR platforms used with UCCE are the Unified IP IVR and Unified CVP; however, almost any IVR that is compatible with the Cisco GED-125 interface can be used. Database lookup does not only have to take place within the call-routing script. When the call is connected to an IVR resource, the IVR can be programmed to perform a database lookup and return database values to the UCCE router as call variables.

For both IP IVR and CVP, each has its own IVR script development environments, Cisco Unified Contact Center Express (Unified CCX) Editor and CVP Studio, respectively. Both of these development environments have native tools that can be used for database lookups. Each environment also provides the ability for a skilled developer to create his own database lookup functions if required.

Note   You can find detailed information about CVP Studio at http://www.cisco.com/en/US/products/ps7235/index.html.

The Cisco Developer Network also provides several example application development files and guides for the UCCX Editor at http://developer.cisco.com/web/ccxs.

Agent Desktop/CRM Integration

For database values to influence call routing, the database lookup needs to be performed before the call is delivered to an agent. However, it is common for data retrieval to occur when the call arrives at the agent's desktop to obtain CRM data. In this scenario, the caller might have been prompted to enter an account number at an IVR, or perhaps the caller's ANI is used. Rather than perform the database lookup in the call-routing script, the call is delivered to an intelligent agent desktop application. On call arrival, the desktop application uses one of the UCCE call variables as a key value to perform the lookup. The data returned from the lookup is then populated onto the agent's screen.

Performing CRM lookups at the desktop can save the agent repetitive work and also minimizes errors by not requiring the agent to request initial data from the caller and then manually enter the data into the CRM tool.

CRM lookups are usually performed in custom desktop applications written using the CTI OS Toolkit, using native CRM-enabled desktops, or through the features available with the Cisco Agent Desktop (CAD), including keystroke macros and the embedded web browser.

Configuring UCCE Database Lookup

The example in the following sections explores the steps required to implement a simple database lookup using the DB Lookup node in Script Editor. In the example, the database contains a list of integer account numbers and the associated first names and surnames of the account holder.

The high-level activities to be performed can be summarized as follows:

Step 1.   Create a database (DB) and database table to store the account data.

Step 2.   Enable the DB Worker process through router setup.

Step 3.   Configure the database connection with Database Lookup Explorer.

Step 4.   Create a simple test script to prove DB lookup functionality.

Step 1: Database Creation

Several tools exist for creating a database within Microsoft SQL Server. I used Microsoft SQL Server Management Studio in MS SQL Server 2005 to create a database on both logger servers called customerName.

The logger servers have been used in this example because it is only a lab demonstration system. On a production platform, an external database server is likely to be used.

Table 13-1   tblCustomerName *Database Table*

Column Name	Type	Description
accno	INTEGER	The customer's account number
fname	VARCHAR(20)	The customer's first name, stored as a string
sname	VARCHAR(20)	The customers surname, stored as a string

To store the custom data, a database table is required. I have created this database table with the information detailed in Table 13-1, using the SQL query in Example 13-1, and populated it with the sample data from Table 13-2. The account number column (accno) will be used as the primary key to retrieve the name values during database lookup.

Example 13-1   *SQL Query to Create the Database Table*

```
create table tblCustomerName
(
accno INT NOT NULL PRIMARY KEY,
fname VARCHAR(20),
sname VARCHAR(20)
)
```

The databases and associated tables must be present on both database servers, assuming that a redundant database is required. The data can be manually entered into both databases, or database replication can be enabled to automatically synchronize both databases.

Step 2: Enable the DB Worker Process

The DB Worker process is one of the processes that makes up the UCCE router. The process is not enabled by default, so it requires the installation engineer to select the database routing check box during both Router A and Router B installation setup.

Table 13-2   *Database Routing Data*

accno	fname	sname
1234	Gary	Ford
2345	Mark	Jeggo
3456	Hein	DeBeer
4567	James	Hughes

By default, the DB Worker process assumes that the database it connects to will use the internal "sa" account with a blank password. It is highly unlikely that most database administrators will allow this. A registry key needs to be changed to define a specific username and password if the sa account is not to be used. The location of the registry key is as follows:

HKEY_LOCAL_MACHINE\SOFTWARE\Cisco Systems, Inc.\ICM\<customer instance>\RouterA\Router\CurrentVersion\Configuration\Database\SQLLogin

A specific format is used in the registry key to instruct the DB Worker process which servers and username/password combinations to use. The setting used for this demonstration database is as follows:

\\CCOCUS01LGRA\customerName=(UCCE\administrator,password),\\CCOCUS01LGRB\customerName=(UCCE\administrator,password)

From this setting, it is possible to determine that the DB Worker process will connect to the Logger A and B servers using the database customerName. The user account that will be used by the process to connect to the database is the administrator account for the UCCE domain. The password has been set to "password."

The SQLLogin registry key value needs to be configured only on Router A. The first time both router processes are started after the configuration has taken place, Router B automatically populates its registry with the SQLLogin values.

Step 3: Configuration Manager: Database Lookup Explorer

The Configuration Manager tool Database Lookup Explorer is used to configure the actual database table and its respective columns of data.

This example uses a database called customerName on both loggers. The database has a single table called tblCustomerName.

Within Database Lookup Explorer, define the name that will be used by Script Editor to identify the database. For simplicity, I have also called this customerName. The default access type is SQL, which cannot be changed. You must then define the Side A and Side B database connections. Table 13-3 details the connections used in this example. The connection defines the server, database, and database table.

Table 13-3 *Database Lookup Explorer Connections*

DB Side	Connection Definition
Side A	\\CCOCUS01LGRA\customerName.tblCustomerName
Side B	\\CCOCUS01LGRB\customerName.tblCustomerName

Within Database Lookup Explorer, a column must also be created for each column in the database table. In this example, three columns are created: accno, fname, and sname. The names of the columns must be identical to the column names in the database.

After the Database Lookup Explorer configuration is complete, the DB Worker processes should connect to the databases. Router A connects to the Side A database, and Router B connects to Side B.

Step 4: Simple Call Script and Testing

To retrieve data during a call, the DB Lookup node in Script Editor must be used. Figure 13-1 details a simple call-routing script that uses a Set node to configure peripheral variable 1 to equal the integer value of 1234. The script then checks that the database is online through the use of an IF node with a simple formula to check the "available" flag for the database.

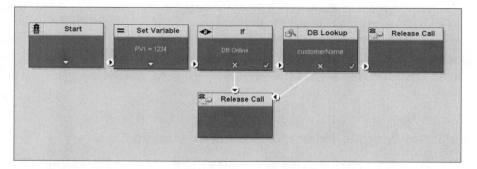

Figure 13-1   *Call Flow with DB Lookup Node*

When the DB Lookup node is called, the lookup value of 1234 is searched for in the accno column. This column is the primary key for the database, so each accno value should be unique. When the lookup value is found, the DB Lookup node returns the values of the fname and sname columns into their respective variables in the script. These values can then be used for further processing or perhaps delivered to the agent as a screen pop. In the example script, you simply release the call because you are only demonstrating the actual retrieval of the values.

Figure 13-2 shows the results of using the Script Editor Call Tracer tool to send a simulated call through the call script. It is clear to see the retrieved database values.

Figure 13-2 *Script Editor Call Tracer Output*

Summary

This chapter covered why data-driven routing should be used to enhance call routing and the callers' experience. Using an external corporate database or application to provide caller-specific data allows the contact center engineer to tailor the call flow and caller experience. This chapter introduced many of the methods available within UCCE to provide a data-driven call flow. In particular, the learning points from this chapter can be summarized as follows:

■ Cisco UCCE features many built-in methods that provide data-driven routing.

■ Agent screen pops, customized IVR applications, and data-driven routing can enhance the caller's experience of the contact center and also make life easier for the agent.

■ A simple database lookup can be easily configured, yet provides powerful routing enhancements.

Chapter 14

UCCE Databases

This chapter covers the following subjects:

- An introduction to relational databases

- An overview of the UCCE database schema

- A selection of useful SQL queries and ideas for UCCE administration

The Cisco Unified Contact Center Enterprise (UCCE) platform uses information stored in a series of relational databases to determine call routing and maintain a copy of the system configuration. The UCCE databases are integral to the correct functioning of the platform and should be administered with care. This chapter covers the following database aspects:

- **Relational databases:** What a relational database is and how the relationships are formed

- **UCCE databases:** What the different databases that make up the core UCCE platform are

- **Database schema overview:** An overview of the popular database tables used for troubleshooting and reporting

- **Example queries:** Several example queries used to retrieve common data requests

Relational Databases

A relational database consists of a collection of several two-dimensional tables, with each table containing unique rows and columns of data. A database record is stored as a single row of data of one or more columns. Tables are organized logically based on a particular purpose to minimize duplication and reduce data anomalies. Doing this reinforces data integrity by simplifying the way the data is defined. This process is called *normalization*.

Figure 14-1 shows an example of two tables, consisting of several columns.

Agent		
SkillTargetID	EnterpriseName	PeripheralNumber

Agent_Real_Time		
SkillTargetID	AgentState	AvailableInMRD

Figure 14-1   *Simple Example from a Relational Database*

Tables can be related to each other in a variety of ways with dependencies being formed when an attribute of one table relates to attributes of other tables. Within a relational database, several different relationships are possible. Table 14-1 details the four possible relationship types.

Tip   Many-to-one and many-to-many relationships can cause problems, so cross-reference tables are often used to reduce the relationships to one-to-many. An example of this within UCCE would be the relationship between agents and skill groups. An agent can be in several skill groups, and a skill group can contain many agents. Within UCCE, the tables ending in the name "Member" are cross-reference tables that can be used to simplify these relationships.

Figure 14-1 shows the relationship between both of the tables by using a *key* in each table. The key is an entity in a table that distinguishes one row of data from another. The key might be a single column, or it might consist of a group of columns that uniquely identifies a record. The key that links the two data records is of identical type and value.

The data stored in the databases is manipulated using a common programming language called Structured Query Language (SQL). A typical UCCE administrator need not understand SQL as all the UCCE tools or processes provide an interface between the user and the databases. A user should not attempt to directly alter any part of the UCCE database using SQL queries as this could have severe consequences on the integrity and functionality of the platform. However, performing read-only SQL queries can be useful when troubleshooting or performing reporting functions.

Tip   The core UCCE databases run on Microsoft SQL Server. Many books and tutorials exist that can teach the reader the basics of SQL and how to administer MS SQL Server.

Table 14-1 *Database Relationships*

Relationship	Description
One-to-one	This is the simplest relationship in which one record in a table is related to another record in a different table.
One-to-many	This relationship occurs when a record in one table has a relationship with multiple records in another table.
Many-to-one	Many-to-one is the reverse of the one-to-many relationship, with several records in one table being related to only a single record in another table.
Many-to-many	Many-to-many exists when more than one record in a table has a relationship with several records in another table.

UCCE Databases

An entire UCCE platform uses many different databases on various different components. Examples of these databases include the Cisco Unified Communications Manager (Unified CM) configuration and call detail records (CDR), the database that is used by Cisco Agent Desktop to store all the information relating to agent and workflow group configuration, and even custom databases that have been created for use during call-routing scripts to populate Computer Telephony Integration (CTI) data variables or influence call delivery destinations.

The central controllers at the core of the UCCE platform require only the logger database to function because this provides all the configuration data to the routers to process calls. To manage and configure the platform, the configuration database on the administration workstation (AW) is required. To store long-term reporting data, a Historical Data Server (HDS) database is necessary.

Table 14-2 provides an overview of the different databases found at the heart of a UCCE deployment. All three of these databases use Microsoft SQL Server.

Note For deployments that use Cisco WebView, a database is created that resides on the HDS. This database does not contain a copy of any reporting data. It is purely used to store the configuration data for WebView, such as a user's favorite reports and any scheduled reporting jobs.

Tip The Configuration-only Administration Server is used with the Customer Contact Management Portal (CCMP) and should not be confused with the administration client.

Table 14-2 *UCCE Databases*

Database	Purpose
Logger	The logger database is stored on both logger servers. The name of the database is of the format *<instance>*_Logger*<Side>*, where *<instance>* is the customer instance name and *<Side>* is either A or B. The logger database stores all the configuration data required for the routers to create an image of what the contact center looks like and describes how to handle route requests. The logger database also has a short-duration historical database that retains call records for a recent time period.
AW	The AW database contains a copy of the configuration data from the logger database. When a configuration tool makes a change to the settings used by UCCE, such as a change to a routing script or the addition of a new agent, the change takes place in the AW database and then is replicated back to the logger database. The AW database is also used for real-time reporting. The name of the AW database is of the format *<instance>*_awdb, where *<instance>* is the customer instance name. Not all AWs have a database. See Table 14-3 for a list of the five types of AW that were introduced in UCCE version 8.0.
Historical Data Server (HDS)	The HDS database is a store of long-term reporting and call detail records used when historic reports are created. Traditionally, the HDS database was always deployed on the same server as an AW, but several different deployment options were introduced with UCCE for enhanced scalability. The name of the HDS database is of the format *<instance>*_hds, where *<instance>* is the customer instance name.

Database Purge

Typically before UCCE software installation takes place, the contact center designer calculates an estimated database size for the logger and HDS databases. Several tools are available to make this estimation, and the results are based on the number of configuration items, such as the number of agents and skill groups, and on figures such as the expected number of call attempts and the duration for which the data should be retained. The database-sizing figures are just estimations as the contact center might grow or shrink in size as the business changes. It is therefore recommended that you factor in the expected growth when calculating the initial sizing.

Database problems can occur when a database reaches its full capacity. To prevent this from happening, the UCCE databases are configured with data purge settings to remove old data and prevent the database filling.

At a specified time (usually 0030 on a daily basis, although this can be changed if required), the purge process deletes old data from the database. Data is deemed to be old based on the specified retention period for the specific table to be purged. Table 14-4 details the default retention periods for the tables in the logger database. You can see that the majority of tables have a 14-day retention period, with some tables having a default of 30 days.

Table 14-3 *Administrative Workstation Types*

AW Name/Type	Purpose/Database
Administration Client	Ability to view and modify the UCCE configuration, but it has no database
Administration Server and Real-time Data Server (AW)	Configuration Real-time reporting
Configuration-only Administration Server	Configuration
Administration Server, Real-time and Historical Data Server, and Detail Data Server (AW-HDS-DDS)	Configuration Real-time and historical reporting Call detail extraction, call variable, and agent detail Cisco Unified Intelligence Suite Feed
Administration Server and Real-time and Historical Data Server (AW-HDS)	Configuration Real-time and historical reporting
Historical Data Server and Detail Data Server (HDS-DDS)	Historical reporting Call detail extraction, call variable, and agent detail Cisco Unified Intelligence Suite Feed

Note   You can also set purge cycles for the galaxy tables, but these settings have been omitted from this table.

The purge settings can be modified in the registry, but the more intuitive way is to run through web setup for the respective servers. Figures 14-2 and 14-3 display the data retention settings and purge settings during logger setup. If you change the settings on one logger, it is recommended that you also mirror the changes on the second logger.

Data retention periods for the HDS are typically much greater than for the logger, and usually run into several years rather than a number of days or weeks. The purge cycle will still run on a daily basis, however, and delete data that is older than the retention period.

Another purge mechanism that operates on the UCCE databases prevents the database from growing beyond 80 percent of capacity. Should a database grow beyond this size, system performance can degrade. The database-sizing purge also occurs on a daily basis at the scheduled purge time. Administrators should be aware that if the database is much greater than the 80 percent threshold, the purge process continues until the database capacity is back to below 80 percent.

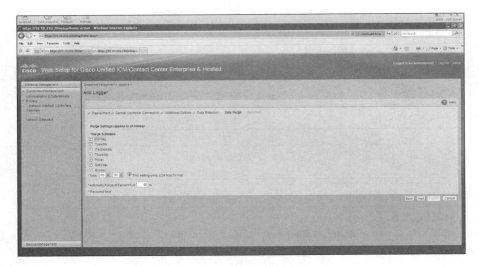

Figure 14-2   *UCCE Logger Data Retention Settings Defined During Web Setup*

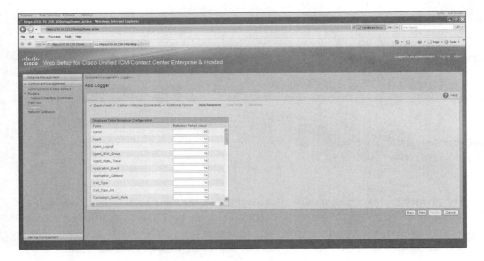

Figure 14-3   *UCCE Logger Data Purge Settings Defined During Web Setup*

Database Schema Overview

The *Database Schema Handbook for Cisco Unified ICM/Contact Center Enterprise and Hosted* (search for this title at Cisco.com) is a comprehensive document that details all the tables and their relationships for the Unified Intelligent Contact Manager (UICM) and UCCE platforms. This document discusses all the database tables that should be used for reporting purposes. Although the schema handbook uses the words *database tables*, the items discussed in the handbook are actually database views.

Table 14-4 *Default Logger Purge Cycle*

Table	Duration (Days)
Admin	30
Agent	14
Agent_Logout	14
Agent_Skill_Group	14
Agent_State_Trace	14
Application_Event	14
Application_Gateway	14
Call_Type	14
Call_Type_SG	14
Campaign_Query_Rule	14
Config_Message_Log	14
Dialer	14
EventDetail	14
Event	14
Import_Rule_History	30
Import_Log	14
Logger_Meters	14
Network_Event	14
Network_Trunk_Group	14
Peripheral	14
Persistent	30
Physical_Controller	14
Recovery	30
Route_Call_Detail	14
Route_Call_Variable	14
Route_Five_Minute	14
Route	14
Routing_Client_Five_Minute	14

Table 14-4   *Default Logger Purge Cycle*

Table	Duration (Days)
Schedule_Import	14
Script_Five_Minute	14
Service	14
Skill_Group_Five_Minute	14
Skill_Group	14
Skill_Group_Logout	14
Termination_Call_Detail	14
Termination_Call_Variable	14
Trunk_Group_Five_Minute	14
Trunk_Group	14

This can be confirmed through the use of the Microsoft SQL Server Management Studio. The tables discussed in the handbook can be found in the Views folder. The actual database tables are listed in the Tables folder. All tables that are prefixed with t_ are replicated as views in the Views folder. Several other tables also exist without the t_ prefix.

A table is a logically organized collection of related columns and rows. A view uses the same structure of related columns and rows but is actually created from one or more tables. The structure and data in a view could be a subset of a single table, an entire table, or an amalgamation of several tables. Views are useful for SQL queries that commonly join multiple tables. Rather than frequently performing a query spanning several tables, a view can be constructed that produces the required data on a regular basis. The user then creates simpler SQL queries against the view. Views also help ensure data integrity, as the data contained in the view is a one-way replication from the tables. Any accidental changes to the views will not affect the integrity of the data in the table. The view could then be reconstructed from the table, correcting the erroneous change.

Tip   Many contact centers use existing reporting methods in addition to WebView/CUIS, including tools such as Excel and MS Reporting Tools. Many of the people that create these non-Cisco-based reports have an understanding of contact center reporting but are not familiar with the UCCE database schema. Database views can be used to overcome this issue. A popular method is to have a scheduled stored procedure that performs an SQL query to export specific reporting data from multiple tables into a single view in another database. The reporting team then uses the sanitized data in the view for their reports.

SQL Queries

It is possible to fully administer a UCCE platform with the tools provided during software installation. However, occasionally it can be necessary to delve into the actual database tables to retrieve some useful information that cannot easily be found with the available toolset.

As all the data is contained in a SQL relational database, a SQL query tool is required to retrieve data. Cisco does not provide a tool to write SQL queries; this functionality is part of the toolkit available with MS SQL Server.

Tip For older UCCE installations that use MS SQL Server 2000, the installation of SQL Server also installed MS Query Analyzer. SQL queries can be executed in MS SQL Server 2005 using MS SQL Server Management Studio. This application is only installed if it is selected during SQL Server software installation.

You might want to write a SQL query against the UCCE databases for many reasons, such as the following:

- **Custom report creation:** Creating custom reports with WebView and Sybase InfoMaker requires a strong knowledge of how to manipulate data using SQL and a detailing understanding of the database schema.

- **Troubleshooting:** When troubleshooting problems with individual calls, the database schema contains two tables (Termination_Call_Detail and Route_Call_Detail) that can provide specific details about the individual call.

- **Reduction of manual effort:** Occasionally, you might be required to find out how certain items are configured, for example, which agents are configured with a certain agent desk setting. It would be possible to do this by stepping through each agent in Agent Explorer, but this would take considerable manual effort. A smarter solution would be to write an SQL query against the configuration database to return a list of the required agents.

Tip Unlike the UICM/UCCE databases, the Unified CM database is an Informix database and cannot be directly accessed with SQL queries. Instead, the Unified CM platform provides an application programming interface (API) called the Administrative XML Layer (AXL). The AXL API methods, known as requests, use a combination of HTTPS and Simple Object Access Protocol (SOAP). SOAP is an XML remote procedure call (RPC) protocol. Users perform requests by sending XML data to the Unified CM server. The server then returns the AXL response, which is also a SOAP message. The AXL SQL Toolkit is available for download from each Unified CM server and contains several SQL methods for accessing the Informix database.

Although writing SQL queries against the UCCE databases is a powerful method of retrieving data that you might be unable to easily find elsewhere, it is important to understand two basic rules that should be followed when accessing the data directly:

- **Do not modify the data.** The data contained in the databases should be considered as read-only. SQL provides several commands that can be used to modify data, but these commands should not be used against the UCCE databases. If you notice that a piece of configuration data is incorrect (for example, the spelling of an agent's name), use the specific UCCE tool to correct this mistake. Do not attempt to modify the database directly.

- **Do not attempt to retrieve extremely large amounts of data.** The UCCE databases support a live production platform and are in constant use by the UCCE software processes. Modest SQL queries can be executed against any of the databases without generating any performance impact. However, writing queries that return excessive amounts of data can have a negative impact on the system and should be avoided. It is often the most simple of queries that can have the biggest impact. For example, Select * from Termination_Call_Detail executed on an HDS database with 7 years of historical data would not be advisable!

The sections that follow examine several useful SQL queries that can be used when administering a UCCE platform. Some of these queries are written against the Termination_Call_Detail (TCD) table, so be careful not to specify too large a DateTime range.

Finding a Call with a Specific ANI

Occasionally, it will be necessary to find the details about a specific call that occurred on a certain day. Sometimes this call is the subject of a complaint, perhaps if the caller has complained that she has been in a queue for a long period of time or if she were extremely unhappy with the specific agent that handled her call. If the caller's Automatic Number Identification (ANI) is known, it is easy to find all the call details from the TCD table.

The SQL query detailed in Example 14-1 can be executed against the HDS database to quickly locate all the call details stored in TCD table. The DateTime range needs to be adjusted to approximately the time of the call, and the ANI value should be changed to reflect the ANI of the caller.

The result of the query returns all the columns from the TCD table for the specific record or records.

Example 14-1 *SQL Query to Locate a Call with a Specific ANI*

```
select * from Termination_Call_Detail
— Substitute the XXXX field for the specific ANI
where ANI = 'XXXXXXXXXX'
— Substitute for the correct DateTime range
and DateTime between '12/1/2010' and '12/31/2010'
```

Listing the Most Popular Callers by ANI

Many business units want to identify who their most frequent callers are and how many times they have called the business over a certain time period. The query in Example 14-2 returns the caller's ANI and the number of times he has called during the defined DateTime period. The query also specifies a list of the call type IDs that should be included in the search. This allows the returned data to be specific to certain business units. Increasing the value in the "having count(*) > 1" line allows the engineer to specify a minimum call frequency. Setting this value to 10, for example, would only return the callers who had made more than ten calls to the business.

Example 14-2   *SQL Query to List the Top Callers*

```
select ANI as CallerID, count(*) as CallFrequency
from Termination_Call_Detail
— Modify the DateTime range as required
where DateTime between '11/1/2010 00:00' and '11/30/2010 23:59'
— Modify the Call Type list to include only the required Call Types
and CallTypeID in (5518, 5519, 5523, 5525, 5526, 5527, 5529, 5531)
and ANI is not null
group by ANI
— Count > 1 to avoid listing single calls
having count(*) > 1
order by CallFrequency desc
```

Finding Unassigned Call Types

Call types are used for reporting purposes. In many cases, call types are mapped to a call script so that the call type changes as the call flows through the various scripts, giving the business analysts a more detailed view of the call flow in their reports. It is possible to define a Requalify Call Type node within a call-routing script but accidentally not associate the chosen call type with a script. This "hanging" call type would cause an error for any calls that reach it.

The query in Example 14-3 returns all the call types that are not associated with a call script. This can be used as a starting point when performing regular housekeeping and cleanup. However, it is important to note that not all call types should be mapped to a call script as some are used in the middle of a call script purely for reporting purposes.

Example 14-3   *SQL Query to Locate Unassigned Call Types*

```
select Call_Type.EnterpriseName as CallType from Call_Type
where CallTypeID  not in (
select CallTypeID from Call_Type_Map)
```

Finding DNs Associated with a Call Type

Dialed numbers (DN) often form a many-to-one relationship with call types. The simple query in Example 14-4 returns a list of the dialed number digits, the DN's description, and its associated call type.

Example 14-4   *SQL Query to Locate the DNs Associated with a Call Type*

```
select Dialed_Number.DialedNumberString as DN, Dialed_Number.Description as
'Description',
Call_Type.EnterpriseName as 'Call Type'
from Dialed_Number, Dialed_Number_Map, Call_Type
where Dialed_Number.DialedNumberID = Dialed_Number_Map.DialedNumberID
and Dialed_Number_Map.CallTypeID = Call_Type.CallTypeID
```

Locating Agents Against Agent Desk Settings

When creating an agent, it is necessary to allocate an agent desk setting value to the individual agent. Unfortunately, none of the configuration tools provide the UCCE administrator with an easy method of producing a list of all agents that are assigned a specific agent desk setting.

The query in Example 14-5 returns a grouped list of agents against their respective agent desk setting.

Example 14-5   *SQL Query to Locate Agents Against Agent Desk Settings*

```
select Agent.EnterpriseName,  Agent_Desk_Settings.EnterpriseName
from Agent, Agent_Desk_Settings
where Agent.AgentDeskSettingsID = Agent_Desk_Settings.AgentDeskSettingsID
group by Agent_Desk_Settings.EnterpriseName, Agent.EnterpriseName
```

Locating the Last Script Node

When troubleshooting call flow problems, it is often useful to know at which part of the call script the call failed. In Script Editor, it is possible to enable script node IDs, which assign an individual ID to each node within the call script. Figure 14-4 shows a call script with this enabled.

The Route_Call_Detail (RCD) table in the UCCE logger and HDS database stores records for every route request attempt made by the router process. The FinalObjectID column in this table lists the value of the last Call Script node that was executed before the call ended or failed.

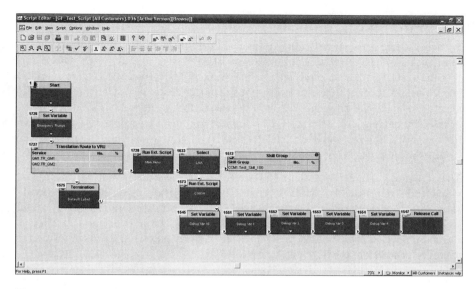

Figure 14-4 *Script Editor Call Flow with Node IDs Displayed*

When troubleshooting an individual call, it is possible to locate the call record in the RCD table and therefore obtain the FinalObjectID. Referencing this ID with the actual call script gives the UCCE administrator a good starting point for fault finding.

The SQL query in Example 14-6 was used to locate an individual RCD record for a caller with the ANI of 5015 within a specific DateTime period.

Example 14-6 *SQL Query to Locate the Last Node in the Call Script*

```
select DateTime, ANI, FinalObjectID
from Route_Call_Detail
where DateTime between '12/21/10 09:37' and '12/21/10 09:40'
and ANI = '5015'
```

Example 14-7 shows the results of the query. Using the value from the FinalObjectID column allows you to determine the final node the call passed through in the call script from Figure 14-4.

Example 14-7 *Results of the SQL Query to Locate the Last Node*

```
DateTime                 ANI
FinalObjectID
— — — — — — — — — —. — — — — — — — — — — — — — — — — — — — —.
2010-12-21 09:37:44.437 5015                             1573
(1 row(s) affected)
```

Agent State Trace

An agent's state is his current work status as defined through the agent software he is currently using to handle calls. For example, the READY state signifies to the UCCE router that the agent is available to receive a call. The Agent State Trace (AST) table is updated every time an agent changes state. For a busy contact center with a large number of agents, this table can grow quickly. For this reason, the Agent State Trace flag is not enabled by default. Instead, the UCCE administrator needs to enable AST for each agent individually. Cisco recommends that AST is used only for a small number of agents for troubleshooting purposes, and disabled when troubleshooting is complete.

The SQL query detailed in Example 14-8 returns the DateTime, Event Name, Reason Code, and Agent State for a specific agent. The query results detailed in Example 14-9 show the exact times that the agent changed state. Knowing this information is useful when troubleshooting issues where an agent did not receive an expected call. The *Database Schema Handbook* details the different agent states and events in relation to the values returned from the SQL query.

Tip   Enabling Agent State Trace can have a performance impact on the database, especially for contact centers with a large number of agents. Before making any changes that could have a potential performance impact, it is advisable to perform a baseline analysis of the current database performance. This can be achieved using the SQL Server performance counters available in Microsoft Perfmon. After a baseline has been established, future changes can be compared against the baseline to determine whether a negative impact occurred when the feature was enabled.

Example 14-8   *SQL Query to Display the Agent States*

```
select DateTime, EventName, ReasonCode, AgentState
from Agent_State_Trace
where DateTime > '12/21/10'
and SkillTargetID = '5665'
```

Example 14-9   *Results of the SQL Query to Find the Agent State*

```
DateTime                  EventName   ReasonCode   AgentState
-------------             ---------   ----------   ----------
2010-12-21 07:55:42.003 1               0            1
2010-12-21 07:55:42.010 1               0            1
2010-12-21 08:06:32.003 3               0            3
2010-12-21 08:07:15.000 8               0            8
2010-12-21 08:07:24.000 4               0            4
2010-12-21 08:08:39.000 6               0            6
2010-12-21 08:08:53.000 3               0            3
2010-12-21 08:17:35.000 9               0            4
```

```
2010-12-21 08:17:35.003 4            0            4
2010-12-21 08:17:37.000 3            0            3
2010-12-21 08:17:38.000 9            0            4
2010-12-21 08:17:38.003 4            0            4
2010-12-21 08:18:50.000 3            0            3
2010-12-21 08:22:54.000 2            33           2
```

Summary

This chapter examined the different uses of relational databases within the UCCE environment and on which servers these databases exist. The chapter concluded by working through a series of example SQL queries that can be used when administering UCCE. The learning points from this chapter can be summarized as follows:

- UCCE uses several different databases. The role of the database determines the type of data stored within it. Typically this type will be either configuration data, real-time data, or historic data

- SQL queries can be created against the relational databases to retrieve data that is difficult to find using the configuration tools or standard reports.

Chapter 15

Management and Administration

This chapter covers the following subjects:

- Roles of platform management and application administration
- Implementing backup procedures
- Real-time platform monitoring

After a Cisco Unified Contact Center Enterprise (UCCE) platform has been installed and is processing live call traffic, the deployment has transitioned into a fully operational state and is now typically supported by the end customer's IT department, with the Cisco partner providing third-line support.

With a large-scale deployment (for example, a service provider's hosted platform), several operational support teams can work together to manage the various different elements of the deployment. Each team can have a tightly defined role and consist of engineers specifically trained for the role they need to perform. With a smaller, single-customer enterprise deployment, the operational support team is likely to consist of employees who have multiple roles or support several platforms. Typically, these engineers have been present during the UCCE deployment, have attended various Cisco-approved training courses, and might have received knowledge transfer from the Cisco partner performing the initial installation.

Unless the platform has been deployed as a fully managed service, it is be the responsibility of these engineers to provide first- and second-line support after the platform has gone live.

The day-to-day tasks for these engineers can be split into two main activities:

- **Platform management:** This includes performing system backups, monitoring platform performance including hardware performance, monitoring software resource availability and capacity, planning for upgrades and applying service packs, and replacing faulty components when necessary.

■ **Application administration:** This includes general platform support for end users, creating new services to support business requirements, and ensuring that the platform configuration remains in a manageable state and that old configurations are removed.

It is important to distinguish between system administration and platform management. Application administration involves a range of activities including the provisioning of new configuration or configuration changes as the business changes. Often termed MACD (moves, adds, changes, and deletions), these changes typically involve adding new agents, administering call flow changes, and generating specific reports for business users. System administration could be considered to be "keeping the wheels turning" as seen from the end user, whereas platform management is more the art of "keeping the lights on." Without a fully working platform, the business cannot function, so it is imperative that the platform management and system administration are both performed correctly.

Platform Management

Platform management is an ongoing process with the sole aim of ensuring high reliability and high availability. The following sections look at some of the common causes of platform problems and describe what you can do to minimize the impact of these issues.

Potential Failures

All real-time IT systems are vulnerable to various different types of failure. When designed and deployed properly, UCCE performs as a highly redundant platform easily capable of surviving quite significant system failures. The required server specifications detailed in the bill of materials (BOM) call for the medium- to higher-end Microsoft Windows servers to have disks allocated as RAID arrays and dual power supplies. The deployment architecture of UCCE also requires software functions to be split over multiple servers. Even the network infrastructure on which UCCE is deployed will use diversely and redundant routed networks to support distributed process communication in the event of a network failure. Even with this level of redundancy, all platforms are susceptible to some form of failure. The most common failures are as follows:

■ **Loss of power:** Losing power to a system can take several forms. The most common is the malfunction of a server or network appliance power supply. Dual power supplies installed in servers and the use of Cisco Redundant Power System (RPS) for routers and switches can help minimize the potential for an outage. Loss of power on a large scale occurs when an entire building suffers a power outage because of a problem with the power company. Uninterruptible power supplies (UPS) and generators can be deployed to allow the company to gracefully shut down the systems.

■ **Disk crash:** The space available on storage devices has grown exponentially over the past decade. Disk drives are physically smaller than ever, and their capacity is huge. Coupled with a low price point, this gives the platform management team the potential to deploy multiple disk arrays and distribute the system data so that the failure of a single disk does not result in any data loss. Many of the servers supported by

UCCE also support hot-swappable disks, allowing an engineer to swap out the failed disk and enabling the server to automatically rebuild the data on the new disk.

- **Network failure:** A network failure can occur because of several reasons. Sometimes the failure of a physical device such as a switch or router can affect part of the network. It is therefore important that when planning and deploying a UCCE platform, the architect use multiple redundant network components to account for the loss of a device. The majority of the UCCE core servers can have several network connections, typically one for the public and one for the private network, which should be distributed over multiple switches. Occasionally, WANs fail and affect the link between both sides of the UCCE platform. Having diversely routed links to split the private and public traffic reduces this risk.

- **Failed upgrade:** The software lifecycle dictates that all platforms require regular updates to remain current and error-free. Updates regularly contain fixes to known problems but can also contain enhancements and features unavailable in previous versions. With a distributed platform like UCCE, an engineer is often required to deploy the new software release over multiple servers using a predetermined upgrade methodology. Occasionally, software upgrades can go wrong. This can occurs for a number for reasons, such as if the engineer did not follow the instructions correctly, the software image was corrupted, or another process running on the server prevented the software from being applied correctly.

- **Human error:** Not all issues are caused by hardware or software failures. Many issues are caused by accident when a human operator performs a task that he should not have, such as the accidental deletion of a part of a configuration that is important to the system or accidentally shutting down a server instead of logging out. As many UCCE administrators know, it is actually quite hard to delete configuration items from UCCE as they always seem to be referenced by another part of the configuration, and you will often see an error message to say that the item cannot be deleted. However, it is easier to accidentally reassign call types to different scripts or make changes that can have a negative impact on the contact center.

- **Malicious intent:** Unfortunately, not all engineers use their skills for the greater good. There exists a minority of people determined to cause problems for IT departments by creating malicious software designed to attack IT systems. Computer hacking and viruses can cause issues for IT platforms. Cisco provides extensive guidelines on platform security to greatly reduce the chance of being affected by a malicious attack. Several tools, including Cisco Security Agent and server hardening, should be deployed and are specific to UCCE.

Much of the impact caused by the problems detailed in the preceding list can be reduced by having a proper system backup and monitoring strategy in place.

Backups

Software backups are an essential part of platform management. With so many servers, applications, and databases it would be a common mistake to assume that the entire UCCE platform is required to be backed up. In reality, because of the distributed and replicated nature of UCCE, it is possible to restore and rebuild an entire system from relatively few backups.

Cisco no longer recommends any specific backup software in the bill of materials to perform a full server backup. The most critical part of any restoration process is the actual database data and application configuration items. With many organizations having standard server rebuild processes and the inevitable shift toward server virtualization (whereby servers can be subjected to a snapshot image and restored quickly), some organizations prefer not to perform a full server backup using third-party backup tools. These companies have a quick rebuild process that allows a new Windows server with the required name, network configuration, and database applications to be installed rapidly, even on new hardware if required. After this is complete, the UCCE software is installed and any service packs are applied. If necessary, database backups are restored using the Microsoft SQL Server tools, or the database is synchronized from another UCCE server.

As a minimum, you should strongly consider the following UCCE components to be subject to a frequent backup strategy:

- **UCCE server software:** Each of the core server components, such as the logger, router, real-time distributor administrative workstation (AW), historical AW, and peripheral gateways should receive an operating system backup that includes the UCCE application installed on that server. As discussed previously, there are various ways to implement this type of backup depending on whether the server is physical or virtual.

- **UCCE registry keys:** During the installation of the UCCE software, the local server has different registry keys set based on the options chosen during setup. Should a server need to be restored, these registry settings are vital for the platform to remain functional. Many third-party backup tools allow the administrator to include registry keys as part of the backup. The UCCE Support Tools application also allows the administrator to perform a manual backup of the UCCE registry keys.

- **UCCE databases:** The UCCE platform contains three key types of databases: the AW DB, the logger DB, and the Historical Data Service (HDS) DB. It is not necessary to back up the AW database as the data it contains can be generated from the logger DB. Either or both of the logger DBs can be backed up as these databases are duplicated with a Side A and Side B, and either side can be used to recover the other side. Although it is common practice to have multiple HDSs, the databases are not synchronized using the Side A / Side B mirroring process used by the loggers. The HDS database can also grow to a considerable size depending on how the database purge cycle is set. All HDS databases should receive a backup.

In addition to the preceding backups, you should strongly consider implementing the following backup strategies:

- **ICMDBA export:** Use the ICM Database Administration (ICMDBA) tool to export a backup of the configuration of the Side A logger. The exported configuration is usually quite small and can easily fit on a CD/DVD or USB drive. Although it is not possible to fully restore an entire platform from the ICMDBA export, it is possible to rebuild the core platform if necessary.

- **Installation spreadsheet:** When planning a UCCE deployment, it is common practice to create a spreadsheet that details all the options set during the initial installation. An installation spreadsheet is useful if a server needs to be rebuilt and a recent registry key backup is unavailable. The spreadsheet should also include a list of the software version, service pack revisions, and any engineering specials that are installed on each server.

- **Backup-related servers and applications:** Cisco Unified Communications Manager (Unified CM), IP Interactive Voice Response (IP IVR), and Customer Voice Portal (CVP) should all be part of the regular backup schedule, as should the Cisco Agent Desktop (CAD) servers, WebView database, WebView custom templates, and copies of the voice gateway/switch/router running config.

- **Rebuild software pack:** Have a software server share, set of DVDs, or source available to rebuild the server. The software pack should include all the installation media, service packs, engineering specials, and third-party tools required. You should also assume that you might not have access to the Internet during the rebuild. I have been caught before when vendors' websites have been unavailable because of a maintenance period.

Note If you perform a manual backup of the registry keys on each server, ensure that you copy all the Cisco registry hives. Depending on the Cisco software installed on the server, not all the applications are under a single Cisco hive. Occasionally, you might see two or more different Cisco hives with slightly different names.

Platform Monitoring

Managing a large distributed platform can be a daunting task to the inexperienced engineer. Without the correct tools and systems in place, the effort required to perform this monitoring is incredibly time-consuming. The aim of platform monitoring is to not only ensure that all the servers, network appliances, and applications are up and running but to also ensure that they perform optimally. With a distributed and resilient platform like UCCE, without any monitoring in place, an end customer might be unaware that part of the platform might have failed as the platform has automatically continued processing and is now running in partial service.

With so many servers, applications, and their subprocesses, it would be an impossible task for an engineer to frequently check each part of the system for issues. Fortunately, the Simple Network Management Protocol (SNMP) was developed in the late 1980s as a standard protocol for monitoring devices on an IP network.

SNMP

Consider a simplex UCCE lab deployment as an example. The simplex solution has only a single logger and a single router. If the lab deployment consisted of several test agents receiving calls and the router process failed, you would have an instantly visible idea that a fault had occurred. You would not necessarily immediately know that the router had failed, but you would see that call traffic had ceased and probably that the agents had been logged out. An investigation of all the UCCE servers would result in the discovery of the failed router.

Now consider the example of a full-duplex UCCE deployment distributed over multiple sites. Assume that one of the router processes fails. This time, however, the opposite side router process is actually processing calls in parallel, so the calls continue, and there are no obvious signs to the agents or administrators of a fault. Although this resilience is great from an engineering point of view, that a part of the system has failed needs to be communicated to the platform management team.

The use of SNMP allows a system to autonomously report problems to a central management system without the need for human intervention. SNMP uses two entities to perform notification—SNMP agents and SNMP managers. A manager or Network Management Station (NMS) is typically one or more servers that host the SNMP management software responsible for handling the management tasks for the platform being monitored. The agent is a piece of software that runs on the individual devices or servers being monitored.

The NMS is responsible for querying an agent to find out information. This query process is called *polling*. The NMS can also receive information sent to it directly from the agent without a poll; this message is called a *trap*. The NMS performs actions based on the information received during polling or when a trap is received. The actions usually take the form of notifying a human that a potential error has occurred. Modern NMSs support various notification methods, including on-screen alerts, email, and SMS.

Figure 15-1 details the polling request generated from the NMS and the associated response. It also shows a one-way trap message sent from the agent to the NMS.

Within a UCCE environment, SNMP polling is often performed by the NMS to query performance metrics about the individual servers on which the UCCE applications run. These metrics are general server statistics, including memory and disk usage, CPU utilization, and network card performance. UCCE can generate a range of SNMP traps when errors or informational alerts occur. Trap sending is managed by the Customer Support Forwarding Service (CSFS) process that runs on the logger after being enabled in the UCCE setup. Figure 15-2 shows the logger receiving notification messages from the other UCCE nodes and generating a trap that is sent to the NMS by the Cisco SNMP agent.

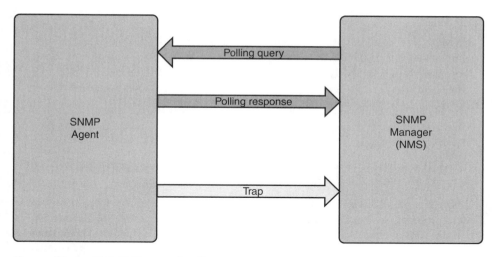

Figure 15-1   *SNMP Trap and Polling*

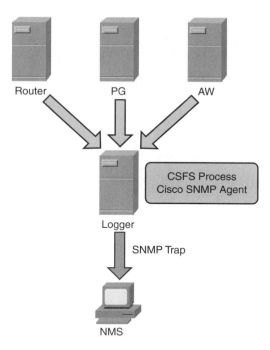

Figure 15-2   *SNMP Trap Flow from Logger to NMS*

SNMP MIBs

SNMP is a standard defined by the Internet Engineering Task Force (IETF), and as such, the standardization of SNMP ensures that it can be implemented across many applications and platforms. SNMP uses a standard definition called the Structure of Management Information (SMI) to define objects and their associated behavior.

The Management Information Base (MIB) is similar in structure to a database of managed objects that are tracked by the agent. The managed objects represent the status and information about the agent.

The SMI provides a mechanism to define the managed objects, whereas the MIB is the actual definition of the object.

Many generic MIBs exist that can be used by vendors. For example, MIBs exist for standard protocols such as Domain Name System (DNS) and Frame Relay and server statistics such as CPU, memory, or uptime. Therefore, the vendor is not required to create a new MIB if the generic MIB is sufficient. However, many products have custom features or functions that are not covered by the generic MIB but still require monitoring. When this happens, the vendor creates a proprietary MIB that implements the objects required for his specific product.

UCCE has a proprietary MIB called CISCO-CONTACT-CENTER-APPS-MIB that can be found in the *<drive>*:\icm\snmp folder after installation.

The creators of the Cisco Contact Center Apps MIB have gone into great detail to explain all the different objects contained in the MIB. I would recommend that any engineer who is implementing UCCE monitoring should open the MIB with a text editor and read through the comprehensive descriptions of each defined object. Example 15-1 details a managed object that was extracted from the MIB and that can be used to determine the number of agents logged on.

Example 15-1 *Example MIB Object*

```
cccaRouterAgentsLoggedOn OBJECT-TYPE
SYNTAX          Gauge32
UNITS           "agents"
MAX-ACCESS      read-only
STATUS          current
DESCRIPTION
    "The router agents logged on object represents the number of
    contact center agents currently managed by the enterprise
    contact center application.  This does not necessarily
    represent the number of contact center agents that can receive
    routed calls, but rather the number of agents for which the
    application is recording statistical information."
::= { cccaRouterEntry 3 }
```

The CISCO-CONTACT-CENTER-APPS-MIB needs to be installed on the NMS that will be used to poll the UCCE platform and receive traps. Without the MIB installed, the NMS will be unable to interpret the message data contained in the SNMP packets.

After the MIB is installed and compiled, each possible trap should be configured and assigned a behavior based on its severity. This can be quite a lengthy process depending on the chosen NMS.

Note The Cisco Contact Center Apps MIB actually requires the installation of several other MIBs before it compiles. Some of these are standard MIBs that might already be present in your chosen NMS, and others might be specific Cisco MIBs. The additional required MIBs are detailed in the IMPORTS section of the MIB, or usually the NMS prompts you with the names of the missing MIBs during attempted installation.

You can find Cisco MIBs at http://www.cisco.com/public/sw-center/netmgmt/cmtk/mibs.shtml.

Enabling SNMP and SYSLOG

Traps are sent from the UCCE logger to the NMS by the Cisco SNMP Agent Management. The SNMP agent is installed during UCCE setup and needs to be configured before use. The SNMP agent is configured with the Microsoft Management Console (MMC) (<Windows root>\System32\mmc.exe) by following these steps:

Step 1.   Open the Microsoft Management Console.

Step 2.   Choose **File > Add/Remove Snap-in**.

Step 3.   Click the **Add** button, and a new window appears with a list of available snap-ins.

Step 4.   Highlight the **Cisco SNMP Agent Management** snap-in and click **Add**.

Step 5.   Click **Close** and **OK**. The MMC should now have the snap-in displayed, as shown in Figure 15-3.

Note The installation steps for the Cisco SNMP Agent Management snap-in can also be applied to all the Cisco voice servers that run Microsoft Windows, including CVP, IP IVR, and version 4.X CallManagers.

After the SNMP snap-in has been installed in the MMC, it needs to have some basic configuration applied for it to send SNMP traps to the NMS. Many of the fields are already populated using default values. Table 15-1 describes the essential items to configure.

UCCE and the Cisco SNMP agent also support Syslog. Like SNMP, Syslog is also a standards-based tool that allows the logging of application messages. Although the syslog messages are generated in real time by UCCE, Syslog is typically used as a record of events that occurred rather than being a terminal that is watched by the support team.

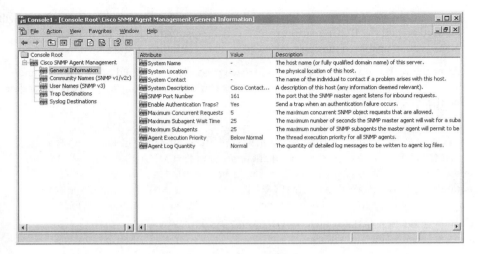

Figure 15-3   *MMC with Cisco SNMP Agent Management*

Table 15-1   *Cisco SNMP Agent Configuration*

Attribute	Description
Community names (SNMP v1/v2c)	SNMP versions 1 and 2 use a name string that is transmitted in plain text to group devices. The device can also be configured to have SNMP read or read/write access. Enabling write access allows other devices to make changes by only knowing the community string. This can be a security risk as the community string is unencrypted and carried over the network in plain-text format.
Usernames (SNMP v3)	SNMP version 3 requires specific user accounts with passwords to be created to access the SNMP information. This authentication is encrypted rather than being transmitted in plain text.
Trap destinations	The Trap Destinations section allows the engineer to define the IP address of one or more NMSs along with the version of SNMP in use.
Syslog destination	Use this to enable the Syslog feature to export syslog messages to an external server.

Benefits of Using SNMP

After SNMP is installed and configured, the NMS becomes an integral part of platform support. Frequent polling of the UCCE servers coupled with the instant notification of failures through SNMP traps provides the support team with a comprehensive view of what is actually happening within the UCCE environment. The flexibility of SNMP enables almost any aspect of the UCCE platform to be monitored with the data captured and stored over a period of time to establish a baseline. The most common monitored items are as follows:

■ **Server performance:** General server statistics, including CPU utilization, pagefile memory usage, available disk storage, NIC utilization, and server temperature.

■ **UCCE node and process availability:** SNMP traps are sent if a UCCE node such as the router terminates or if individual processes within the node terminate. Should the latter occur, the Node Manager will attempt to restart the process, but notification that this failure occurred is still important.

■ **UCCE resource usage:** Includes the number of calls in progress, agents logged in, and database storage.

Application Administration

The application administrator has different monitoring requirements to the platform management team. Although the administrator requires that the underlying platform is available and functioning correctly, she is more concerned that the system configuration is performing as required by the business teams.

The application administrator is typically concerned about the correct routing of calls, thereby ensuring that calls are not being dropped by the platform or accidentally delivered to a script or resource where the call could never be answered correctly. The administrator is also often interested in resource utilization, such as the number of calls in progress at an IVR or on a trunk.

An important role of the application administrator is to provide feedback to the contact center manager when he observes changes that could be made to enhance the performance of the platform. Rather than using network-monitoring tools like SNMP, the application administrator typically uses the client tools available within the UCCE Administration Tools. One of the most useful of these tools is the Router Log Viewer.

The Router Log Viewer, as shown in Figure 15-4, is a standalone application found on an administrative workstation. The main window has two panes, with the upper pane showing all the calls in near real time as they are processed by the router. The lower pane displays errors as they occur.

The common errors that are seen in Router Log Viewer are generated when the router cannot return a destination label for the call. In most cases, the error message shown in the Router Log Viewer is self-explanatory and leads to a swift resolution of the problem.

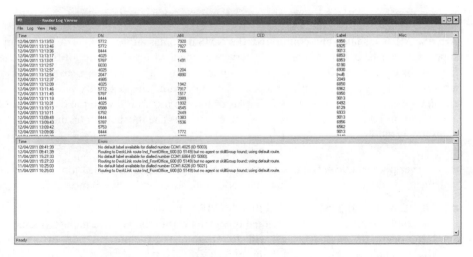

Figure 15-4   *Router Log Viewer*

Within the System Information tool in Configuration Manager, it is possible to define a default call type for error handling. It is good practice to run a WebView report against this call type on a regular basis to see whether calls have been routed to it. If calls have been delivered to the default, it is possible to search through the Route_Call_Detail and Termination_Call_Detail tables in the HDS database to determine more information about the call and why the fault occurred, and to potentially prevent the fault from happening again.

WebView can also be used to produce real-time and historical reports for resource utilization on items such as the services used for translation-routing calls to IVRs.

Summary

This chapter covered different types of platform failures and their causes, how you can guard against a prolonged service outage by taking different platform backups, and the monitoring options available with SNMP. In particular, the learning points from this chapter can be summarized as follows:

■   Cisco UCCE is inherently resilient and can survive many different failure scenarios when deployed correctly.

■   The higher-end servers often have features that enhance reliability, such as dual power supplies and RAID arrays.

■   Various different backup strategies can be deployed to allow a quick platform recovery.

■   SNMP platform monitoring should be used.

Chapter 16

Troubleshooting

This chapter covers the following subjects:

■ What troubleshooting is and why you need it

■ A generic troubleshooting approach

■ Various tools and techniques to be used while troubleshooting issues

Integrating Unified Communications (UC) products that support voice, video, and data over a diverse IP network is a challenging task, both for deployment and management. The level of service the UC products provide to its users and to the end customers contacting the organization depends on the health and status of the underlying platform applications and the IP network on which they are based.

To ensure that these platform service levels are attained, the Cisco Unified Contact Center Enterprise (UCCE) support engineer must be aware of the range of management tools used by each of the components that make up UCCE. Many of these tools are specific to an individual component, with the UCCE support engineer potentially having to use several different tools to perform successful troubleshooting.

Troubleshooting is a logical and systematic process that is followed when trying to solve a problem, typically relating to a fault. Troubleshooting a fresh UCCE installation or upgrade can encompass a wide range of different faults usually caused by interoperability issues or misconfiguration. General business as usual troubleshooting of an established contact center platform is usually focused around agent problems, such as being unable to log in, or contact routing issues as call flow scripts are modified.

This chapter examines how to approach an issue or fault and describes the different tools and techniques available when troubleshooting UCCE.

A key problem found by engineers when troubleshooting a distributed platform such as UCCE is that the engineer must frequently use many different tools to capture logging information from multiple systems to diagnose the fault. UCCE is also guilty of this. However, Cisco has worked hard to develop a serviceability framework shared by all the

Unified Communications components (Unified Communications Manager [Unified CM], UCCE, Customer Voice Portal [CVP], and Unified Contact Center Express [UCCX]) to set tracing levels and collect troubleshooting data through a single user interface. This tool, covered later in the chapter, is called Analysis Manager.

In addition to reactive troubleshooting, proactive monitoring should take place to pre-warn the support team of any impending problems. Chapter 15, "Management and Administration," covers UCCE platform monitoring in detail.

Fault Logging and Handling

All medium to large enterprises (and many small companies, too) have a dedicated IT support team that manages the IT infrastructure used by the organization. With the convergence of voice and data technologies, many companies have seen their voice and data groups merge into a single team capable of supporting a wide range of communications platforms.

In addition to having a dedicated communications team, large organizations also have many other teams that are assigned to the other technologies in use. These teams typically include a server infrastructure team, desktop support, and assorted applications specialists.

For office users to raise problems with these IT teams, the organization typically has a first-line support team that answers the initial fault call, logs the necessary fault details and contact information, and in some cases, even diagnoses the fault with the caller. If unable to resolve the issue, the first-line support team passes the fault onto a specialist for fault resolution. Table 16-1 explains a typical tiered support model.

Fault Logging

During my time spent working with UCCE, I have also performed the role of second- and third-line support. One of the greatest pains experienced during these roles is when the fault description documented by the first-line engineer is incredibly vague or does not contain information of any use. I have regularly seen fault descriptions that are little more than the comment "A user is having a telephone problem."

Faults logged with this type of fault description are incredibly frustrating for a skilled engineer as they clearly demonstrate that the first-line engineer has not performed his role correctly and is simply passing the fault on without even trying to resolve the issue.

The simplest method of ensuring that the first-line support team obtains the correct information is for them to work from a script or prepared series of questions to ask the caller when the fault is reported. The caller might not have all the answers, but the first-line engineer should still be prepared to ask the questions and uncover as much fault-specific information as possible.

Table 16-1   *Tiered Support Model*

Tier	Description
First-line	First-line, or front-line, support is usually performed by a team that has a wide range of technical skills, but perhaps possibly not the depth of knowledge to solve complex issues centered around a specific technology. The first role of the first-line support engineer is to document the caller's information and determine the type of issue that the caller is experiencing. Many straightforward problems, such as password resets, are resolved by the first-line support engineer. For issues where the solution is outside the knowledge of first line, the engineer typically escalates the fault to a specialist second-line team.
Second-line	Most organizations have several second-line support teams, with each team having a specific technical or product focus rather than the generic approach employed by the first-line team. The second-line technical support team contains more experienced and knowledgeable personnel. The second-line engineer uses the details collected by the first-line team as a starting point when attempting to diagnose the fault. It is therefore important that the first-line engineer perform a thorough capture of the relevant information. Otherwise, the second-line engineer might waste valuable time having to request that more information is provided, or might have to directly contact the person who raised the fault to obtain the required data. Many of the issues escalated to the second-line team can be problems that have occurred before and solutions already exist. However, if new, time-consuming, or complex issues have been found, the second-line team has the opportunity to escalate the issue to tier three.
Third-line	Third-line or tier three is the highest level of support responsible for handling the most complex or advanced issues. The tier-three engineers typically have access to lab equipment or additional tools that can be used when troubleshooting issues. The engineers that make up the third-line team are also unlikely to exclusively perform a support role; perhaps as much as half of their time is spent performing research or product deployments elsewhere. When an organization engages with a Cisco UC partner, the role of third-line support is likely to be performed by the partner. The partner also has direct access to the Cisco Technical Assistance Center (TAC). This gives the partner the ability to query the Cisco TAC knowledge base and raise TAC cases if necessary.

The answers to the questions should be documented in the fault management software shared by the support teams. Many fault-logging applications have the capability to use structured forms for simple data entry.

An added benefit of using a fault management platform is that solutions to frequent issues can be turned into a knowledge base, therefore allowing the first-line team to search through the knowledge base and potentially solve the issue without having to escalate to the specialist support teams. This provides a quicker fault resolution and better customer service to the caller. Many fault management platforms also have the capability to create reports about specific areas that faults have been raised against. This information can be used by the business to understand whether certain products and services are having a large number of specific issues and whether they are technical problems or whether they can be solved through better training for the end users.

When documenting a fault, the first-line support engineer should determine the following:

- A problem statement detailing the users and products or platforms affected by the issue.

- A problem analysis of the user's experience. For example, is it a major issue preventing the user from performing any work?

- An analysis of the impact the issue is causing. This could include details of how often the fault is occurring.

- Details, if known, of what is causing the problem and when the problem first occurred. For example, does the fault occur every time the user performs a certain action?

Note One thing that always concerns me is whether to have the first-line support team's service on the same contact center platform as the one it supports. The obvious potential downside for not doing this is that if the UCCE platform goes down, it will be difficult for users to report any faults to the first-line support team. I have seen this problem happen in more than one organization, and it is often a point of embarrassment for the communications team.

Cisco Technical Assistance Center (TAC)

The Cisco Technical Assistance Center provides 24/7 support throughout the world for the entire range of Cisco products and services. The major global support centers are complemented by many satellite and regional centers of excellence. Cisco TAC usually becomes involved when the end customers and their partners cannot resolve an issue. However, Cisco TAC is not just there to provide vendor support for product faults. The Cisco TAC website and its tools provide a wealth of knowledge and documentation that can be used at all the different stages of a product's lifecycle.

Should a fault be raised with Cisco TAC, the TAC engineer uses Cisco tools, including WebEx, to share desktops and gain access to the customer's platform to investigate the fault and retrieve log files if required.

Occasionally, the issues cannot be fixed by the TAC engineer and require the input and potential development skills of the Cisco engineering departments. For UCCE-specific problems, the engineering resources of the Cisco Contact Center Business Unit (CCBU) would get involved.

The Cisco TAC also has access to a series of virtual worldwide laboratories that can be used to replicate a customer's environment to try and reproduce faults and for testing purposes.

When a TAC case is raised, it is assigned a priority from one of four severity levels. These four levels are detailed in Table 16-2, reproduced from the Global Cisco Technical Services Guide.

Table 16-2   *Cisco TAC Severity Levels*

Severity	Definition
Severity 1 (S1)	Your network or environment is down, or there is a critical impact on your business operations. You and Cisco will commit all necessary resources around the clock to resolve the situation.
Severity 2 (S2)	The operation of an existing network or environment is severely degraded, or significant aspects of your business operation are negatively affected. You and Cisco will commit considerable resources during normal business hours to resolve the situation.
Severity 3 (S3)	The operational performance of your network or environment is impaired, while most business operations remain functional. You and Cisco are willing to commit resources during normal business hours to restore service to satisfactory levels.
Severity 4 (S4)	You require information or assistance with Cisco product capabilities, installation, or configuration. There is little or no effect on your business operations.

Note   Often after you have raised a TAC case and the issue has been resolved, you might receive an email survey offering you the chance to give feedback on how your TAC case was handled. The results of these surveys have a direct effect on the performance reviews of the TAC engineer who handled your case. If the TAC engineer did a good job, please reward him with good feedback.

Troubleshooting Methodology

Many different troubleshooting methodologies exist. A popular model that the Cisco TAC engineers follow is the Kepner-Tregoe analytical troubleshooting methodology. This methodology provides a logical framework for troubleshooting that can be enhanced and adapted for specific technologies.

The role of a troubleshooting methodology is to provide a clear, concise framework that gives the support engineer a logical flow for information gathering and problem solving.

The methodology needs to be rigid enough that it can be repeatable and be taught to junior engineers, yet be flexible enough to adapt to problems that occur outside of normal boundaries.

Key Point   A specific troubleshooting methodology should not be forced on an individual or team. Often skilled support engineers will adapt a troubleshooting approach to their specific style of troubleshooting. More often than not, this hybrid approach can be more successful as it has been adapted to be more relevant to the underlying technology.

A generic troubleshooting methodology could consist of the following steps:

1. Understand what the perceived problem is. This can be achieved by reading through the trouble ticket if one has been raised by a user. Hopefully the trouble ticket will contain specific details of the fault if it has been documented correctly. Occasionally, it might be necessary to contact the user directly to obtain further information.

2. Create a list of concerns. While beginning to understand the fault, it might be evident that this could be part of a larger issue about to manifest itself.

3. Sometimes the reported fault can actually be several issues that have happened simultaneously. If this is the case, a good approach is to separate the faults into individual issues. This makes the fault easier to deal with. Should the individual issues be of considerable size, it is probably worth raising further trouble tickets for each of the issues. Doing this assists with fault tracking and management.

4. If the fault were raised by a user, the user is likely to have requested a specific priority or urgency to the fault. This priority level should be evaluated and reassigned to a different priority if required. This step is important for busy or small support teams that are likely to be investigating several faults simultaneously.

5. Plan and schedule the next steps, and then allocate resources as required. Simple faults such as locked accounts or password resets could be allocated to junior resources.

6. Explore the knowledge base. All previous issues and their resolution processes should be documented in a knowledge base. Therefore, solutions to common issues should already be available to the support engineer.

7. If the issue is previously unseen, an investigatory process needs to take place to determine the cause of the fault. Table 16-3 details some specific areas of investigation for UCCE. Investigation requires the use of available tools and techniques. This can be considerably complex depending on the type of fault.

8. After the issue has been diagnosed, ideally the support engineer will be in a position to prove how the fault occurs. This proof can be through the ability to reproduce the issue on demand.

Table 16-3   *UCCE Troubleshooting Investigation*

Approach	Description
Know the UCCE toolset.	This chapter details a small subset of the tools available with UCCE that can assist when troubleshooting issues. As a support engineer, you should be aware of these tools and have used them in anger before a problem occurs. If you find yourself reading the instructions for how to use these tools while trying to fix a priority 1 fault, you could potentially slow the fault resolution process.
Understand the fault escalation process.	UCCE is a large platform with many areas of integration for several different products. It would be difficult for a single person to be extremely knowledgeable in all aspects of UCCE. This is where your Cisco partner should be used if you cannot fix the issue yourself. You should familiarize yourself with the process required to escalate a fault to your Cisco partner and understand how it will be dealt with and the potential access requirements they might have to your system.
Understand the UCCE process integration.	Many problems can be solved through an understanding of how the processes communicate with each other. Knowledge of the communication paths allows the support engineer to quickly narrow down to components, nodes, or processes that might be causing the issue.
Know your platform.	At the heart of UCCE, nearly all the deployments share the same components. However, at the scripting or application layer, every UCCE deployment is different. Many faults that occur are related to scripting or configuration changes that have an adverse impact elsewhere on the platform. This type of fault can be prevented only when the engineers involved have a thorough understanding of their UCCE environment.

9. After the root cause of the issue has been identified, the next step is to find a solution and create an action plan. Often issues can be solved with many solutions; therefore, a low-risk solution might be required. Before implementing a solution, the support engineer should assess the impact of the proposed solution to ensure that it does not adversely affect other areas of the platform. Occasionally, a low-risk solution is only a short-term fix and what is actually required is an overhaul that has a higher risk and impact. Situations like these should be assessed as a team and are likely to involve a representative from the management structure as the solution might need to implemented as a project. As example of this could be the deployment of a software upgrade to several servers.

10. After the solution has been implemented, a series of tests should be conducted, first to determine whether the solution resolved the issue and second to ensure that the solution did not negatively impact other areas of the platform.

11. When proven to be successful, the original trouble ticket can be closed and the knowledge base updated with details of the solution. Operating procedures or other documentation might also need to be updated.

Tip Occasionally, a large service-affecting fault will happen, and the initial instinct of all support engineers is to resolve the fault as quickly as possible. It is good practice to get a copy of all the logs for the fault window before attempting to fix the fault. Using an application such as the Support Tools Dashboard makes this a relatively quick process. You should do this immediately because the log files can overwrite quite quickly in a busy contact center, meaning that you might be in a position where you cannot later determine what caused the fault.

UCCE Process Tracing

Nearly all the processes running on a UCCE node have an individual process window that details what the process is currently doing. The textual content within the process window is known as a trace output and can be considered to be a running log of the tasks that the process has performed and is currently attempting to perform. Figure 16-1 shows a snapshot from a Unified CM Peripheral Interface Manager (PIM) that has just started and has gone into an active state. By default, the process windows show 25 lines of text output. The sizing and fonts used for each process window can be tailored if required, but often the information the support engineer is looking for is not displayed in the current window as it is likely to have scrolled by previously because the window is constantly being updated as the process performs more tasks.

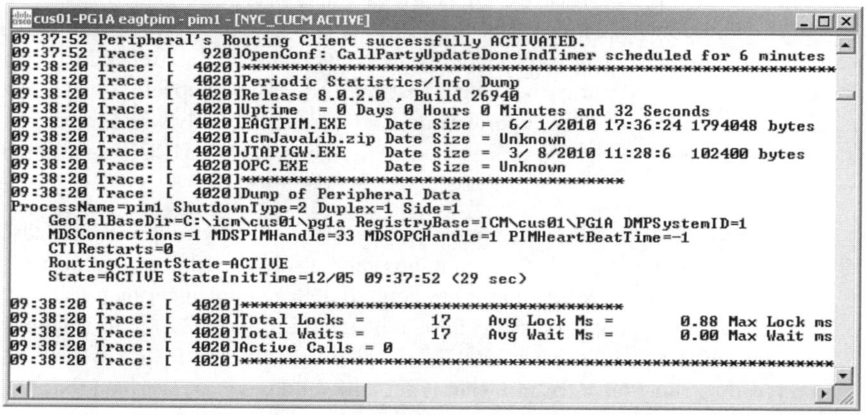

Figure 16-1 *Typical Process Window with Tracing*

The tracing output reveals a lot of information about the health of the process. When used in conjunction with the output from several processes, the support engineer can determine the health of the overall UCCE platform; therefore, the tracing output is frequently used when troubleshooting problems. Typical information that can be obtained from tracing includes the following:

- **Process startup information:** Each time a process starts, it displays data including the software version and connectivity to other processes. Many of the processes require the download of configuration data from other processes or databases; the status of this download is often displayed.

- **Periodic data updates:** Several processes, such as the peripheral gateways (PG), observe time periods in which they report collated statistics to the central controllers.

- **Configuration changes:** Updates to routing scripts or platform configuration affect the way calls are delivered. These changes need to be distributed to the necessary components of the platform. The processes frequently display when they have received a change and updated this configuration accordingly.

- **Error conditions and debugging messages:** Many error conditions can be critical to the performance of the platform. Debug messages can usually only be seen when they are specifically enabled by a support engineer.

The tracing output is written to log files on the local server. The log files are specific to the individual process. These log files are not permanently stored on the server indefinitely but are overwritten when the allocated disk space is used up. They are overwritten on a rolling basis, which means that the oldest data is discarded with latest tracing information. The log files are stored in a binary format. Later in this chapter, you explore the use of the dumplog utility to convert the log files into text.

Each process has a default level of tracing. The tracing level determines the amount of detail that is written to the log file. Often when troubleshooting an issue, the support engineer will need to increase this trace level to obtain further detail about what the process is doing.

The default levels are a compromise between server performance and enough tracing information to perform daily platform management.

Key Point   Increasing the trace level increases the performance hit on the server. For a PG or Computer Telephony Integration (CTI) server, this could mean that it supports less simultaneous agent logins. For a router, it can mean that the number of calls per second is reduced.

Fortunately, tracing levels are not an all-or-nothing approach. It is possible to enable different levels of tracing for different specific areas. Using a selective approach to tracing minimizes the performance impact and also reduces the amount of logging information the support engineer needs to work through when fault finding. In addition, raising the tracing level too high can result in the log files being overwritten too quickly, resulting in the loss of the interesting data.

Tip The log files can also be overwritten quickly if the platform is particularly large or processes a high volume of calls. The default file sizes and number of allocated log files are suitable for the majority of enterprises. However, it is possible to increase the allocated storage on a per-server and -process basis by editing the registry. The log file settings are stored under the following registry hive:

HKEY_LOCAL_MACHINE\SOFTWARE\Cisco Systems, Inc.\ICM\<instance>\<node>\EMS\CurrentVersion\Library\Processes

The individual processes are listed within the registry hive. Setting the following registry keys increases the disk space allowed for log files, the number of log files retained, and their associated size:

EMSAllLogFilesMax

EMSLogFileCountMax

EMSLogFileMax

Figure 16-2 shows an example of a log file directory containing several .ems files for the processes running on a Unified Communications Manager peripheral gateway. The first few characters of the filename are used to easily identify which process the log file is for.

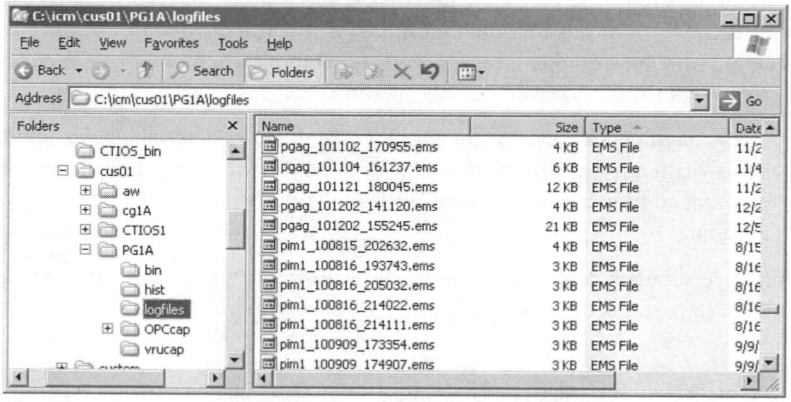

Figure 16-2   *Example Logfiles Directory*

In recent versions of UCCE, some of more verbose processes have their displayed tracing disabled by default. The tracing is still logged to a file, but it is not displayed to the process window. Figure 16-3 gives an example of a PIM process with Display to Screen disabled.

The Display to Screen can be enabled by editing the EMSDisplayToScreen registry key and setting the value to 1.

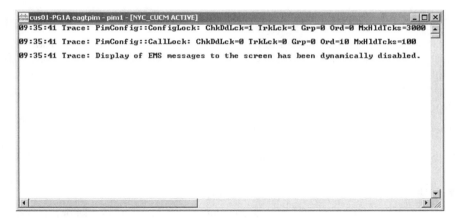

Figure 16-3 *Process with EMSDisplayToScreen Set to Off*

Setting Trace Levels

Different trace settings are used to troubleshoot different problems. For example, if you were troubleshooting an agent login issue, you would probably not be concerned with increasing the tracing level for call routing for that peripheral. You would therefore use only trace settings relevant to the problem under investigation. Applying irrelevant tracing would greatly increase the amount of data in the log file and likely obscure the information that you are looking for.

Several different methods exist for setting the trace levels:

■ Use of a Windows or web-based tool such as the Support Tools Dashboard, Analysis Manager, or Router Trace

■ Use of one of the traditional command-line interface utilities such as procmon or opctest

■ Directly setting a trace level value, normally in hex, into the registry on the respective server

Many of the preceding methods have a degree of overlap between them. For example, several tools can be used to set the same tracing levels for the router process; however, some processes require a specific tool or can only have their tracing set through registry modifications.

Later sections in this chapter examine some of the more common tools used during troubleshooting.

Analysis Manager

Analysis Manager is a component of the Unified CM Real-Time Monitoring Tool (RTMT). RTMT is a plug-in available for download from the administration pages of a Unified CM server. The Analysis Manager component was introduced with Unified CM version 8.0 and is used for troubleshooting call failures across a wide range of Cisco UC products, including Unified CM, UCCE, and UCCX.

The main features provided by Analysis Manager include

- The ability to individually configure all the UC servers (nodes) in the inventory and allocate the servers into groups.
- The ability to configure and determine trace settings.
- The ability to perform ad hoc collection and also schedule the collection of trace files. These trace files can then be sent through FTP to the Cisco TAC servers, if required.
- The ability to apply templates for setting trace levels, allowing the support engineer to easily reapply trace settings for future troubleshooting of similar problems.
- The ability to perform call tracing through several UC components from a single application. This greatly reduces the time and cost required to troubleshoot issues.

Support Tools

Long before the release of Analysis Manager, the majority of troubleshooting tools were all command-line-based and also specific to the single server on which the command was executed. This resulted in the support engineers having to individually access all the servers they were troubleshooting to set trace levels and retrieve log files. Cisco then released a web-based support suite called Support Tools.

Support Tools provides a web front end for many of the proprietary command-line tools available within UCCE. It also provides many useful networking tools, including ping, traceroute, and the **shutdown** command. Collating all these tools through a single web interface (called the Support Tools Dashboard) revolutionized UCCE support by providing the support engineer with a single graphical user interface to perform the majority of his troubleshooting.

Support Tools performs using a client/server architecture, with the Support Tools NodeAgent being installed by default when the core UCCE components such as the router, logger, and peripheral gateways are installed. Figure 16-4 shows a screen shot taken from the Router A Service Control tool, which shows that the Support Tools NodeAgent is installed and running. Communication between the Support Tools Server and the NodeAgents is through TCP/IP. The Support Tools NodeAgent is compatible with many of the Cisco UC products outside the core UCCE platform. The Support Tools user guide gives a detailed compatibility list of the products that it can be used on.

Support Tools provides a wealth of useful utilities that can greatly improve the supportability of a UCCE platform. These features are too vast to fully document in this book.

When troubleshooting UCCE issues, you can use Support Tools to perform the tasks detailed in Table 16-4.

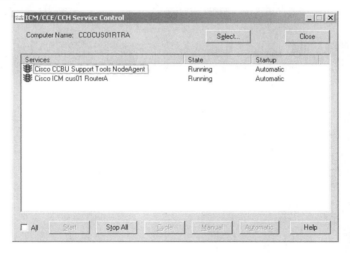

Figure 16-4   *Support Tools NodeAgent Running on Router A*

Table 16-4   *Useful Features of Support Tools*

Feature	Description
Registry comparison	The support engineer can select two servers, for example, Router A and Router B, and perform a registry comparison to check for differences between the two servers. I often use this feature to check that the correct maintenance releases have been applied to both servers. Figure 16-5 gives an example of the difference between two UCCE routers. From this tool, you can see that both have had SR8.0.2 installed and the time of the installation.
Stop/starting UCCE processes	It is possible to list all the processes and services running on a UCCE node, including native Windows services and other third-party applications. These can all be stopped and restarted (with the exception of the Support Tools NodeAgent!), if required.
Setting trace levels and log collection	With the large number of UCCE nodes and the processes running on these nodes, setting the correct trace levels for each process and the collection of the resulting log files can be a daunting task; however, Support Tools greatly simplifies this process. Individual traces and logs can be quickly set and collected using the Interactive Mode. If the support engineer is required to perform this task for multiple servers, the Batch Mode allows the setting and collection process to be scheduled.
Checking network routing and name resolution	Support Tools provides a large third-party toolset, including ping, traceroute, and NSLookup. It is incredibly useful to run these tools remotely through the Support Tools Dashboard rather than have to directly access the respective machines.

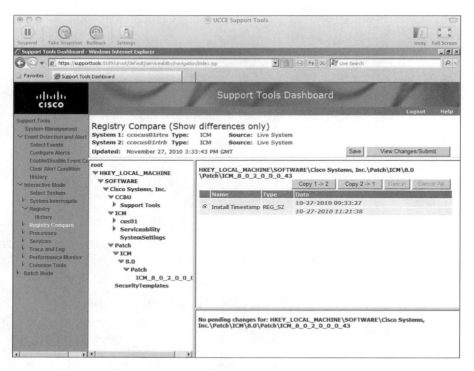

Figure 16-5   *Registry Comparison with Support Tools*

Tip   Thinking about performing a full UCCE audit for a customer? If so, Support Tools is an excellent tool to gather all the system and application information required for a full audit. The System Interrogate function within Batch Mode can be used to retrieve all the really useful platform configuration details for all the UCCE servers that have the Support Tools NodeAgent installed.

Router Trace

Router Trace is a Windows-based tool that allows an engineer to turn up tracing on the UCCE routers without having to use the various command-line utilities. This tool is ideal for quickly enabling or disabling the required trace levels when the engineer is consoled onto the router server.

The Router Trace tool is located at *<root>*:\icm\bin\rtrtrace.exe and can be executed by double-clicking its icon or running from a command-line prompt. After the application is open, the engineer must enter the router host name and customer instance and click the Connect button. The engineer is then presented with a simple application that allows specific trace settings to be set, as shown in Figure 16-6.

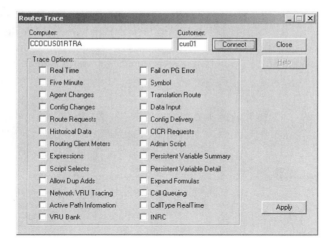

Figure 16-6 *Router Trace Main Application Window*

To set the specific trace settings, the engineer can select one or more of the check boxes next to the required trace and then click the Apply button. Router Trace simultaneously sets the specified trace settings on both routers. Example 16-1 shows output from both Router A and Router B when the Route Requests, Translation Route, and Call Queuing trace options are set.

Example 16-1   *Router Trace Settings for Both Routers*

```
Router A
14:24:55 Router has verified that the logger still has the correct
config sequence number of 578461830003.
14:24:55 All configuration operations complete.
14:25:00 DBWorker configuration delivered.
14:25:38 Trace: Debug turned on: Route,TranRoute,CallQ
14:25:38 Trace: Current debug flags: Route,TranRoute,CallQ


Router B
14:24:54 Router has verified that the logger still has the correct config sequence
number of 578461830003.
14:24:54 All configuration operations complete.
14:25:00 DBWorker configuration delivered.
14:25:38 Trace: Debug turned on: Route,TranRoute,CallQ
14:25:38 Trace: Current debug flags: Route,TranRoute,CallQ
```

The trace settings enabled by Router Trace remain in place even after the Router Trace tool is closed. The trace settings can be reset to their default values either through Router Trace or one of the other trace tools. Figure 16-7 shows a screen shot from the Support Tools server that also displays the current router tracing values for Router A.

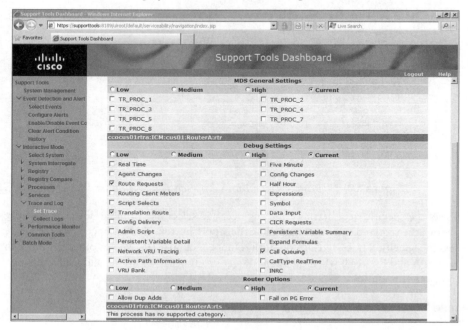

Figure 16-7   *Support Tools Showing the Current Router A Trace Values*

UCCE Command-Line Tools

Before the recent introduction of several Windows or browser-based troubleshooting tools, the majority of the debug and fault-finding tools for UCCE were driven from a command-line interface. These tools are still present on modern UCCE installations. The support engineer should be aware of these tools for the following reasons:

- Not all UCCE installations have Analysis Manager or Support Tools installed, so the command-line tools need to be used instead.

- If the support engineer is consoled onto a UCCE server, or even physically present at the machine, it is likely to be quicker and easier to use the command-line tools unless a large amount of logging is required.

Tip   Many command-line troubleshooting tools exist, most of which can be found in the *<root>*:\icm\bin directory. The tools detailed in this section are the ones most likely to be used when troubleshooting the majority of issues. Occasionally, a Cisco TAC engineer might ask you to use a different tool to set tracing or gather information. If you are required to do this, the engineer always provides detailed steps on how to perform the task.

dumplog Utility

The dumplog utility is probably the most useful command-line tool. It certainly is the one my colleagues and I use most often.

When the core UCCE processes write out logging information, it is stored locally on the respective server in a binary format with the file extension of .ems (Event Management System).

The .ems files cannot be read in a normal text editor and need to be converted into a text format before being human-readable. Each process running on the UCCE node creates a log file, and these logs are typically split over multiple files for performance and storage reasons. It would be awkward for the support engineer to have to manually concatenate multiple log files when searching for information. Fortunately, the dumplog utility takes care of this automatically.

After a text log file has been created, it can be opened with any text-editing program. When performing a quick analysis at the console of a UCCE server, most support engineers use Notepad.exe as it can be easily run from the command line and can typically be found on every UCCE installation.

> **Tip**   To use many of the command-line tools such as dumplog, you need to change the directory to the log file directory. In Windows, this would be performed using the **cd** command, for example, **cd :\icm\cus01\pg1a\logfiles**.
>
> Occasionally, some installations might not use the default directory structure, so there is an alternative or shortcut way to change the directory using the **cdlog** command.
>
> Usage: **cdlog** *<instance> <node>*
>
> For example, **cdlog cus01 pg1a**

Example 16-2 shows the command-line options for the dumplog utility.

Example 16-2   dumplog *Command*

```
C:\icm\cus01\PG1A\logfiles> dumplog /?
Version: Release 8.0.1.0 , Build 26931
Usage: dumplog [ProcessName(s)] [/dir Dirs] [/if InputFile] [/o]
               [/of OutputFile] [/c] [/bd BeginDate(mm/dd/yyyy)]
               [/bt BeginTime(hh:mm:ss)] [/ed EndDate(mm/dd/yyyy)]
               [/et EndTime(hh:mm:ss)] [/hr HoursBack] [/all] [/last]
[/prev]
               [/bin] [/m MatchString] [/x ExcludeString] [/ms] [/mc]
[/debug]
               [/ciscoLog] [/help] [/?]
```

Table 16-5 details the meaning of some of the popular command-line options available with the dumplog utility, and Example 16-3 shows an example usage.

Table 16-5 *Popular dumplog Command-Line Options*

Option	Description
ProcessName(s)	The particular process or processes for which you require the dumplog command to parse.
/of OutputFile	OutputFile specifies an output text file, for example, c:\temp\mylog.txt.
/bd	BeginDate (mm/dd/yyyy) specifies the begin date. If used with /bt, this specifies a range of dates. Otherwise, dumplog dumps events for only the specified date.
/bt	BeginTime (hh:mm:ss) specifies the begin time. Use with /et to specify a range of time.
/ed	EndDate (mm/dd/yyyy) specifies the end date. Use with /bd to specify a range of days.
/et	EndTime (hh:mm:ss) specifies the end time. Use with /bt to specify a range of time.
/last	Displays information from the most recent log file for the process.

Example 16-3 *Example Usage for the* **dumplog** *Command*

```
Change the current directory to be that of PG1A:
cdlog cus01 pg1a


Dump the PIM1 process to a text file for a specified date and time
range. The dates are in the format /mm/dd/yyyy:
dumplog pim1 /bd 12/03/2010 /bt 19:00 /ed 12/04/2010 /et 10:00 /of pg1a_pim1.txt


To perform a quick PIM1 process dump of the most recent events. The
output file created with the /o option is the process name suffixed
with .txt:
dumplog pim1 /last /o


When troubleshooting a problem such as CUCM PG registration, it is
often useful to combine multiple processes into a single output file.
```

```
This command combines both the PIM1 and JTAPI processes by specifying
both process:
dumplog pim1 jgw1 /last /of pim1_jgw.txt



Rather than using the /o or /of options, it is also possible to use
the > redirect:
dumplog pim1 /bt 12:00 /et 13:00 > pim1.txt
```

Tip   Each line of the output file available from dumplog has the first eight characters specifying the time the output was created. For example:

09:36:41 PG1A-pim1 Trace: Uptime = 12 Days 5 Hours 0 Minutes and 46 Seconds

When using the **dumplog** command over multiple days, the support engineer needs to understand from the log on which day the output occurred. dumplog achieves this by inserting a blank line break and then an additional line as the date changes. For example:

Events from December 4, 2010

signifies that the events following this line are now for the date December 4, 2010.

opctest Utility

The Open Peripheral Controller (OPC) process runs at the heart of each peripheral gateway. The **opctest** command-line utility can be used on each PG to find out its current state, including real-time information such as the overall PG's health and communication with its duplex pair and the central controller, and useful information such as the current state of the agents associated with the PG.

The **opctest** command can also be used to turn up tracing levels so that additional debug information is stored in the EMS logs.

Example 16-4 shows the command-line options for the opctest utility.

Example 16-4   *Example Usage for the* opctest *Command*

```
C:\> opctest /?
Version: Release 8.0.1.0 , Build 26931
Usage: opctest [/f InputFile] [/system SystemName] [/cust Customer]
               [/node ICRNode] [/pipe OutputPipe] [/debug] [/stop]
[/help] [/?]


C:\>opctest /cust cus01 /node pg1a
OPCTEST Release 8.0.1.0 , Build 26931

opctest:
```

Example 16-5 details the outout of opctest. The output shown in this examples was created using the **status** command. Notes have been added and highlighted.

Example 16-5   *opctest Usage with the* **status** *Command*

```
** Time information, very useful if the PG is in a different time zone

OPC Current Time:    12/02 21:54:27
OPC Local Time:      12/02 21:54:27 (0 sec)
OPC Version: Release 8.0.2.0 , Build 26940
Release Date:    06/01/10 17:57:40



Current Time:    12/02 21:54:27
Local Time:      12/02 21:54:27 (0 sec)
** This shows the PG's uptime and side synchronization

OPC Up:      12/02 15:53:16 (6.0 hr)
OPC Sync:    12/02 21:28:14 (26.2 min) (A->B)



** The PG processes and their respective states. We can see that PGB has only recently
come on-line, perhaps from a restart

Process              LastStateChange              LastHeartBeat
A pgag       OK M- 12/02 15:53:21 (6.0 hr)       —
A pim1       OK M- 12/02 15:53:21 (6.0 hr)       —
A pim2       OK M- 12/02 15:53:21 (6.0 hr)       —
A ctisvr     OK M- 12/02 15:53:21 (6.0 hr)       —
A opc        OK  H —                             12/02 21:54:16 (11 sec)
B pgag       OK M- 12/02 21:28:16 (26.1 min)     —
B pim1       OK M- 12/02 21:28:16 (26.1 min)     —
B pim2       OK M- 12/02 21:28:16 (26.1 min)     —
B opc        OK  H —                             12/02 21:54:16 (11 sec)
B ctisvr     OK M- 12/02 21:28:16 (26.1 min)     —



** The information in this section is truncated on three lines but has been sepa-
rated
in this example for clarity.


** It is possible to determine that the PGAgent process is connected to SideA
central
```

```
controller, but not SideB. This means that the PG is not in communication with
SideB.
Perhaps the SideB Router process is down or there are network connectivity
issues.
PGAgent      LastStateChangeTime            ConnectATime                Status
SideA      PIA 12/02 21:25:49 (28.6 min)  12/02 21:25:45 (28.7 min)   CONNECTED
SideB    P— 12/02 21:28:16 (26.1 min)                                 IDLE AGENT


PGAgent      ConnectBTime                        Status
SideA     12/02 21:25:45 (28.7 min)         DISCONNECTED
Side B                                        IDLE AGENT

** This output also shows that the PG is not in communication with either
Peripheral
5001 (CUCM) or 5002 (IP IVR). If they were in communication, the Side column
would
reflect which side of the PG pair (A or B) is active and the State column would
have
the value PIM_ACTIVE.
PeripheralID  Side    State            LastStateChange
LastHeardFrom
  5001          ?    PIM_NULL      —   12/02 21:53:46 (40 sec)
12/02 21:53:48
(39 sec)
  5002          ?    PIM_NULL      —   12/02 21:54:03 (24 sec)
12/02 21:54:11
(16 sec)


CTIServerNo   Side    State            LastStateChange
LastHeardFrom
  1            A    CTI_ACTIVE        12/02 15:53:31 (6.0 hr)
12/02 21:54:20
(6 sec)
```

Table 16-6 details the meaning of some of the popular commands available within the opctest utility. A full list of the available commands can be obtained using the **help** command within opctest. Many of the commands also have shortcuts. For example, **list_agents** has the shortcut of **la**.

Example 16-6 shows all the trace levels that can be set with the **opctest debug** command.

Table 16-6   *Popular* opctest *Commands*

Command	Description
expression	Use this command to evaluate an expression against the current router configuration. For example, in a call-routing script, you can have a formula that checks to see whether a certain number of agents are available before trying to deliver a call. The **expression** command can be used to test this formula in real time.
list_calls	This command displays the OPC call state.
list_agents	This command details a state summary of agents for a specific peripheral by skill group.
status	This command displays the real-time status of the PG.
debug	This command allows the support engineer to set specific trace levels.

Example 16-6   opctest debug *Command Usage*

```
Usage: debug_control [/realtime] [/agent] [/halfhour] [/rcmeter]
[/routing]
                     [/skillgroup] [/closedcalls] [/cstaecr]
[/cstacer]
                     [/pimmsg] [/ctimsg] [/rcmsg] [/dmpmsg] [/icmsg]
[/opcmsg]
                     [/mdsmsg] [/pdmsg] [/inrcmsg] [/passthru]
[/tpmsg]
                     [/physctrlr] [/periph] [/dailydata]
[/missingdata] [/task]
                     [/diskio] [/simplified] [/calls] [/NCT]
[/autoconfig]
                     [/default] [/callstatus] [/all] [/help] [/?]
```

Tip   Be sure to issue the **opctest: debug /noall** command when you have finished troubleshooting with opctest. This command resets all the debug tracing back to default levels.

Tip   When quitting the opctest utility, be sure to use the **exit** command and not the **exitopc** command. The latter command forces a simultaneous reload of the OPC process on both PGs. This is a great command to perform a quick restart of both PGs if you need to flush all real-time information. (No state transfer will take place between the PGs, which would happen if you restarted one at a time.) However, be careful not to accidentally run this command as it also bounces the CTI Server and any PIM processes.

rttest Utility

With functional similarities to opctest, the **rttest** command-line utility can be run on the UCCE routers to allow you to find out the current state of the central controllers and configured peripherals, and it can be used to set tracing and view debugging information.

Example 16-7 shows the required parameters for the rttest utility.

Example 16-7   rttest *Parameters*

```
C:\icm> rttest /?
Version: Release 8.0.1.0 , Build 26931
Usage: rttest [/f InputFile] [/system SystemName] [/cust Customer]
              [/node ICRNode] [/pipe OutputPipe] [/debug] [/stop]
[/help] [/?]


C:\icm> rttest /cust cus01 /node routera
RTTEST Release 8.0.1.0 , Build 26931
rttest:
```

Example 16-8 detail the command usage of **rttest**. The output shown in this example was created using the **status** commandNotes have been added and highlighted.

Example 16-8   rttest status *Command Output*

```
rttest: status

Router Version: Release 8.0.2.0 , Build 26940
Release Date:    06/01/2010 17:45:38


Current Time:    12/04 14:41:26
Local Time:      12/04 14:41:26 (0 sec)
Router Up:       12/04 12:42:04 (119.3 min)
Router Sync:     12/04 14:29:52 (11.5 min) (A->B)
State size now: 1,419,672 bytes
State size max: 1,423,624 bytes


** The following output lines detail the status of all of the UCCE processes run-
ning on Router A


Process                LastStateChange                LastHeartBeat
A agi                  - —                            —
```

```
A basv           - —                              —
A cic            - —                              —
A clgr        OK MH 12/04 12:42:13 (119.2 min)  12/04 14:40:57 (30 sec)
A crpl           - —                              —
A csfs        OK M- 12/04 12:42:04 (119.3 min)  —
A dba         OK MH 12/04 12:42:04 (119.3 min)  12/04 14:40:58 (28 sec)
A dbw         OK MH 12/04 12:42:04 (119.3 min)  12/04 14:40:59 (27 sec)
A hlgr        OK MH 12/04 12:42:13 (119.2 min)  12/04 14:41:26 (0 sec)
A nrpl           - —                              —
A rcv         OK M- 12/04 12:42:04 (119.3 min)  —
A rtr         OK MH 12/04 12:42:04 (119.3 min)  12/04 14:41:04 (22 sec)
A rts         OK MH 12/04 12:42:08 (119.3 min)  12/04 14:41:06 (21 sec)
A ssim           - —                              —
A tsyr        OK M- 12/04 12:42:04 (119.3 min)  —
** The following output lines detail the status of all of the UCCE processes run-
ning on Router B


B agi            - —                              —
B basv           - —                              —
B cic            - —                              —
B clgr           —                               12/04 14:29:55 (11.5 min)
B crpl           - —                              —
B csfs           - —                              —
B dba         OK MH 12/04 14:29:55 (11.5 min)   12/04 14:41:20 (6 sec)
B dbw         OK MH 12/04 14:29:55 (11.5 min)   12/04 14:41:21 (5 sec)
B hlgr           —                               12/04 14:29:55 (11.5 min)
B nrpl           - —                              —
B rcv            - —                              —
B rtr         OK MH 12/04 14:29:55 (11.5 min)   12/04 14:41:04 (22 sec)
B rts         OK MH 12/04 14:29:55 (11.5 min)   12/04 14:40:58 (28 sec)
B ssim           - —                              —
B tsyr        OK M- 12/04 14:29:55 (11.5 min)   —


** This section gives details of the logical controller, we can see that only a
single logical controller is defined
Controller          LastStateChange           LastHeartBeat
NYC_PG,1         CFO 12/04 12:42:16 (119.1 min)  12/04 14:41:23 (3 sec)


** This section gives details of the configured peripherals, the NYC_IVR1 periph-
eral is out of service
Peripheral          LastStateChange           LastHeardFrom
NYC_CUCM         COS 12/04 14:31:02 (10.4 min)  12/04 14:41:16 (11 sec)
```

```
NYC_IVR1          CO   —                      12/04 12:42:17
(119.1 min)
```

From the status output detailed in Example 16-8, it is possible to see that the results are split into three sections:

- The first section details all the process status on both routers.

- The second section gives details about the logical controllers.

- The third section gives details about the individual peripheral gateways.

Tip   By observing the Router Sync value in the **rttest** status output, it is possible to determine which side sent the last state transfer. In Example 16-8, you can see that the state transfer occurred from Side A to Side B. It is also possible to determine the size of the state transfer. If one side of the platform has been down or unreachable for a long period of time and many configuration changes have taken place, the size of the state transfer can be considerable. An exceptionally large state transfer to be copied over a restricted WAN link can cause problems.

Example 16-9 shows all the trace levels that can be set with the **rttest debug** command. These are the same debug settings available with the Router Trace utility. Table 16-7 details several of the popular **rttest** commands used when troubleshooting call flows.

Table 16-7   *Popular* rttest *Commands*

Command	Description
expression	Use this command to evaluate an expression against the current router configuration.
set_variable	This command sets the value of a variable in the router. This is often useful when you are troubleshooting a call flow scenario that uses several variables to determine public holidays or emergency scenarios.
test_route	This command allows the engineer to check for a valid return label for a particular routing client and dialed number. Note: When specifying the routing client, enter the name of the peripheral, not its peripheral ID.
status	This command displays the real-time status of the both routers.
debug	This command allows the support engineer to set specific trace levels.

Example 16-9   rttest debug *Command Usage*

```
rttest: debug /?
Usage: debug_control [/realtime] [/5minute] [/agent] [/config]
[/route]
                     [/halfhour] [/rcmeter] [/expr] [/select] [/dupadd]
                     [/failpgerror] [/symbol] [/tranroute] [/datain]
                     [/delivery] [/cic] [/admin] [/pervarsumm]
[/pervardetail]
                     [/expform] [/vru] [/callq] [/activepath]
[/calltypeRT]
                     [/vrubank] [/inrc] [/all] [/help] [/?]
```

procmon Utility

The Process Control Monitor (procmon) is another command-line utility that can be used on the peripheral gateway to determine status information and set tracing levels. Although **opctest** and **rttest** are specific in the processes that they investigate, **procmon** is slightly more generic and can be used for the Peripheral Interface Manager (PIM), the Open Peripheral Controller (OPC), the Java Telephony Application Programming Interface (JTAPI), and the Computer Telephony Integration (CTI) Server processes.

Example 16-10 shows the required parameters for the **procmon** utility.

Example 16-10   procmon *Parameters*

```
C:\> procmon /?
Version: Release 8.0.1.0 , Build 26931
Usage: PROCMon CustomerName NodeName ProcessName [SystemName] [/f InputFile]
              [/wait] [/stop] [/help] [/?]


C:\> procmon cus01 pg1a pim1
>>>>


C:\> procmon cus01 pg1a jgw1
>>>>


C:\> procmon cus01 cg1a ctisvr
>>>>
```

Tip   Typing **help** at a **procmon** prompt does not give much information. A better command to use is **mhelp** as this details all the commands that can be used to perform monitoring and troubleshooting. As the **procmon** utility can be used for a number of processes, the commands available shown with **mhelp** differ depending on the process being investigated. For example, the commands available with the PIM process are different than the commands available with the CTI Server process.

UCCE Script Editor

UCCE Script Editor has two features that, while not strictly troubleshooting tools, are often useful when investigating a call-routing issue.

Monitoring

UCCE Script Editor has the capability to perform real-time, script monitoring accessing from the Script menu. This real-time monitoring displays the calls as they flow through the routing script. The display is almost real time, but does lag slightly behind what the router is actually doing as the data displayed actually comes from the distributor and not directly from the router. Several monitoring options are available, with the capability to display data from the start of the day, display starting now, or display the calls for each reporting interval.

Figure 16-8 shows a screen shot from Script Editor in Monitor mode. It is possible to see the path that calls are taking through the script. This is invaluable for larger and more complex routing scripts as it narrows down the potential area that is causing a problem.

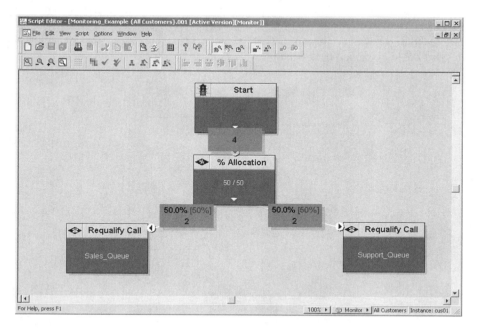

Figure 16-8 *Script Editor Real-Time Monitoring*

Tip Chapter 15 briefly discusses the use of Router Log Viewer for displaying a real-time view of the calls being router by UCCE. The lower pane in Router Log Viewer displays all the routing errors experienced by the router process. Occasionally, it is possible to observe apparently successful calls with Script Editor real-time monitoring, with the call reaching the intended destination in the script, yet the call does not physically reach the correct destination. These types of errors regularly happen because of misconfiguration such as missing call type mappings or incorrectly configured agent device targets. Router Log Viewer is helpful in uncovering this type of fault.

Call Tracer

Another useful Script Editor feature that can be used for troubleshooting basic scripting is the Call Tracer tool, also found under the Script menu.

Call Tracer simulates a route request to the router process just as if a peripheral had performed the request. This allows the support engineer to see how the router would process a real call.

Using Call Tracer does not have an impact on the reporting metrics stored in the UCCE database, but it does increment the real-time counters seen within Script Editor.

Figure 16-9 demonstrates an example call setup for Call Tracer to simulate. As Call Tracer does not interact with an Interactive Voice Response (IVR), it is necessary to simulate this interaction. In this example, it is possible to see that two responses to the Run External Script node have been set. These responses simulate to Call Tracer example values that could be passed back from the IVR.

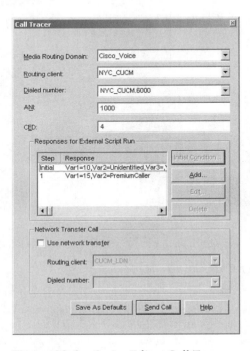

Figure 16-9 *Script Editor Call Tracer*

Tip   Call Tracer works only for UCCE/UICM scripts; it cannot simulate calls through the Unified CM platform. If a support engineer needs to test a call flow involving Unified CM, Analysis Manager or the Dialed Number Analyzer should be used. Both of these tools are available on Unified CM, with the latter tool being excellent for troubleshooting issues with partitions and calling search spaces.

Summary

This chapter covered the different troubleshooting techniques and tools that can be used to help administer a UCCE platform. In particular, the learning points from this chapter can be summarized as follows:

- When trying to solve issues, have a documented troubleshooting methodology that can be followed.

- Collect log file outputs as soon as practically possible so that their detail is not accidentally overwritten because the tracing levels are high or the contact center is busy.

- Consider installing a Support Tools server or using Analysis Manager to assist with troubleshooting.

- Be aware of the different trace levels, know how to set them, and know where the resulting log files are produced.

Index

I

J-K-L

M